Cipher/Code of Dishonor

Aaron Burr, an American Enigma

————

TRINITY

The Burrs versus Alexander Hamilton and the United States of America

By

Alan J. Clark, M.D.

authorHOUSE™

1663 LIBERTY DRIVE, SUITE 200
BLOOMINGTON, INDIANA 47403
(800) 839-8640
WWW.AUTHORHOUSE.COM

First published by AuthorHouse 08/23/05

ISBN: 1-4208-4639-6 (e)
ISBN: 1-4208-4638-8 (sc)
ISBN: 1-4208-4637-X (dj)

Library of Congress Control Number: 2005903676

Printed in the United States of America
Bloomington, Indiana

This book is printed on acid-free paper.

Cover design by Mercedes D. Bujans
Research assistance by Norma Perdue

Dedicated to Mom
Barbara Ramsdell Clark Tesch
August 30, 1918-May 20, 2005

In Memoriam

Rindak

February 15, 2005

He was this reenactor's war horse for 13 years, and eight movies, loyal companion for 27 of his 32 years, race horse, polo pony and gentle diplomat of his Arabian breed.

"Old soldiers never die, they just fade, fade away."

Though these Views of American History are much at Variance with Historians of Today, a Quotation from the Puritan Richard Baxter states the case, *"As long as men have liberty to examine and contradict one another, one may partly conjecture, by comparing their words, on which side the truth is like to be."*

This book contains its own modern day cipher. Hint: To decode one must read the whole book.

TABLE OF CONTENTS

Part One: The Loyalists

Part Two: The Principals' Principles

Part Three: The Mechanics of Manhattan

CHAPTER SUMMARY

<u>Preface: The British are Coming, The British are Coming, The British Never Left</u>

The preface introduces the author to the audience of genealogists and historians alike. He enumerates his past publications from listing the casualties of the Battle of Lake George, an opening to the French and Indian Wars, to the extensive investigations of the origins of British and Loyalist families of the Revolutionary Period. He even delves into the history of an American family during the War of 1812.

The author traces the extensive information on these families gleaned from the genealogical archives of the Mormon Church and local town historical libraries. He puts together a nearly complete story of the heretofore unknown wartime experiences of these Loyalist families which eventually fled to Ontario, Canada to found a new colony. Some of these stories find their place as examples in the text of this book.

The author gives his reasons for studying history and the relevance to the present descendants of another time. He takes a recent PBS television documentary as an example of the significance of historical investigation.

The author cites a brief unpublished example of his self-coined form of historical investigation, Genealogical Historian. Using time-line analysis the example corrects an error in the important genealogical literature of the founder of American Genealogy, Donald Jacobus. The author connects this example with the current recent historical revelation on the capture of Nathan Hale.

Introduction: God's Divine Gift, (Aaron Burr's Theodosia(e), or The Supremacy of Royal Heredity).

The introduction poses the question how did some of the Tories of New York avoid confiscation of their property during the Revolutionary War. It establishes their continual influence on American political and economic foundations. The source of this wealth and power, originating in the Crown of England, still exists today.

New York City as the hub of the continental economic wheel is the key to a successful business venture in the United States. The old real estate saying, location, location, location is as prescient today as in the beginning of our nation and colonial heritage. The location became a privilege of the few. The selection of the chosen elite as it turns out rested with the Feudal European system of the Monarchies, in this case the Crown of England.

Prologue: The Blockhouse; Death of General Montgomery at Quebec, 1775. This is a fictional account of the death of General Montgomery from the Canadian perspective of the commendation of John Coffin in 1776.

Part One: The Loyalists

Chapter One: The Dispossessed

The confiscations of Loyalist properties during the Revolutionary War reached its peak in the final year of the war, 1783. Before that in 1779 legislation was enacted to punish the principal leaders of the Loyalist resistance by disenfranchisement of the wealthy officers of the Loyalist Legions, many from Manhattan and Long Island. The confiscations of 1783 were few in Manhattan and Long Island compared to the rest of the state. Also the people most affected were the ordinary craftsmen, merchants, laborers, farmers and tradesmen of society. How did the aristocracy of New York fare so much better?

Chapter Two: The Loyalist Families

The De Lancey and Heathcote families, descendants of the Duke of York, King James II, had joined before the War of Independence with the wealthy Dutch families of New York, Van Cortlands. These families were prominent in much of early New York political and economic life. From them descend many other loyalist families by intermarriage. These families continued to maintain close ties with and served the Crown of England in other parts of the world.

PART II   The Principals' Principles

Chapter Three: Alexander Hamilton and the Cruger Family

Alexander Hamilton is introduced to the world of international trade and business by the Cruger family first in the Caribbean and then in New York City. The Cruger family was and still is involved in world trade.

Chapter Four: Prelude to the Duel

The career of Alexander Hamilton from college to artilleryman, to aide-de-camp of General George Washington, to lawyer, to founder of the Bank of New York, to Secretary of the Treasury in President Washington's first administration, to the Reynolds Affair, to the duel with Aaron Burr are briefly reviewed for the reader as background to the following chapters.

Chapter Five: The Affair of State

The Reynolds' Affair between Alexander Hamilton and Maria Reynolds is first described as most historians have thought about it. Then a novel suggestion is made that the affair was originally a scheme to confirm the intent of Hamilton in paying old obligations of the Revolutionary War by Congress at 100% so that speculators in purchasing the notes at discount from the weary original holders would reap a profit. But Hamilton had turned the tables on the Reynolds schemers, one of whom was Aaron Burr, and used Maria as a courier for his negotiations with wealthy American and British investors in his Bank of the United States and industrial espionage for the United States. Maria was known to Hamilton during the Revolutionary War. He had intimate contact with her half brothers on nearly a daily basis. Her brother was also a courier for Washington.

Chapter Six: The Political Assassination

Alexander Hamilton and Aaron Burr sparred politically but remained social friends as lawyers and politicians are known to do today. But there was a special something about Burr that Hamilton detected that made Hamilton bulldog Burr. Alexander could not let go of the notion that Aaron was up to no good in every sense of the word. It seems Hamilton dedicated his life, and gave it also for the sole purpose of checkmating Burr. Aaron Burr showed no remorse at the outcome of the duel, that even his cousin could detect.

Chapter Seven: Another Plan of Secession

Hamilton's last checkmate of Burr in the 1804 election for governor of New York led to Hamilton's death. But Burr was undeterred. He forged a new scheme with Charles Williamson and Minister Anthony Merry that would lead to the secession of the western United States and conquer Mexican territory for himself with the help of England.

Chapter Eight: Burr, Hamilton, the Loyalists, and Trinity Church

Alexander Hamilton attended King's College, a loyalist stronghold which got its beginning from a grant of land from Trinity Church. Aaron Burr had many dealings with the Church including helping renew its corporate charter with the state of New York. He subsequently had many land leases from Trinity Church over the years. Hamilton was counselor for Trinity on several occasions and his part time partners were full time attorneys for Trinity yet he seems to not have had any land transactions with the Church.

Aaron Burr came from a prominent Presbyterian family of Princeton, New Jersey, and Fairfield, Connecticut. His mother, an Edwards, is related to the Robert Edwards who deeded him 80 acres during the Revolution, which he turned over to the Church. Aaron in 1777 began an association with the wife of a British Officer of the southern campaign, Theodosia Bartow Prevost, whom he eventually married. Theodosia seemed to be the connection between Burr and Robert Edwards, the Shippens and Benedict Arnold. The lease of 80 acres by Robert Edwards to Burr just prior to the Battle of Monmouth becomes the focus of further investigation.

Chapter Nine: Burr and Washington and the Beginning of Schemes of Power

After the Battle of Monmouth, Washington sends Burr on detached duty as a spy on Manhattan while he tries to figure out which of his officers he could trust after the court martial of Charles Lee and the almost disastrous exposure of the left wing of Washington's army by Burr. Aaron is sent on various errands to escort Tories into their lines in Manhattan; he later landed a sedate position at Westchester where his true leanings toward the Tories became more evident. Burr resigned his commission under a cloud of suspicion and no truthful regrets from Washington.

In late 1780s Burr began plotting with his brother-in-law to create a toll road through lands they owned in West Farms area of south Westchester County, New York. The road at the expense of the local land owners provided convenient access to their lands from Manhattan thus increasing their value. With the money acquired from these lands Burr and Dr. Brown purchased the leases of Richmond Hill of 150 acres in upper Manhattan and started a water project to supply the City with pure water. The profits from which financed the new Bank of Manhattan.

Chapter Ten: Burr, John Jacob Astor, and Trinity Church

Aaron Burr's home, Richmond Hill with 26 acres was *"well sold"* to John Jacob Astor. Burr was successful in including his daughter and son-in-law, *"two bottles of Madeira wine"*, in the deal with John Jacob Astor and England (Astor's landlord) which was the secession plan of the Federalist New England from the United States, with Burr at the helm from the governor's seat in New York. Trinity owned the land that Burr subleased to John Jacob Astor. In the final year of his life Burr married a second time, and continued right on scheming with his wife's money.

Chapter Eleven: Burr's Counselor, Theodosia

The letters between Burr and his daughter, Theodosia contained cipher codes. Analysis of the time-line coincident with the letters brings to light a plot to assassinate Hamilton six months before the duel and probably hatched by Theodosia herself. Burr continues to plot secession with the British Minister Merry in the guise of an affair with old flame Celeste. The letters from Theodosia reveal knowledge of the assassination of Montgomery at Quebec in 1775 before her birth and Burr suggests knowledge of the still secret Culper Ring of Long Island in his letters to her. Burr plays all wild cards, Spain, France, and England to his advantage.

Montalto becomes the code for summit conference with Merry. By transference Richmond Hill becomes Montalto the equivalent of Jefferson's Monticello as Burr anticipates the outcome of the duel with Hamilton. The development of the code word for Hamilton, La G., reveals the plot began as far back as November, 1803.

Chapter Twelve: Alexander Hamilton and His Gravestone by Trinity Church Corporation

The inscription on the gravestone is analyzed and the conclusion is obscuration of complicity in his death.

Chapter Thirteen: Theodosia Burr Alston, God's Divine Gift; Her Portrait Artist and the Myths.

The many stories of the disappearance of Theodosia Burr Alston in December, 1812 are recounted. The myth has clouded the truth. Accounts of her portraits by John Vanderlyn and the relationship to Aaron Burr follow.

Chapter Fourteen: Aaron Burr's Spy Ring

Aaron Burr's *Memoirs* are strangely silent on his two wives and relationships with other women. His publisher admits to destroying much of the evidence of his affairs of love or state with these women. But we know of the pivotal role women played in the espionage of the Revolutionary War on both sides. Burr's Theodosias, wife and daughter, are no exception.

Aaron's resignation from the American army takes on new light in a letter from Theodore Sedgwick. Then what ensues is a nearly complete sequence of letters from Robert Troup to Aaron Burr, and between Peter Colt and Aaron Burr, which implicate them in the treason of Benedict Arnold. In fact the monetary arrangements are made before Major Andre returns from Charleston, South Carolina. It is supposed that Burr meant for us to find this connection by publishing this complete series of letters from 1778-9.

The incident at New Haven, Connecticut, is supposed to be a ruse to enhance Burr's credibility as a Rebel even after his resignation. Again there is a revelation of the Culper Spy Ring and Rivington's Press.

The date and time of the turn over of West Point by Arnold is made in these same correspondences. Even coded in the letters is the decision of Washington to almost not post Arnold to West Point command which was reversed by the protest of Peggy Shippen Arnold.

Troup reveals the plans to trap Cornwallis at Yorktown one year prior to the event. Why General Clinton does not act is surmised.

Burr ultimately gained from his espionage with leases from Trinity Church.

Chapter Fifteen: Burr the Revolutionary War Hero or Traitor

The truth about the Battle of Monmouth, New Jersey, is told. Burr does not look the part of a hero. In fact, he avoids three possible court-martials. His exposure of Margaret Moncrief as a spy has a new meaning.

Chapter Sixteen: Guilt by Association

Letters from William Paterson and James Monroe included in Burr's *Memoirs* suggest Burr is getting back at his old friends turned enemies. Monroe especially spoiled Burr's plans to conquer the Louisiana Territory from Spain or France by the purchase of it from Napoleon. Burr asked his son-in-law, Joseph Alston, to interfere with the nomination of Monroe for President in preference to Jackson. Charles Lee and the Conway Cabal involve Burr also.

Chapter Seventeen: Burr's Counterespionage

New interpretation of Burr's involvement in the Revolutionary War comes from his use of the Culper Spy Ring code names. Burr's exemplary performance in the evacuation of Manhattan might have another purpose. He could have been privy to the attempt on Washington's life hatched by Governor William Tryon. And at Quebec did Burr lead General Montgomery to his death? A reference by Theodosia to a J. McPherson might lead one to think so. A Major Coffin at the blockhouse where Montgomery was ambushed was related to people Burr knew. He had the opportunity to set up the trap while passing through the enemy lines in disguise.

Chapter Eighteen: A Second Plan of Secession

Andrew Jackson foiled Burr's plans to seize the Louisiana Territory and parts of Mexico. Burr was unaware of Jackson's actions when he proposed Jackson to replace Monroe for Presidential candidate in 1816. The origin of the blank commission is analyzed. A revealing exchange between Harmon Blennerhassett and Aaron Burr shows Burrs character and the extent of those involved with Burr, willingly or not.

Another reason for Burr's dislike of Hamilton was Hamilton's opposition to Matthew L. Davis' appointment as naval officer of the port of New York, a plum opportunity for graft. Matthew Davis was Burr's thirty year friend and editor of his *Memoirs*.

Chapter Nineteen: Burr Agent of the Crown

Burr retreated to Europe after the treason trial. He was housed by the father of British Intelligence, Jeremy Bentham. He was unsuccessful in obtaining assistance from other governments for his schemes and returned to the United States via Boston under an assumed name. In Boston, he gained further assistance from the Essex Junto, a group dedicated to the return of British rule in the Americas, which supported him in the 1804 governor's race in New York and would later favor the South in the Civil War. Burr involved his son-in-law once again during the War of 1812.

Chapter Twenty: Burr vs. Hamilton Once Again

Aaron Burr was offered positions of rank and power in Mexico and South America, but declined. Burr died in debt and alone, never attaining his goals of his childhood to show his uncle who was boss. Hamilton became the favorite champion of Loyalist causes in the United States. Robert Frost sized up the situation of Theodosia's death, *"twas to punish her, but her father more"*.

The close interconnectedness of the upper classes of the United States lies in politics, education, economics as well as religion.

Part Three: The Mechanics of Manhattan

Chapter Twenty One: The British Bankers

John Jacob Astor was the agent of the Crown, the paymaster through Trinity Church leases. The way Astor was compensated tells how others may have been also. The global network of an empire with vast and varied holdings can swap favors with its loyal subjects anywhere on the earth.

The succession of ties to the Crown of England through Astor and his agent, Moses Taylor, and his family lead straight to the current banks of New York and London, John D. Rockefeller, and J.P. Morgan. Although some feel this influence of Britain too strong, there are set in place checks and balances in the Federal Reserve Bank of the United States, the successor to Hamilton's First Bank of the United States. For good or bad Hamilton was the champion and originator of our present economic system. He did not personally gain from this endeavor which makes the Reynolds Affair seem less selfish and more selfless. Hamilton emulated wealth, but never attained it for himself. Only his double, Edward Stevens, could claim that.

Chapter Twenty Two: The Land

The land of Trinity Church Corporation consists of four large parcels in lower Manhattan on land used for Wall Street and the World Trade Center. The line of ownership and locations are discussed. The meaning and use of Quit Rents is discussed.

Chapter Twenty Three: The Church

The legal charter of the Trinity Church Corporation is followed. The Church revealed its income and outflow in 1856 to the State Legislature of New York. The figures don't completely explain the vastness of the holdings and the cash flow generated. An 1885 GSGA survey map plots the holdings corresponding with the leases held by Trinity in the 18th century.

Some of this land is traced to the Port Authority of New York and New Jersey. A recent transaction of property between Trinity Church and Rupert Murdock is used to illustrate a possible method of disposition of some of the property and by which the Queen of England may derive some of her income.

Epilogue: The Crown's Jewel; the Twin Towers

The economic interests of the royalty of Europe are global and non-nationalistic. The formation of secret economic summits in Europe and the United States by the wealthy international business families seem to pledge a goal of free trade and unified currency and global governments to simplify their lives of international hegemony.

Hamilton succeeded in stopping Burr's use of this international system for his own aggrandizement. Aaron Burr came very close to accomplishing his goals of overthrowing the fledgling government even before it really got going. Thanks to fate and Hamilton, we are a free country today.

We have a staunch ally in Great Britain because it still has a stake in the United States.

PREFACE: The British Are Coming! The British Are Coming!

The British Never Left

What is a preface but to explain the how, why and wherefore of that which follows.

History is not a collection of facts and dates, the fear of which kept me from taking courses in history early on in my schooling. The perception of history by those whose lives are ultimately affected by it molds how it is interpreted.

The following story, a digression, of recent historical discovery revealed on PBS-TV demonstrates how important history is to the average person. Amateur scuba divers discovered the wreck of a World War II German U-boat 60 miles off the New Jersey coast. For seven years they attempted to identify the wreck. They found a knife of the captain and a box with the label of the vessel U-869 in the engine room. The German U-boat archivist was incredulous since his records indicated it was lost off Gibraltar having been diverted there for refueling from a course to the United States. The orders were intercepted by British intelligence, but the captain of the U-boat never acknowledged its receipt. The divers located a sister, not yet born at the time of the loss, of a crewmember now living in New Jersey, and the son of the captain. The woman received the new facts with much emotion, for the lost brother yet nearer to her than first thought. A survivor of the crew who had missed the embarkation of the U-boat because of illness came forward upon viewing the program. An ocean no longer separates the sister and brother's watery grave, while the new facts give answers to old secret questions for the others as to the fate of the U-boat.

Likewise in this book new facts and perhaps some old facts reassembled give a different story to history than what has been the official record. Nothing new may be revealed in these pages that can't be found elsewhere. Yet the interpretation from reassembling these facts into a logical history is new. The Atlantic Ocean has never separated us here in America from our mother country. She is closer than we think. The British never left the colonies. Only their army and direct political rule left. What remain are the people, their laws, religions, money and traditions. Participants of the War of Independence will come forward in these pages to tell a different story than has been told up to now.

Why rewrite history? Truth is history. Does not our generation await the truth of the Kennedy assassination? This history will certainly be rewritten someday if and when new facts are unearthed. My experience of 15 years as a Living History Reenactor with the 7th Illinois Volunteer Cavalry (another story) gave me an appreciation for how the people of the time endured, suffered and lived as best they could in a now popular time. More than once I had a deja vu experience. I had taken my mother to see Joshua Chamberlain's home in Maine and visited the hospital in City Point, Virginia with her. Subsequently, I learned from the internet that her father, George A. Ramsdell, had been named for an uncle who fought in the 20th Maine under Colonel Chamberlain. He was a corporal in company H of the Union Army at the time of the Little Round Top at Gettysburg. Company H was positioned in the middle of the defensive hook at the top of Little Round Top. He had as a sergeant died at City Point hospital of wounds received at Peebles Farm just before the surrender at Appomattox Court House. She never knew, nor did her father also, what significance his name had with American history. How great a discovery this was for me! After so long as a reenactor to find a relative so close to home and family is a tremendous adrenalin rush. A man without a legacy had finally left his mark on history, my personal history. Thus was born my respect for all that precedes us.

I grew up in the shadow of the famous authors Kenneth Roberts and his mentor, Booth Tarkington. My mother's close friend was Mr. Roberts' niece and secretary for many of his books, Marjorie Mosser Ellis, of Kennebunkport, Maine. Roberts wrote *Arundel* about the march of Benedict Arnold through the Maine woods with Aaron Burr to Quebec in 1775 during the American Revolution, a story retold here later. I sailed daily past the old docks where Booth Tarkington had used a coastal schooner, like the ones my ancestors built and sailed. I remember the old hulk before it was scuttled. My grandmother cherished her antique decorated chairs and a Tiffany Lamp from their estates. Although I did not know it then, the seeds of historical inquiry were sown.

My respect for truth and learning have its roots in my schooling at The Phillips Exeter Academy and the Harkness round table form of discussion and analysis as a method of education. Subsequently my Yale College education through the then pass fail grading system left no extraneous competitive rewards for learning. Then my Yale Medical School education without grades or exams instilled the last desire for truth for its own sake. My interest in history started my senior year at Yale where the elective Russian Communist and Chinese History courses were the rave of the undergraduate. But not until a seasoned genealogist, John Hunt, encouraged me to publish a listing of the casualties of The Battle of Lake George, the first, and often neglected by historians, battle of the French and Indian War, did my interest in writing history begin. The absentees from the muster rolls of the British colonist militias did not reflect their ultimate sacrifice. Only upon delving into the individual town histories were the names of the losses revealed for compilation. James Fenimore Cooper's, *Last of the Mohicans*, relates a story set a year later than this battle in the same arena, where many of my ancestors fought and some died. The opening scene of the popular movie version shows a friendly Indian racing through the woods towards history. The rhythm of the music resonates with the beat of my heart. This is history coming alive for me.

Subsequent publications in the Connecticut Nutmegger were treatises on interesting family history. One, a widow of an American surgeon who died at Fort Ticonderoga early in the Revolutionary War, married a British seaman during the war, surely a story needing revelation. Two Michael Smiths emerged. One sailed with John Paul Jones around the British Isles while at the same time the other across the Atlantic fought with the Massachusetts Navy at the Battle of Penobscot Bay. One was a prisoner of the British and the other captured by the Americans. Another paper told of the movements and persecution of the early Baptist Church and the Fullers and Fairchilds who fought with the British and lived near the Battle of Saratoga. They tried to remain in northern New York after the war was over, but the hatred of the Tory forced them to flee to Ontario, British Canada. Then the United Empire Loyalists of Canada, the equivalent of the Sons of the American Revolution, both groups to which I have belonged, had no knowledge of the New York origins of another early settler of Ontario, Abraham Smith. The Genealogical and

Historical Quarterly of Orange County, New York published my Hegira in four installments. Abraham had told a small white lie to help his family establish a homestead in Ontario. He claimed a loss of 1100 acres in the War. In fact his mother had lost that land in 1771 before the War of Independence to a border dispute between New Jersey and New York. He had spent the war trying to survive imprisonment by both the Americans and the British and helped Loyalists cross hostile lines in his wagon and even drove in the hospital corps of the French army in New York. He had to flee persecution and threat of death by his neighbors and own family in New Jersey after the war first to Nova Scotia and then Ontario. These Loyalists, or Tories as we Americans call them, half of my blood line, could not survive the war and its aftermath unscathed. As you will soon read other Loyalists fared much better, including the ultimate Loyalist of all.

What does history tell us? Often, we must read between the lines in order to get the gist. Other papers of mine illustrate this point. A relative, 40 at that time, enlisted with his son in the American army in Boston to fight the British and Canadians in the War of 1812. He neglected to list his birthplace which his son readily stated on his next line as Boston; an oversight, perhaps, or purposeful deception. At 20, this man may have participated in Shays' Rebellion of western Massachusetts, to which some attribute the formation of a permanent federal army, universal currency and more powers to the federal government. Being born in Connecticut, Cornelius Wheeler had emigrated Eastward toward the rural suburbs of Boston, rather than the usual Westward pull of most ordinary emigrants of Connecticut. The one omission on an enlistment roll gave the clue to the reason for his location. A man so adventurous at age 20 to participate in a most popular insurrection, would then leave his 12 children and wife intestate for a War further afield at a then ripe old age of 40. Cornelius literally lost his life on the fields of my Canadian ancestors, Greens and Haughns at the Battle of Lundy's Lane near Niagara, Ontario, Canada. Massachusetts had pardoned the Shay's rebels but not the neighboring states from whence he came to hide among his old line of Concord Wheelers.

Why attempt to correct history? The following as yet unpublished revelation illustrates that point. I told you about my grandfather's name originating in a granduncle lost during the Civil War without a family. The often considered father of modern American genealogy, Donald Lines Jacobus, published a genealogy of the Bulkeley Family considered a significant source for New England families, including the Presidents

Bush family, tracing heritage to mother England. The study of history is the never ending search for the truth.

In the book on the *Bulkley Genealogy* Jacobus states that a Captain Charles Bulkeley, born 28Oct1724 at Littleton, Mass., died unmarried at Halifax, Nova Scotia in 1757. (Charles' brother, Joseph was killed at the battle of Lake George in 1755, referenced above). Actually, Charles was the same Captain Bulkley who survived the Louisburg campaign in 1757 and died at the Battle on Snow Shoes near Crown Point, New York, under Robert Rogers Rangers in 13Mar1758 one month before his will was proved in Littleton, Mass., not as stated in Jacobus' *Bulkley Genealogy*. The full documentation is below as an addendum.

An interesting story discovered in 2000 of the encounter between Yale University graduate, Nathan Hale, and Robert Rogers during the Revolution on Long Island led to the former's capture and execution as a spy. It is reported that Nathan met Robert Rogers on Long Island during Nathan's infiltration behind British lines. Nathan mistook Rogers for a Rebel and confided in him about his mission. Rogers, a Loyalist, turned Hale over to the British. Hale was hung on September 22, 1776 on Manhattan Island just after the Americans had relinquished it to the British. His last words have been reported as, *"I only regret that I have but one life to lose (give) for my country."* This quotation originated from the play, *Cato*, by Joseph Addison, 1713.

Some attribute the conflagration of New York City which consumed one quarter of the city including Trinity Church on the same day as his capture on September 21, 1776 to Nathan Hale whose identical statues stand at Yale University Old Campus in front of Connecticut Hall and at C.I.A. Headquarters and in front of City Hall on Manhattan with the above inscribed words. It was General Washington's desire to deny the British Army the comfort of New York housing during their occupation of the City which Continental Congress vehemently overruled. As the new nation's first spy casualty, was Hale the instrument of Washington's wishes to start the fire, our nation's first covert action? To this day no one knows for sure if Hale caused the fire.

Robert Rogers' Rangers were about as popular during the French and Indian War as our Navy Seals or Green Beret are today. Though he died a destitute and fallen man after the Revolutionary War, Robert Rogers was a war hero of mythical proportion, much like General Joshua Chamberlain became during and after the Civil War and their memoirs were popular reading. Robert Rogers neglects to name Lieutenant and then Captain Bulkley's first name in his accounts of the battles. But I reveal it to you here.*

To my collaborator and tireless researcher, Norma Perdue, a rightful heir to the Robert Edwards land, I owe the seminal idea for this book and the initiative for its creation. To Mercedes Bujans, I owe many thanks for her motivation and tireless encouragement, and my deepest love, and a special accolade for the creation of this book's cover. To Professor emeritus Donald B. Cole, PhD of the History Department at The Phillips Exeter Academy, alma mater of authors Gore Vidal and Dan Brown, I give my fondest respect for his constructive criticism of this text. I shared four memorable years with his lovely family at Langdell Hall. To Walter Penny B.B.A., doctor of amateur historians, my special thanks for an enthusiastic read of this book. To Blair Bergstrom and her consort, Donald Needham D.V.M., my dearest friends, I give my thanks for their tireless ears. From Norma Perdue our thanks go to librarian, Mary Merenda and staff at Dunnellon and Lorain and staff at the Genealogical Library of Palm Beach County, Florida Public Libraries and the Family History Center Library at the Church of Latter Day Saints in Ocala, Florida.

I have coined the descriptive title for what I do, Genealogical Historian. In this way I shall attempt to show you that through names, family ties, and good old fashioned patronization, blood is thicker than water. Through this will history unfold for you as well. Happy reading.

*Addendum:

CAPTAIN CHARLES BULKELEY AND ROBERT ROGERS' BATTLE ON SNOWSHOES
A review of *The Battle on Snowshoes*, Bob Bearor, author
By Alan J. Clark, M.D.

Bob Bearor of French descent brings a fresh interpretation of Major Robert Rogers from the perspective of the French Canadians who fought him. In particular Jean-Baptiste Levreault de Langis de Montegron, or Langy, was victorious over Rogers in three out of four engagements between their forces. In the final encounter in 1760 Langy ambushed Rogers at the same five-mile point between Ticonderoga and Crown Point where Rogers had been so successful in earlier years and took his party of unarmed recruits with muskets stored in the sleigh. Rogers left behind 3,961 pounds of his own money, from which, although not said, one could imply led to the debts which placed him ultimately in debtors' prison in England where he died in 1790.

Even more refreshing is the description of conditions at the time of the battle and all the factors of equipment, clothing, supplies, and personnel from the perspective of a reenactor who has endured the same conditions. Bob Bearor, as reenactor, historian, and woodsman brings to life the people and events of this time. He analyzes the truth and mythmaking of history. His description of Rogers' Rock puts to bed any hope that Rogers could have slid down its face. This is not a dry retelling of Rogers own bravado.

But even more, the genealogist has an opportunity to correct some inaccuracy of the past. In particular a Captain Bulkeley is said to have perished in the Battle on Snowshoes when the second French and Indian force subsequently engulfs the initially victorious British Colonial force in the battle's notorious turn of events. Noted genealogist, Donald Lines Jacobus, in his Bulkeley Genealogy, pages 147-8, relates a Captain Joseph Bulkeley, born 7 Sep 1670 at Concord, MA, died at Littleton, MA, 24 Sep 1748; married 2nd, 25 May 1713 Silence Jeffrey who survived at Harvard, MA. in 1778.

Their children:

Silence, born 1716, m. Simon Davis, tanner of Harvard

Joseph, born 1719, killed 8Sep1755 at Battle of Lake George

Charles, born 28 Oct 1724, died unmarried at Halifax, Nova Scotia, in 1757. His will, dated there 1 Aug 1757 was proved 12 Apr 1758 in Middlesex Co. MA., where-in he styled himself of Littleton, "Captain of a company of Rangers in His Majesty's service in the forces commanded by the Earl of Loudoun."

Jacobus does not cite proof that Captain Charles Bulkeley died at Halifax in 1757, at the attempt to take Fortress Louisbourg. On page 32, Bearor states that Rogers and most of his Rangers embarked on that same abortive campaign in the summer of 1757. This placed both men in the same theatre under the same command of Lord Loudoun. The fact that Charles' will is not proved until one month after the death of Captain Bulkeley on 13Mar1758 at the Battle on Snowshoes at Ticonderoga supports the idea that both the Captain Bulkeley of Robert Rogers' command and Jacobus' Captain Charles Bulkeley of Louisbourg are one and the same.

Further investigation reveals Charles Bulkeley of Littleton, Mass. served on the Eastern Frontier 8/1-8/30/1748 under Captain Elisa Meldon, and 4/23-10/1/1754 as 1st Lieutenant on the Eastern Frontier in Captain Phineas Osgood's company in the regiment of Colonel Winslow. No mention of later service is given. But Robert Rogers himself mentions Lieutenant Buckley (sic) of Captain Hobbs Company of Rangers at Lake George on January 23, 1757. Later Rogers calls him Lieutenant Bulkley, whom he promotes to Captain upon the death of Captain Hobbs in a letter to Major General James Abercrombie before April 22, 1757. The best evidence is that Rogers mentions Captains Stark's and Buckley's companies with his own embarked from Sandy Hook, New Jersey for Halifax, Nova Scotia, June 20,1757 arriving by July 3rd upon the instructions of Lord Loudoun made through James Abercrombie, Aide de Camp. This places Captain Bulkley of Rogers Rangers at Halifax, Nova Scotia at the time of the making of the will of Captain Charles Bulkeley of Littleton, Massachusetts on August 1st, 1757.

Citations:
Bob Bearor, The Battle on Snowshoes, (Heritage Books, Bowie, Maryland, 1997)

Donald Lines Jacobus, Bulkeley Genealogy, (Tuttle, Mcreehouse and Taylor Co., New Haven, Conn.1933)

Robert Rogers, Journals of Major Robert Rogers, (London, England, 1765, 1966).

Nancy S. Noye, ed., Massachusetts Officers in the French and Indian Wars, 1748-63, (Boston, Mass., 1975)

Robert E. Mackay, ed., Massachusetts Soldiers in the French and Indian Wars, 1744-55, (NEHGS, Boston, Mass., 1978).

Alan J. Clark, M.D., Casualties of the Battle of Lake George, 8September1755, The Connecticut Nutmegger, (Connecticut Genealogical Society, Glastonbury, Conn, Dec.1997).

INTRODUCTION: God's Divine Gift, (Aaron Burr's Theodosia (e), or The Supremacy of Royal Heredity)

Popular history has it that when the Revolutionary War was over the British Army left the American Colonies and with it went most all Tories or Loyalists to the Monarchy. Those that remained were forced to leave later at the threat of losing their lives. Most also lost their holdings and real estate in the colonies by confiscation. Less widely known is the fact that many Loyalists slipped back into the United States in later years and took up where they had left off before the War of Independence. The economic benefit to the Crown derived from the colonies likewise one would imagine ceased with the end of the war as did the economic responsibility or drain on the Monarchy.

The prolonged hatred between the British sympathizers in Canada and in the original colonies below erupted into the War of 1812. Before that there were many confrontations upon the high seas between ships from both countries. Given these two facts one wonders how the return of the British sympathizers to their former financial status in the colonies would go unnoticed or commented on by the newly formed United States Government, its representatives and executives.

One wonders who was in the know or should have been. Was there collusion or at the very least a turning of a blind eye and a deaf ear to what was going on in Manhattan, the economic center of the new United States, then and now. Especially, why did The King of England warmly receive the first emissary to England from the new United States in the form of the most rabble rousing of the Rebels, John Adams of Boston. Was there something going on behind the scenes that even today no one talks about? A little in-joke or dirty little secret that only those in the know knew but never talked about.

When the current Queen of England visited Manhattan in 1976, she was likewise warmly received especially by the Crown's former religious charges in the Episcopal Church in Manhattan, Trinity Church. She was given a symbolic basket of produce and many unusual, perhaps knowing smiles. The basket contained exactly 279 peppercorns representing the one peppercorn rent charged by the lease of the Queen's Farm for each year of the Royal charter of the Trinity Church Corporation in 1697. The symbolism of payment of back rent cannot be dismissed as quaint. Rather it has profound significance under the Feudal European system of Quit Rent; the representation of allegiance and subservience to the all powerful and all determinant Monarchy from which all privilege of ownership derives. The Trinity Church Corporation is demonstrating its deference to and recognition of the ultimate authority and ownership of its holdings in the North American continent. *"A pepper-corn, in acknowledgement of the right, is of more value than millions without it."* said George Grenville, adviser to King George III in the 1760s. In other words the symbolism of fealty to the Crown granted more rights than possession of the fruits of gain in that one holding at the behest of the Crown. Thus the right to do business in Manhattan far outreached the monetary value of that transaction which led to the right of location in the heart of North American Commerce. From the very beginning, the fur trade, then the Erie Canal deposited the wealth of the expanding United States in the early 19th Century at the doorstep of Manhattan. With its railroads and seaport and most of all as the money center of the New World for the Dutch and the English who swallowed them up, the place to do business was on a small island at the mouth of the Hudson River.

The favor of doing business on Manhattan Island has no value but in the acknowledgement of its originator, the Crown of England. Without that privilege to locate one's business there was no advantage. Without the favoritism of the Crown there was no privilege. If one understands this one fact then all else makes perfect sense. What flows from the Crown must ultimately return there however circuitous a route. This is the essence of the feudal system forever invoked by the Royal owners of Europe.

What we do know is that the colonists kept many of the old traditions, laws, religions and forms of government of the mother country. It would then make sense that there still remained a twinge of feeling for the roots of the populace then dominating the United States. Even today the

American people watch in curiosity if not in awe the marriage of a Prince and Princess, the drama of their lives and sorrowful deaths.

At the close of the American Revolution there were no official laws of separation. In fact the confiscation laws of Tory property of the colonies were revoked by the new Congress and the Treaty of Paris. The reinstatement in 1784 of the corporate charter of Trinity Church in New York State left essentially everything previous to the war intact except its reference and deference to the Crown of England as an extension of the Anglican Church of England, yet even today many of the ministerial heads, priests and bishops, of the separated American Episcopalian, once Anglican Church are trained in Scotland. This reinstated corporate charter of Trinity Church was engineered by none other than the notorious Aaron Burr of The Duel and Treason Trial fame.

Then when can one date the separation of the economic power of Europe especially England from the United States? The end of the Revolutionary War in 1783? The end of the War of 1812 in 1814? The end of the American Civil War in 1865? The Crash of the American Stock Market in 1929? The 9/11 Attack on the World Trade Center in 2001? Who's to say that it doesn't still exist? How is the question? By what means? And to what extent? We shall see that the principal players of the American Revolution were instrumental in maintaining the status quo and even encouraged further investment of Europe in the United States in spite of the popular dislike and distrust of the average American for all that was European. There still remained pockets of wealthy Americans who wished to revert back to the close ties of America and England because they had and still were gaining economic advantage in trade with Europe. One such group was called High Federalists. In contrast at the close of the 18th century there were the agrarian based economists or Jeffersonian Republicans who wanted nothing to do with European power or wealth and wished America to remain bucolic. In the next century these same Jeffersonians would support trade with Europe. They abhorred the centralization of the American economy and government and resisted the industrialization of North America in the guise of Emancipation of the Slave.

Both Aaron Burr and Alexander Hamilton played to the drums of these groups, but for different goals. Burr sought personal aggrandizement in carving out an empire for himself with the High Federalists in New England in the governor's race of New York in 1804 and alternately in 1805 from the western lands of North America once owned by Spain and France. Alexander Hamilton had a vision of a strong United States dependent on the wealth of Europe to sustain itself as an industrialized nation with a centralized banking system and Federalist government.

Both men were founders of the New York State Manumission Society, yet Aaron Burr never freed his many slaves, not in his will in anticipation of the Duel nor thirty years later. Alexander Hamilton also owned slaves at his death in 1804 but espoused their gradual release which in fact had begun in 1799 for all blacks born after that year.

If Aaron Burr was tried for treason in 1807, when did he become treasonous? Certainly anyone who becomes a traitor is one far before he is caught, usually years. This uncertain fact we shall see weighs heavily on the character of one key player, Aaron Burr.

What this book will attempt to show is that there is still a serious financial dependency between the two countries that really never ended nor even temporarily ceased with the end of the Revolutionary War. English brethren kept close watch over each other, as even today. Blood is thicker than the gulf of the Atlantic Ocean that separates us. Wealth and family ties or breeding meant everything then, as it still does today. A foreign publisher is quoted, *"It would not be possible to trace ownership of corporations and the power structure in the United States... The Government control... functions through a maze of personal contacts and tacit understandings."*

A word of direction and explanation about the organization of this book is warranted. I have written this book not only to reveal new original theory on the interactions of Aaron Burr and Alexander Hamilton during the Revolutionary War and during the early formation of the United States up to the famous duel and Treason Trial of Aaron Burr, but to give relevance to the present time of what history preceded. Thus, I will not only interject current locations of property discussed as I feel they are important to the reader's understanding, but from a genealogical frame of reference give the reader sources to do one's own research about one's own family. As a classical historian might object to the antithesis of the chronological approach to the facts, a genealogist might understand that research is often done in reverse and not in sequential time. I feel I must introduce the reader with average or no special knowledge of the period and prominent figures to the story, yet I also assume anyone interested in this period of American History would have already read the current most recent bibliography and thus find the reorganization of the facts refreshing and unique. Likewise, I must work in the reverse from common ground, such as the facts of the Treason Trial of Aaron Burr and sometimes his letters to develop the theories and show how they evolve. Some chapters will investigate relationships of several people or groups and seem out of sequence, but it is the theory not the history that dictates placement.

To this end the book has chapter summaries for one to pick and choose and three major divisions. The first part is introductory and sets the theme of the book. The second chapter is genealogical. The third and fourth chapters are introductory to bring the reader up to speed with the principal characters especially without the current bibliography under one's belt. The remainder of the second section is the meat of the story for amateur and professional history buffs. This is where you will get the most novel and stimulating, hopefully intriguing arguments. The last section will be inclusive, but the epilogue will leave you gasping for air. The latter is where I am allowed to play with your mind a little and stir your imaginations. This book represents my interpretation of facts and letters revealed in my research and the piecing together of seemingly disparate events into a story plausible to me. What if I'm right! Or will we ever know? Don't miss the prologue!

Note: This book contains its own cipher. Hint: To decode one must read the whole book.

Prologue: The Blockhouse

Light was falling in the late afternoon. It was bitterly cold on the last day of the year, 1775. Snow was falling steadily all day and lay lightly over the icy base at least three feet deep upon the riverbank.

Inside the home of John Coffin were gathered men from many backgrounds, French artisans, a silversmith, weaver, a British sea captain and his band of sailors. John, himself recently arrived from Boston that last August bringing with him his family and business aboard his own ship, was a merchant and brewer. He had purposely purchased the home on the banks of the St. Lawrence for his brewery, outside but at the base of the walls of the City of Quebec.

They could see their breath as they talked ever so lowly as to not be heard beyond the walls of this stone house. The smell of brewing beer permeated the home. There was no fire because smoke would give away their presence.

Someone, perhaps Francois Chabot, whispered in French, *"They're coming."*

John Coffin approached the slit in the wall and peered out into the blinding snow. Forms of men were struggling to raise their knees forward in order to make a path in the waist deep snow. *"Let them approach so I can see the whites of their eyes."* He was mocking the valiant stand of the Patriots at Breed's Hill earlier that year before he left his hometown, Boston.

Captain Adam Barnfare interjected, *"I'm in charge here."*

"Lieutenant-colonel Allan McClean has given you your orders." John Coffin suppressed his objection.

"See there Louis (Louis Alexander Picard), *the tall man on the right is your target. God make you accurate. On the left the tricorner hat is yours Picard. The man in the white coat, the shorter one in front is not to be harmed on punishment of death. Is that clear?"*

Captain Barnfare, *"They make their way towards us as if we are a mirage!"*

"They expect no resistance, since they have had none to now. Captain, make your sailors shoot at the crowd behind but no one is to attempt to injure the lead. Am I clear?" Coffin insisted.

Barnfare, *"I never would have expected a British naval officer to take orders from a new recruit in the militia."*

Coffin, *"I have special intelligence no one else is to know about."*

"John, they are near enough to snuff out an eye." Picard reported.

"Oui, allez nous on." The two French marksmen squeezed off one round apiece and both the men flanking the shorter man in the white coat and beaver hat dropped to the ground like fallen trees. The rest of the block house erupted in flames and smoke as the rest of the mass of men either dropped in their tracks or turned to flee a few paces before being dispatched in the back. Only the white coat now imperceptible in the blizzard remained standing. Immediately the crack of riffles from the walls of the city broke the silence from within the blockhouse. The man in white picked up the fallen comrade to his left and draped both arms over his shoulders from behind and turned toward the riverbank from whence they had come, laboring under the weight of the massive limp body draped over his back. The dull thud of spent bullets pocked the back of the moving target to no effect on the locomotive. He disappeared over the crest of the rise of the bank and dropped the body unceremoniously behind him.

"Aaron, Aaron, are you all right? Where are the others? Your arm is bleeding. Let me help you back to camp. Is all lost?" The Reverend Samuel Spring of Newburyport, the American chaplain in Benedict Arnold's army helped his friend and former Princeton classmate from the field.

Part One: The Loyalists

Chapter One: The Dispossessed

Something is not right!

Of all the confiscations of Loyalists in New York in 1782-3, some 670 persons, only 16 (a mere two percent of the total confiscations for the whole state) were in Manhattan, Queens or Kings Counties of Long Island. Two of these fifteen were tavern keepers, three military men, and 4 yeomen, 1 farmer, 1 cordwainer or shoemaker, and one a merchant of New York proper, so significant his name is mentioned here as Waldron Blauw, a merchant related to the Cruger family, international Dutch and British merchants pivotal to this story. Several of the others were descendants of families of the original Dutch settlers on Manhattan Island in the 1620s such as Abraham Rapeljie. Others were from Dutch families who had sworn allegiance to the British in 1676, Gerret Williamson, Dowe Van Dyne, Samuel Striker, Johannis Stothoff, and Johannus Remsen. Among all the rest of the 670 only a few at best were professional men, a few physicians and lawyers and a banker, and very few merchants. The majority were farmers and laborers, yeomen, or skilled craftsmen, blacksmiths, wheelwrights, weaver, surveyor, tailors, innkeepers, shoemakers, carpenters, and boatmen. What is conspicuously absent from this list are names from New York City proper or Long Island and especially persons of significant wealth and land holdings. Considering that there were many Loyalists in both places during the war while the British Army maintained control until the 1783 surrender it is inconceivable that the legislature in Albany would overlook this den of British sympathizers, and not be aware of the names of such persons and their property.

How did these people of New York City avoid the backlash of hatred for all that was British sweeping the rest of the newly independent colonies? The hangings and tar and feather denigration of others in public, with subsequent forced emigration to Canada or England, must have happened outside the most populated areas. Well for one, the British Army was present in New York City and Long Island until the end of the war. But not until 1786 did the citizens themselves flee to Nova Scotia at first, and then in the 1790s to Ontario. It seems the countryside populated by the poor and unskilled was where most of these acts of hatred and revenge occurred and where the confiscations were most likely to proceed with vigor.

In October, 1779 Tory lawyers were barred from practice which gave the newly minted lawyers, Alexander Hamilton, Robert Troup and Aaron Burr, more than enough business for their practices after the Revolution. New York passed in 1784 a law banning the right to vote and hold office to those who served in the British Army, officeholders under the British occupation, abandoned the state or joined the British during the war. This disenfranchised two thirds of the inhabitants of the City and Richmund County of New York. Hamilton was instrumental in repeal of this law two years later and in 1792 banished Loyalists were allowed to return to New York but the confiscation of their property by the state was not overturned.

Alexander Hamilton negotiated the withdrawal of the British from New York and was a staunch advocate for moderation in the treatment of the Loyalists, *"make it the interest of those citizens, who, during the revolution, were opposed to us to be friends to the new government, by affording them not only protection, but a participation in its privileges, and they will undoubtedly become its friends",*

There must have been other less obvious reasons for the insulation of the staunch New York Loyalists of wealth and means in New York City. Even the most noted Loyalists, the army of Butler's Rangers, seem to have avoided the list of confiscations by some hand of divine providence, or was it not divine? Many of the notable officers of the Loyalist Army, Oliver De Lancey, John Harris Cruger, John Watts, Edward Jessup, Sir John Johnson, and John Butler had already been named in the Act of Attainder of October 22, 1779 which had been in the works since June of 1778 but not all seem to have lost property. The James De Lancey family owned 350 acres of the north eastern half of the island of Manhattan which was divided up after the war and sold to average American citizens, although nearly half went to about fifteen wealthy Whig or Rebel merchants.

To us now everything should seem black and white, Loyalist or Revolutionary. But like all civil and revolutionary wars there are no clear dividing lines among families and friends, neighbors and acquaintances. Surely, family came first before politics. Most citizens of the day were related to England in some recent past. And the main motivation for separation from England was avoidance of laws and taxation of Parliament and was not total rejection of English traditions or even the King.

The Treaty of Paris in 1783 stipulated fair treatment of Loyalists in America and compensation for loss and cessation of further confiscations. Even the staunchest of principal Revolutionaries, John Adams, wrote repeatedly from Paris to Congress to live up to these peace terms, which Congress refused to do. Adams felt that this neglect would later haunt America with more troubles with England. As a direct result of mistreatment of the Loyalists in the United States, Britain refused to vacate its forts in the Ohio Valley which it was supposed to do by the Treaty. Indeed trouble started to occur upon the high seas when English ships began impressing American seamen into British service leading to a second War with England in 1812.

This looming trouble between Great Britain and the United States encouraged Congress in 1798 to form its first army under retired ex-President Washington with second in command, Alexander Hamilton. Even Abigail Adams along with many others felt this to be a dangerous move. Hamilton was the effective commander of the new army whereas George Washington was too old to be other than a figure head. When Hamilton formed a plan to seize Spanish Louisiana with the help of the British Navy, Abigail thought him an American style Napoleon.

But Hamilton had already shown his stripes. As a lawyer in New York City he had helped many Loyalists regain their property. Washington had chosen Hamilton as his number two in command against outspoken opposition from many in Congress. Hamilton had been instrumental in the first cabinet, forming the first Bank of the United States as first secretary of the Treasury under Washington and before that, the Bank of New York. Both banks had many known Loyalists and Britons as investors and board members. This was the reason in 1811 for Congress not renewing the charter of this first Bank of the United States. America was without a central bank until 1816 for that same reason, fear of foreign control.

Alexander Hamilton, Washington's right hand man had obvious British sympathies. This is so because he owed his allegiance to England, just as the Dutch had sworn in 1676. Both owed their financial wellbeing to English wealth. Hamilton had been brought from the Caribbean at age 15 and adopted by a Dutch family, the Knoxs and Crugers in New York

City, to work in their businesses where he learned the trade of money and English law which he adapted to the first banks of New York and the United States. Hamilton had ties to the Dutch who remained loyal to the Crown of England and the wealthy of New York through these early business experiences. The fact that after the Revolutionary War he continued to help these British loyalists regain their holdings in New York suggests that perhaps during the War he might not have been that partisan or anti-British either. So might he not have been instrumental in helping these same people during the war avoid the same losses he helped these Loyalists regain after the war? How, you ask? He was aide-de-camp of Washington during the war. Was he a traitor? Or did Washington know of these matters and acquiesce. It seems inconceivable that Washington did not know something of the way Loyalists avoided loss of their property during the war, as surely Hamilton did.

There is no indication that either Washington or Hamilton did anything overt to disrupt the lives of peaceful Tories. Washington was not squeamish about enforcing military justice and he hanged many deserters and some of the plotters of his abduction in Manhattan early in the war. He court-martialed his disloyal officers like General Lee at Monmouth, yet he was ready to forgive even General Benedict Arnold after his run in with the Continental Congress and Arnold's own military censure for profiteering from his post as military commander at Philadelphia. This readiness to forgive was out of necessity to keep qualified and aggressive military officers like Benedict Arnold employed in his army. This type of officer he sorely needed. Yet it was also a vulnerability because these same officers with bigger than life egos would almost be his downfall. Benedict Arnold would shortly after this act of compassion disappoint his commanding general at the attempt to turn over his newly appointed West Point Command to the British for money and promotion into the British Army. Other officers as we shall see would play a different but just as dangerous a role to the floundering nascent United States. General James Wilkinson present at both Quebec and Saratoga battle fields with General Arnold would later become secret agent of Spain and plotter of secession with another officer, Colonel Aaron Burr in 1805, who likewise followed Arnold into the Maine woods bound for Quebec in 1775. It is the latter colonel who would be that secret agent of the Loyalist during and after the Revolutionary War, not Alexander Hamilton.

When one looks at the dealings of all these Loyalists, another name keeps popping up, Trinity Church. Trinity Church started in 1697, got its first land grant from Queen Anne of England on June 27, 1704, as an Anglican Church of England. During the Revolution this charter was nullified by Continental Congress in 1775 and when reformed in 1784 as Episcopalian all ties with the Crown and England were supposed to have been broken. But in fact these ties persist to this day. Trinity Church is most likely a land bank for the Crown of England, then and possibly even now. It is no small wonder that Hamilton, who had helped many loyalists and even Trinity after the war, is buried in the graveyard at Trinity Church. The Cruger brothers were merchants, justices of New York and vestrymen of the Episcopal Church of Trinity. During the Revolution the Cruger brothers gave holdings of 80 acres and 77 acres to the church which they had no authority to do as mere leaseholders except by time limited sublease. Colonel Aaron Burr of the American army was co-lessee of the 80 acre transaction just before the Battle of Monmouth in June, 1778. Two days after he retired from the army because of ill health this 80 acre lease was turned over to Trinity Church while its charter was still voided by Continental Congress. After the war that same land was returned to Aaron Burr by a 69 year lease. It seems that in other cases where Revolutionary heirs appear, these holdings were not relinquished except to Loyalist descendants even if they were not a direct lineage.

It is inconceivable that the powers of the day did not know of these transactions and thus turned a blind eye. Where the land was retained by Trinity through the years its value increased with the leasehold improvements which in the Depression years through defaulted loans and leases reverted to the owner until today it represents some of the most valuable land and property in the United States, lower Manhattan near Wall Street. Even today those that should know must be aware of the British leanings of Trinity Church Corporation. And where does the wealth that is generated by these vast holdings ultimately rest? It might very well rest by inference with the original grantor, The Crown of England.

How is this so? Those same trustees of the Bank of New York and later the First Bank of the United States of America formed the Bank of Nova Scotia in 1786 upon fleeing New York City. They came back years later to resume their businesses in New York with the help of Hamilton and Trinity Church and ultimately the Crown of England. Even today the Queen of England acknowledges she gets much of her income from the Bank of Nova Scotia. In the 1984 it appears that Rupert Murdock bought two properties 217 and 225 Broadway Street from Trinity Church with money loaned from the National Bank of Tennessee. He presumably deposited this money in a new closely held Bank or Trust in Nova Scotia Mr. and Mrs. Murdock formed shortly thereafter in 1987. Later these properties were placed in the Trinity Holdings Company of British Columbia in 1993.

What this ultimately shows is loyalty is rewarded. Certainly, loyalty to the Crown is rewarded by protecting and maintaining one's wealth. In this case Trinity Church is likely an agent of the Crown counter to its current charter, but true to its original charter. During the War and shortly thereafter the holdings of Loyalists could have been deposited with Trinity Church in safekeeping from confiscation by the Revolutionary zealots until such time as it was safe to return, whereupon, the property could be returned to the original owners or their loyalist heirs. If loyalist heirs did not exist the property reverted to the original grantor dating back to the Queen Anne era, the Crown through its agent, Trinity Church, acting as land bank. This might then generate income for the Crown in trade in kind with other wealthy Loyalists.

Thus when John Adams first met with the King of England, as America's first ambassador to England, he was surprised at the warm reception and conciliatory attitude of the King. The King already knew he had removed the burden of supporting an army to protect the colonies and the headache of financing it through collection of taxes there. The King probably still retained his financial holdings and growing income from the remaining Loyalists in New York, which he and subsequent rulers fostered through dealings with Trinity Church, still an Anglican arm of the Crown.

What remains to do is show in depth how these dealings occurred and how they might still be occurring.

Chapter Two: The Families

Appendix B lists in alphabetical order over 550 names of those with real estate transactions with Trinity Church between 1760 and 1834. A great majority of these were 21, 69 or 99 year leases and not outright sales. This period involves the Revolution and time leading up to and subsequent to it wherein those families involved in the Revolution were active. The list is broken down into those with family connections with the De Lanceys, VanCortlands, and Heathcotes, descendants of the Duke of York, King James II. The latter two families are the maternal ancestry of the De Lancey family before the Revolution. The De Lancey family held many high offices of considerable influence in New York during this period. Prior to the war James De Lancey had been Judge and Governor of the Province of New York upon his death in 1741.

Stephen De Lancey had been Clerk of the City and County of Albany in 1765. Sister, Susannah (1707-71) was daughter of Etienne (Stephen) De Lancey (1663-1741) the progenitor French Huguenot. Susannah was also sister of James, chief justice, also lieutenant governor of New York. She married in 1731 Admiral Sir Peter Warren who had obtained considerable property on Manhattan adjacent to but just north of the Robert Edwards and Elbert Herring (Haring) property obtained from Wouter Van Twiller who had acquired it before 1638. Sir Warren and Robert Edwards were both British Naval officers and privateers for the Crown of England. They used their three eighths bounty from their prizes to purchase these lands on Manhattan, most of which would eventually be returned to the Crown through deeds or leases to Trinity Church Corporation before and during the Revolutionary War. Admiral Peter Warren had been the commanding naval officer in the Louisbourg Campaign in Nova Scotia in 1745. He retired in 1747, died in 1752. Robert Edwards had seized a valuable Spanish galleon full of treasure about that time which made him very wealthy. He probably acquired the property from Sir Warren's heirs.

Joseph C. De Lancey had been Governor of New York during the confiscations of Loyalist lands in 1783, while Robert Edwards and Brigadier General Oliver De Lancey both were overt Loyalist in the Revolution. This family married into the Barclay, Livingston, Stuyvesant, Watts, De Peyster, Hunt, Cruger, Kennedy, Rynderts, Beresford, Dundas, Fraser, Kearny, Laight, Parsons, Cox, Wickham, Lawrence, Taylor, Franks, Izard, Tippett, Colden, Jones, Yates and Walton families. Son Major Oliver De Lancey Jr. served in the 17th Regiment of Light Dragoons. Cousins Lieutenant Colonel Stephen and Ensign James De Lancey served the Second De Lancey Battalion. Their sister, Susanne married Thomas Barclay, son of the Anglican head of Trinity Church in Manhattan, and Major in the American Loyal Regiment. Anne, daughter of Brigadier General Oliver De Lancey married Colonel John Harris Cruger who served with her father in the First De Lancey Battalion. Her brother Stephen De Lancey was Chief Justice of The Bahamas, and Governor of Tobago. Her sister, Charlotte, married Field Marshall Sir David Dundas. In addition, Brig. Gen. Oliver's sister, Anne, married John Watts, a Kings Council Member. Their daughter, Anne, married Archibald Kennedy at Trinity Church. The son, John Watts, Jr. died at his residence, 3 Broadway, New York City, original home of Oliver De Lancey. He is buried at Trinity Church.

From these connections it is clear that the De Lancey family held considerable power on both sides of the War for Independence and the political and financial health of New York. All these families were closely connected with the Anglican Church of England, especially Trinity Church, where many were married, and buried. They held Royal appointments even after the War of Independence and continued to hold close connections with the supposedly independent Episcopal Trinity Church of New York. Colonel James De Lancey former sheriff of Westchester County retreated to Nova Scotia in 1783 and in 1786 was involved in the determination of the King of England's compensation of Loyalist claims for loss in the colonies as a result of their loyalty to the King during the Revolutionary War.

Notable descendants of the grandparents of Stephen De Lancey, Stephanus Van Cortlandt and Gertruyd Schuyler are Robert Anderson, and Edward Montgomery Clift, Margaret Kemble, wife of General Thomas Gage, Stephen Watts Kearney, Alice De Lancey, wife of Ralph Izard, Anna Livingston Street, wife of Levi Parsons Morton, Susan Auguste

De Lancey, wife of James Fenimore Cooper, and wives of Clement Clark Moore, Walter Livingston, Robert Fulton, Henry Walter Livingston, Alexander Hamilton's wife, Elizabeth Schuyler, Cyrus Robert Vance's wife, Grace Elsie Sloan, Herman Melville, who is grandson of General Peter Gansevoort, Elisha Kent Kane, Caroline Webster Schermerhorn, mother of John Jacob Astor IV, John Jay, General Philip Schuyler, and his daughter Angelica, sister-in-law of Alexander Hamilton, and President Thomas Jefferson. From Stephenus Van Cortlandt's grandfather Jan Loockermans descend Cyrus Hall McCormick, Presidents Theodore Roosevelt and Franklin Delano Roosevelt and from grandson in law Wesel Ten Broeck descend Elizabeth Cady wife of Henry Stanton and Dore Stanton Blatch, wife of Lee DeForest; his granddaughter was wife of Philip Livingston, ancestor of Eleanor Roosevelt, wife of President Franklin Delano Roosevelt and great granddaughter Catherine Livingston mother of Stephen Van Rensselaer. From the Loockermans descend Phoebe Bayard, wife of Arthur St. Clair, Hamilton Fish, John Winthrop Chanler, and sons Lewis Stuyvesant Chanler and William Astor Chanler and wife of George Folsom, Margaret Cornelia Winthrop.

From this extensive but not exhaustive list one can get the extent of the importance and political reach of this early Dutch and English family. Many of these family members and relatives will show continued real estate dealings with Trinity Church (see addendum).

My ancestor, Abraham Smith, had been a spy and double agent for the Crown as a wagon master crossing the military line between the American and English armies in New York City outskirts and had been taken prisoner by both sides. He went to Nova Scotia in 1786 to lay claim to royal land for his loyal service which was denied by Colonel James De Lancey. Was this denial because he was not connected to the wealthy royal hierarchy above? Or was it because his service was so successfully secret to both sides? He was subsequently rewarded in 1790 in Ontario with 200 acres for himself and each of his sons.

The address of 3 Broadway, New York City a residence formerly of Oliver De Lancey which later became the home of the John Watts Jr. family after the War for Independence rests on the Queen's Farm. Next door at 5 Broadway Aaron Burr would make his law office. Aaron Burr would later lease property to John De Lancey on July 23, 1801 (book 114/page 500). Likewise, Peter De Lancey, father of Stephen, the Clerk of Albany before the War, had lived at Rosehill which subsequently became Aaron Burrs' mansion in Albany while he served at the Statehouse in his numerous positions appointed and elected. Aaron Burr was a law contemporary of Alexander Hamilton, who had been taken under the wing of the Henry Cruger family in the Caribbean islands as a boy and subsequently at age 15 in New York City. Nicholas Cruger also had an estate on Manhattan Island named Rosehill just north and east of Aaron Burr's Richmond Hill.

Reverend Henry Barclay was second rector of Trinity Church and died in 1784. His brother, Andrew was a successful New York merchant who married Helena Roosevelt whose brothers, Isaac and Jacobus, and their father, Jacobus, who was fourth great grandfather of President Franklin D. Roosevelt, took over Andrew's sugar works upon his death in 1775. Reverend Henry's wife was Maria Rutgers whose father, Anthony, owned a large farm, (Rutger's Farm granted by King George II, where Nathan Hale was hanged by the British as a spy), which is now East Broadway, and several breweries. Maria Rutgers had a sister, Elizabeth Rutgers, whom after the Revolutionary War in 1784 Aaron Burr and Robert Troup represented against a Joshua Waddington, defended by Alexander Hamilton in a dispute over one of these breweries. Their daughter, Cornelia married Colonel Stephen De Lancey, Chief Justice of the Bahamas and Governor of Tobago, whose sister Anne De Lancey married Colonel John Harris Cruger. Stephen and Anne were children of Brigadier General Oliver De Lancey. Son, Thomas Barclay, major in the loyalist army, married Susanna De Lancey, daughter of Peter, the clerk of Albany.

Thomas Barclay returned to the United States in 1789 and helped settle the boundary between Canada and the United States in Maine and was the first British Consul-General in New York in 1799. He also was American consul to Morocco in 1799 which shows how readily the Loyalists got back into American government and politics. In turn, their grandson Henry married Catherine Watts, daughter of Robert Watts. Their great-great grandchild was Franklin Delano Roosevelt. Bertram Peter Cruger, son of Nicholas, brother of Colonel John Harris Cruger and guardian of Alexander Hamilton, married as his second wife Mary Watts, another daughter of Robert.

The De Lancey family was closely connected to the Barclay and Cruger families who counted deacons and vestrymen of Trinity Church among their members, and incidentally to both Aaron Burr and Alexander Hamilton.

Appendix A is an alphabetical list of the confiscations of Loyalist property on Long Island and Manhattan in the State of New York in 1783 prior to the Treaty of Paris. Many listings show relatives who had subsequent deed transactions with Trinity Church. Of the fewer than 16 confiscations in predominantly Loyalist New York City and Long Island, all but one was returned to these families from Trinity holdings after the formation of the United States. Butler's Rangers were notoriously unpopular with the patriots for their use of Indians and waging war on the civilian population of northern New York in the King's service in northern New York Province. Yet interestingly enough, several of the officers received deeds from Trinity Church after the war as did those who served with De Lancey in Westchester County either directly or through their relatives (Appendix B).

How did this occur, one might ask? The Law of Attainder in 1779 confiscated 54 Loyalist properties in New York City. Later in 1783 the New York legislature chose to ignore by direct legislation the suggestion of the new Congress of the United States to stop all confiscations and seek to restore to the Loyalists that which they had lost before the Peace. It seems Trinity Church became the means by which this restoration was enacted in spite of the reticence of the state legislature. This dichotomy existed because the legislature was made up of representatives from the whole state, most of who were not of a mind to be charitable to any Loyalists especially from these latter groups of militants. Yet the predominantly Loyalist or Tory New York City had to rectify these losses by subterfuge. The former Anglican, now supposedly independent by new incorporation entitlement, Episcopalian Trinity Church of New York became one such vehicle. Essentially, it acted as a land bank.

But who determined the amount of restitution? There are no records forthcoming from the Church. One can doubt they really existed. Most of the records of the British occupation and earlier were removed to Nova Scotia with the withdrawal of the British Army from New York City at the close of the War. One can make a case that the directives of granting deeds to former Loyalists of the War from Trinity Church came directly from the King of England. In 1775-6 over two thirds of the 328,000 acres of land granted from the Hampshire Grants west of the Connecticut River, now Vermont, by the Crown of England through the royal governors of New York went to prominent loyalists. In fact this may have been seen as a safer location for land holdings by the Tories during the increasingly turbulent early war years. In addition Royal Governor Henry Moore in 1767 gave 24,000 acres in future Vermont for future income to King's College as did Governor William Tryon, who gave 10,000 acres in 1774 for the support of a municipal law professorship.

But how did Trinity obtain the land it so deeded afterwards? In 1775 Continental Congress stripped Trinity of its legal status. Further, any holdings turned over to it might be deemed illegal or invalid. In the case of Robert Edwards' land, John Cruger, vestryman of Trinity Church, after obtaining the 99 year lease gave Edwards' land to Trinity Church as if he owned it outright. This mechanism may have been a design of the Loyalists to hide the true ownership to avoid confiscation. Of the 484 transactions by Trinity as grantor to other individuals excluding other corporate entities in the years from 1790 to 1850, no comparable number of grantee records can be found to Trinity before 1790 or thereafter. Trinity Church Corporation is conspicuously absent from the grantee list of the records of the County Clerk of Manhattan! In other words, in the early 1800s Trinity just appears with a great number of grantor records for property that can not be accounted for, listing Trinity as prior recipient. Did Trinity not record these transactions? Were they obtained during the period when Trinity was not a legal entity under New York State Law during the Revolutionary War from Loyalists who wished to hide their ownership of property subject to confiscation acts of the New York Legislature in 1779 and 1783? Were they held by members of the church vestrymen or other members of the church and turned over to Trinity for disposal to the original grantors or their relatives when times were more propitious?

In 1857 Congress passed a law mandating recording of all deed transactions with the county clerk's office in each state. During this decade a flurry of recordings, pages long for a single individual, many as trustee for others now deceased, appears dating back many years even into the seventeenth century in Manhattan. This reveals the use of pocket deeds where the true ownership of land was not public knowledge. One wonders how the tax rolls were accurately administered. The use of triple net leases where the current leasee pays all expenses including taxes on the property probably sufficed to mollify the tax collector.

These deeds do not represent what the current understanding by the average American across the rest of the country thinks of as a warrantee deeds. Rather many of them are actually time limited ground leases. Any improvements on these properties are transferred by recorded deed up to the expiration of the ground lease whereupon all the improvements revert to the owner of the land itself, often with purchase by grantor. This is how one could enrich himself or his heirs with improvements on his land. More importantly one could influence the politics of the city by the subtle reminder of who really owned a large part of the land and whose wishes one had to pay attention to in order to renew the lease in the future. Appendix C shows the many different political influences Trinity Church can bring to bear through its various leases or deeds with nearly all the different religions, schools, fire departments, banks, and politicians of the city of Manhattan.

Just after the close of the war James De Lancey's 350 acre estate on the East River was broken up and sold to common citizens, artisans, and tenants. About fifteen buyers, including the wealthy Whigs William and James Beekman, four Livingstons, sugar refiner Isaac Roosevelt and merchants John Delameter, John Delafield, and Dominick Lynch, bought half of the property. Other Tory property confiscated and sold before 1788 included that of Oliver De Lancey, Isaac Low, Frederick Philipse, John Watts, Roger Morris, and William Bayard. Alexander Hamilton would die in the home of a William Bayard from a wound in the duel with Aaron Burr on July 11, 1804. A Henry Bayard was rector of Trinity Church. The Bayard property was returned to the family in 11 transactions with Trinity Church from 1825 to 1833 to four Bayard family members. Two Bayards, Robert and William, were directors of Hamilton's Bank of New York. A John Phillips in 1800, John L. Morris, and Helen Watts in 1816 also received deeds from Trinity perhaps representing compensation for their family losses at the hands of the New York Committee on Confiscations. Of the 484 listed Trinity grantor transactions in the late eighteenth and early nineteenth century more than 14%, 56 or more, went to direct relatives of the Loyalist De Lancey family and the Van Cortland, and Heathcote matriarchal relatives.

A whole town on the outskirts of then New York City owned and called by the family name of Embury or Embree, had been leased during the War thus avoiding confiscation and wound up deeded back to Effingham Embree in May or June of 1795. The whole town of Embury, all Loyalists, leased their land, left for Canada and came back to their land in March 16, 1809 returned from Trinity Church.

It becomes more obvious that Trinity Church is involved in returning confiscated land to Loyalists after the War of Independence. How it obtained these lands is not always clear, but in many cases leased land was turned over to the church from members of the church, vestrymen or parishioners, perhaps to avoid confiscation during the War. The control or direction of these transactions might have come from England and ultimately the King who originated some of these transactions through his royal governors and mayors. Where the original owners were dead, unable or unwilling to regain possession in the States, loyal descendants, relatives, or heirs were given the deeds. One has to remember that most of this land originated from the Crown of England's grants to loyal subjects of current or prior generations, or validation of Dutch grants. In the case of Robert Edwards' land, it appears that only those descendants of continued Loyalty to the Crown were ever compensated and any patriot descendants of the Edwards family were denied, even in court.

Part Two: The Principals' Principles

Chapter Three: Alexander Hamilton and the Cruger family

We have already seen how the Cruger family is connected to the important families of early New York City. John Cruger was mayor of New York City from 1739 until his death in 1744, interred in Trinity Church Graveyard. His son Henry met with Prime Minister Lord North in 1775 to ask acceptance of the Petition of Conciliation from the Second Continental Congress to no avail. The name of Philip Schuyler future father-in-law of Alexander Hamilton came up in his conversation with Lord North in 1775 (a demonstration of the connection between the Crugers and Philip Schuyler). His son, Henry II, was active with his father and brother Nicholas in trade between Jamaica and New York. Henry senior served in the Assembly of New York from 1745 to 1759 and as Council of the Province until 1773, when another son, John Harris Cruger succeeded him. The son, Henry II as a merchant with his father located himself in 1754 in Bristol, England, where he became mayor from whence he carried a petition to Parliament to repeal the Stamp Act on the colonies. Cruger was the first American to sit on the British House of Commons along with Irish orator and statesman Edmund Burke. Henry was branded a supporter of the Revolution and swore allegiance to the United States. After the cessation of hostilities he returned to New York in 1792 where he served in the New York Senate.[1]

---

[1] *The Cruger family today enjoys significant influence in the financial world. Anne Krueger is the current International Monetary Fund, Acting Managing Director.*

John Harris Cruger married Anne De Lancey, daughter of Brigadier General Oliver De Lancey mentioned before. He served as Colonel in the British Army during the Revolutionary War. He was a vestryman of Trinity Church and was instrumental in assigning several land leases in New York City from Robert Edwards in 1778 to Trinity Church in 1779. One of these leases was for 77 acres, another for 80 acres. The latter carried the name of Aaron Burr, who was later to become a law peer of Alexander Hamilton , along with two other names Robert and George Cruger, brothers of John Cruger, as assignees.

The Cruger Family Bible (New York Genealogical and Biographical Record, vol. 6, 74-80, 180-182) records a Myndert and wife Rachel Schuyler as sponsors of Henry Cruger Sr.'s baptism, tying these two families together. This connection between the Schuyler and Cruger families suggests a plausible introduction of Alexander Hamilton to his future wife, Elizabeth Schuyler, daughter of Philip Schuyler. They met during the war in the camp of General Philip Schuyler.

Nicholas Cruger established a merchant trade in St. Croix, Virgin Islands, where Alexander Hamilton became an apprentice clerk in 1766. Here Hamilton expressed his opinion to a peer that the surest way to a speedy recognition was through a war. His future involvement in the Revolutionary War as aide-de-camp to General Washington should be viewed with this statement in mind. As his father had essentially abandoned him, he was adopted by the Cruger family. Through these Cruger family connections Hamilton came to New York in 1773 to enter King's College, now Columbia University, having been rejected by Princeton College. Here he developed his writing and oratory skills in defense of natural rights. With this skill for rhetoric he was able to assist his school's president Mr. Cooper escape tar and feathering in 1775 with a speech on his doorstep. Meanwhile Cooper slipped out the back door avoiding the mob lynching. This showed a certain opportunism to be his trademark by helping a Tory to safety while playing to the sensitivities of the Patriotic cause. A war was brewing that would raise his star on high.

Chapter Four: Prelude to a Duel

While rescuing a cannon at the Battery under fire Hamilton distinguished himself enough to be appointed captain in command of the Provincial Company of Artillery. He fought at the Battle of Long Island and first met General George Washington at Harlem Heights, New York. It was here that Aaron Burr rescued Hamilton's brigade commanded by General Henry Knox from the clutches of the British onslaught. Hamilton's artillery company fought at White Plains repulsing the Hessians attack, and later in 1777 at Trenton and Princeton. That same year at Morristown, New Jersey, Hamilton was appointed aide-de-camp to Washington with rank of Lieutenant Colonel at the young age of 22. Alexander Hamilton took the position in Washington's headquarters in which Aaron Burr had lasted only 10 days. This was the beginning of a long competition between the two men.

Alexander Hamilton went on to distinguish himself during the Revolution. He warned Continental Congress of the British approach to Philadelphia where his horse was shot from beneath him. Washington sent Hamilton on a mission to General Gates. Hamilton helped Washington draft a report to Congress on reorganization of the Army. Hamilton was with Major General Charles Lee at Monmouth Court House. Charles Lee's actions at Monmouth infuriated Hamilton so much that he challenged him to a duel which did not occur. During the war Hamilton began writing on the weaknesses of Congress and endured Valley Forge with the army of Washington. He proposed a constitutional convention for a new government with taxing powers and proper executive to correct the ineffectiveness of the Confederation.

Alexander Hamilton was a proponent of using Negro troops and would later help form the Manumission Society for freeing the slave. Aaron Burr likewise was a member of the Manumission Society but kept several slaves even to his death. Burr pushed unsuccessfully for the abolition of slavery in the New York State Legislature. However, his will before the duel with Hamilton did not mention freeing any of his slaves in his instructions to his daughter.

In 1778 Hamilton submitted to Congressman Robert Morris, who later recommended him to Washington for Secretary of Treasury, his first plan to stabilize public finance and to James Duane in 1780 he expressed his views on government. Washington sent him in pursuit of the traitor Benedict Arnold unsuccessfully. Washington did not advance Alexander Hamilton to his liking who then sought over Washington's head the same advancement from Congress. This did not sit well with General Washington. In 1781 Hamilton resigned his position as aide to Washington in order to command a battalion of light infantry. At Yorktown he distinguished himself in the final charge of the Revolution at redoubt No.10.

In 1782 Alexander Hamilton was appointed Receiver of Taxes in New York and admitted to practice law after only three months of study with James Duane. A member of Congress from New York in 1783 Hamilton established his law practice at 57 Wall Street. In 1784 Hamilton founded the Bank of New York of which many stockholders were wealthy Loyalists and Patriots, and from which Hamilton would characterize, as its director, his later formation of the First Bank of the United States. Hamilton represented Loyalist claims to regain confiscated property. He was defense counselor for the Tory Joshua Waddington, who during the British occupation had taken over the Maiden Lane Brewery owned by Elizabeth Rutgers. The suit was brought by none other than Aaron Burr and Robert Troup. Hamilton won on the pretense that the Peace Treaty of Paris he had helped to negotiate, which had specified cessation and compensation for confiscations of Loyalist properties, would be upset if the plaintiff prevailed.

Hamilton's political career continued to shine in 1786 at the Annapolis convention calling for a new constitutional federal government. Seated at the New York State Assembly in 1787 he attended the Federal Convention where he argued for a strong President for life with powers to appoint state governors. This showed his leanings toward a regal dictatorship, if not a benevolent aristocracy. Hamilton perhaps rightly believed that the fledgling government could not succeed without the help of the wealth of Europe. But he led the fight in New York to ratify the new constitution as it stood in 1788. Hamilton became Secretary of the Treasury in

Washington's first Presidency in 1789. The next year Hamilton argued for the assumption of all the state's debt by Congress and the need for a central national bank which was chartered on July 4, 1791. Locating the new capital of Washington on the Potomac River some think won the support of Jefferson who was initially opposed to Hamilton's projects.

The alleged affair of Alexander Hamilton with the young wife of James Reynolds to whom Aaron Burr was also reportedly attached began in the summer of 1791 at the same time the Bank of the United States opened its doors. Hamilton had two projects, the Bank and the Society for Manufactures (i.e. the industrialization of the United States) developing at the same time, while he was encouraging Congress to make good on the I.O.U.s of Continental Congress and colonial states at face value.

Not to be outdone again Aaron Burr sought and eventually obtained a New York charter for The Manhattan Corporation in 1799, ostensibly a waterworks corporation for New York City, which instead turned out to be a competing land bank to Hamilton's Bank of New York. Burr's bank has become the current Chase Manhattan Bank, which curiously owns the dueling pistols of John Church used in the duel between Burr and Hamilton. Burr claimed that Hamilton's Bank of New York had denied the common farmer and merchant access to his bank in preference to the wealthy aristocracy thus necessitating a competing bank. Aaron Burr likewise made Tammany Hall originally formed as a trade union into a political machine for the republican Jeffersonian party and himself in New York. Thus Burr formed the first political party of the United States.

Hamilton was abrasive, overbearing, and very forceful in his arguments. Many in Congress charged Alexander Hamilton with irregularities at the Treasury especially in land bounty dealings. Eventually he resigned as Secretary of the Treasury in 1795, but not out of favor with Washington whose farewell address he drafted in 1796.

Aaron Burr caused Alexander Hamilton's father-in-law, Philip Schuyler much difficulty with the help of his associate Leggett's paper such that he lost the run for New York Senator in 1791 to Burr. Later Hamilton would return the favor by helping Schuyler regain his seat in 1796, and Jefferson win the final 36th vote in the House of Representatives for President breaking the tie with Aaron Burr in 1801. Hamilton opposed Burr's bid for Governor of New York in 1804 with derogatory remarks that led to the famous duel.

During this time the difficulties between the British and the French eventually put the new and still weak American interests on the high seas at risk causing a new American Army to be raised with the old retired General Washington as Commander in 1798. Against many other's misgivings

Washington appointed Hamilton second in command and effectively Commander of the Army in aged Washington's stead. Hamilton opposed a commission for Burr. Hamilton came up with a scheme to conquer the Louisiana Territory from Spain with the aid of the British Navy prompting Mrs. Abigail Adams to call him another Napoleon wannabe. Aaron Burr adopted this plan as his own in 1805 and was awarded a trial for treason in which he narrowly escaped conviction with the aid of Justice John Marshall's strict interpretation of treason in the Constitution. But General James Wilkinson, Burr's accomplice, had preceded them both in 1795 with his own scheme of secession of Kentucky with Daniel Clark. Both Burr and Wilkinson were looking to place themselves in the position of power and control of these vast lands, while Hamilton and ultimately Jefferson were looking to expand the power of their new country by pushing the westward boundaries toward the Pacific Ocean, later to become known as Manifest Destiny.

The framers of the Constitution had not wanted to repeat the European monarchies' loose use of treason to put down political dissent and eliminate political rivals. They defined treason narrowly as an overt act of armed aggression against one's country witnessed by at least two persons. Aaron Burr escaped conviction for plotting secession on this strictly narrow interpretation of treason by Justice Marshall. Some but not all historians think Burr wanted to have the territories west of the Appalachians secede from the United States, and then seek annexation of all of Mexico to form a new country with himself at the throne with the aid of the British, who had their own designs on the Ohio Territories. His published letters to his daughter support this theory. It was Alexander Hamilton who helped alert President Jefferson to Burr's designs in an earlier plot in 1804 of Timothy Pickering and High Federalists like Tapping Reeve, Burr's brother in law, to cause the Northern New England Confederation to secede. Alexander Hamilton had penned a scathing attack on Burr's fitness for public office which ended Burr's bid for Governor of New York. The secessionists had hoped Burr would become governor of New York and add New York to the New England States and secede. Aaron also needed a political office at that time to avoid the collection of his large debts, since holding political office forestalled the bill collectors.

In 1799 Aaron had dueled John Church, Alexander's brother-in-law without damage. In 1801 Alexander Hamilton's son, Philip, was killed in a duel with George Eacker who attacked Alexander Hamilton in support of Burr who may have enabled the duel. Although this soured Hamilton on the institution of dueling but not before six (or 11) prior aborted duels, he accepted his own challenge from Burr. They met on July 11, 1804 on the same ground where Philip Hamilton had died at Weehawken, New Jersey. Reportedly not intending to harm Burr, Hamilton received a mortal wound from his nemesis, a deliberate killing by a known marksman who had been seen practicing before the duel and even before the challenge itself. Hamilton's gun had fired and as late as 1976 found to have a hair trigger which he refused to set. At his deathbed were his wife and sister-in-law, Angelica Church, popular wife of John above and the object of Thomas Jefferson's prior aspirations as well as of both Aaron Burr and Alexander Hamilton. He was buried at Trinity Church with a glowingly inscribed headstone.

Chapter Five: The Affair of State

The reason for the latter duel was reportedly a slight about Burr's personal deportment (some suggest a possible reference to incestuous relationship with his daughter, Theodosia), or Hamilton's political assassination of Burr. Burr had successfully interceded with a call out to duel between Alexander Hamilton and James Monroe in 1797 over the scandalous leak by John Beckley. Beckley, a Jeffersonian republican who had copied Hamilton's and Maria Reynold's letters for Monroe during the Congressional inquest of 1792 into the affair, possibly kept copies for himself. James Thomson Callender published Hamilton's affair with Maria Reynolds in 1797. All three, Monroe, Beckley, and Callender were Republicans and supporters of Jefferson. The reason for exposing the Reynolds sex scandal of Hamilton was to force Hamilton to deny a sexual affair by admitting speculation in discounted notes of the government, or as we shall see corroboration with English money. Even Callender felt the affair a fabrication of Hamilton including the love letters of Maria and suspected a cover-up of some other political intrigue. Instead, Hamilton did the most unexpected sacrifice of his political career. Swallowing his pride he admitted adultery, rather than scuttle his economic plans for nation building. Either way he had already been forced out of office as Secretary of the Treasury in 1795, but his schemes for a central bank and strong central government were intact. Hamilton had most assuredly lost his political career for the good of the country. While Callender who felt unrewarded by Jefferson for his exposure of the scandal would later expose President Jefferson's affair and children with his slave Sally Hemming confirmed recently by DNA testing of the descendants.

General Washington too was unconvinced of any wrongdoing on Hamilton's part and sent him a four bottle silver wine cooler without mentioning the publication of the affair. Eliza Hamilton cherished the cooler for the rest of her life, perhaps as a memento of Washington's steadfast honor and respect of her loyal husband. Eliza had from the start been privy to her husband's political thoughts even in correspondence before their marriage. It is inconceivable that he would not have informed her and consulted her on the way to handle the Reynolds Affair. This is perhaps why Eliza destroyed all the letters to her from her husband after his death.

Hamilton had confided with Monroe in 1792 about the affair in order to avoid political fall out over misinterpretation of bribery allegations with Mr. James Reynolds. The payments to either Reynolds or Maria might well have been for services rendered as contact between Hamilton and the foreign investors for his Bank; the acknowledgement of an affair was to hide the reason for the prolonged association of Hamilton and the Reynolds. Most likely James Reynolds was interfering with Hamilton's and Maria Reynolds' association so they convinced him the meetings were sexual rather than political, paying him to keep him out of the way. The continuation of the affair after discovery by James Reynolds can only convincingly be explained on these terms.

The affair had begun in 1791 just after the time of the Congressional passing of Hamilton's Bank of the United States. Hamilton remained vague as to the dates saying it started in the summer of 1791 perhaps because he was hiding the earlier liaison before the subscription to his Bank of the United States on July 4th which was the initial reason to communicate with interested foreign wealthy investors. The bank being a private corporation did not have to reveal the names of its stockholders, which meant that the identity of the foreign investors needed to be kept confidential.

In support of this argument, Colonel William Stephens Smith, son-in-law to John Adams, and also a former Washington aide, sought British investors in London during 1790-1 well before the supposed affair of Hamilton with Maria. He brought back numerous orders for Bank of the United States stock.

During this time Alexander Hamilton had been urging Congress for the complete honoring at face value of all of the debts of the Continental Congress and the colonies of the Confederacy. This included bounty payments to soldiers for their service during the war plus debts, currency payments for goods, and services rendered to the Revolutionary cause. Speculators, among who were Aaron Burr, Jacob Clingman, and James

Reynolds, were buying up these IOUs of the state and continental and federal governments for pennies on the dollar from frustrated holders.

Did Clingman, a pawnbroker from Philadelphia who had a secret affair some might say even marriage, with Mrs. Maria Reynolds, or her husband, send this fetching woman to seduce Hamilton, Secretary of the United States Treasury under Washington's first administration? It could be supposed the speculators wanted to know how earnest Hamilton was in paying off the debts of the United States at face value and obtain lists of possible holders of these notes. On December 15, 1792 Hamilton was forced to explain the relationship with Maria Reynolds who herself avoided the subject of the affair to the Congressional inquiry of Speaker of the House of Representatives from Pennsylvania, Frederick Augustus Muhlenberg, Representative Venable, and James Monroe, future President of the United States. The accusation by Clingman implied payments by Hamilton to Mr. James Reynolds of several thousand dollars in order for him to buy the speculative discounted IOUs of the government for Hamilton's own gain. Clingman admitted his only friends in high office were Muhlenberg and Aaron Burr! Maria claimed to be abused and abandoned by husband James Reynolds as the reason for her entreaty for help from Hamilton. Hamilton succumbed to the story and seduction. Mr. Reynolds supposedly returned to the support of his wife and learned of the affair. He demanded hush money from Hamilton, who supposedly paid up.

However, what is not believable is the fact that Hamilton would accept a continuance of the affair offered by husband, James Reynolds! That Hamilton, who had resisted so many other temptations in his position of importance in the government, should continue a compromising situation was unlikely. The story hides another truth; not what was thought by his contemporaries, the speculation on government notes for Hamilton's personal gain, but rather what Maria Reynolds was doing for him politically. Maria or Mary Reynolds was the daughter of Richard Lewis and Susannah Van der Burgh whose ancestor, Cornelius or Lucas Vanderberge had sold 24 acres to Dirck Dey who conveyed it to Trinity Church Corporation which leased for 99 years to Abraham Mortier. This land passed to his widow and then their daughter Elizabeth Banyar who then subleased to Aaron Burr as his home, Richmond Hill. The real estate connection to Aaron Burr and the wealthy Manhattan Loyalist landholders is indisputable.

What if Hamilton had figured out the duplicity of Maria and turned the circumstances to his advantage? The payments to Mr. Reynolds were not for Maria's sexual favors to Hamilton but for continuing contacts on his behalf and ultimately the behalf of his government with British wealth needed to support his Bank of the United States. Hamilton wrote *"No society could succeed which did not unite the interest and credit of rich individuals with those of the state."* If the members of Congress, namely the Republicans opposed to his bank bill and his industrial Charter for the Society for Establishing Useful Manufactures on 700 acres on the Passaic River in New Jersey, had knowledge of his corroboration with foreign investors in England not only would his Bank possibly never see the light of day but his position on the Washington cabinet would be tenuous at best. Jefferson as head of the Republicans wrote *"I sincerely believe... that banking establishments are more dangerous than standing armies."*

Hamilton was very familiar with the Van der Burgh family during the Revolution in which several of Maria's uncles had served for the American cause. Her half brothers Henry Dubois and Colonel Lewis Dubois had served in the 5th New York Regiment. Henry had carried messages between his brother, Colonel Lewis, and General Washington throughout the war. Hamilton on Washington's staff would have had personal and frequent conversations with Henry. The Henry Van der Burgh family branch on the other hand had been loyalists. It seems unlikely that Hamilton would have been unaware of her important Dutchess County connections to both Loyalist and Patriot wealth. Her playing destitute and abandoned by her husband would not make sense with such an extensive wealthy family to draw support from. It is unlikely that Hamilton was drawn into an affair unwillingly. Given his cautiousness in his political connections, it is hard to believe he would not have smelled a rat in such a story and withdrawn immediately. Instead one can more rationally conclude that the whole affair was a cover up from the beginning to hide the Reynolds', at least Maria's assistance, in contacts with wealthy European investors in his Bank of the United States.

True, Jacob Clingman, her lover, and James Reynolds, her estranged husband, were both connivers most likely with Aaron Burr in the note speculation of Revolutionary War debt, but that might be incidental or coincidental to the arrangement between Alexander Hamilton and Maria Reynolds. Burr might have sent Maria to entrap Hamilton into an affair, but Hamilton most likely did not take the bait. The connection between Burr and Clingman and thus Reynolds stands on Clingman's statement that his clerkship with Muhlenberg and ties with Aaron Burr were the only important political contacts he had. James Reynolds was closely related to Pierpoint Edwards, Aaron Burr's uncle through the Pierpoint family. After the affair in 1792 Maria, who now changed her name to Mary and Jacob Clingman would marry. James Reynolds must have outlasted his usefulness.   Aaron Burr served James Reynolds with Maria's divorce papers.

It is less likely that Clingman would later marry Maria if he truly believed she had an affair with Hamilton while he was also her lover. Clingman claimed to have observed Hamilton leave a slip of paper with Maria who explained that it was in reference to a payment of some eleven hundred dollars to her husband, James Reynolds. Clingman likewise accompanied Reynolds himself to Hamilton's office where Reynolds received one hundred dollars. These events led Clingman to believe Hamilton was speculating with Reynolds in discounted notes of the government, which Reynolds confirmed. At the time he did not suspect the payments for Reynolds silence in any affair between Maria and Hamilton.

The question of whether or not Maria was a prostitute for her husband is mainly raised by the son of her landlady in Philadelphia, Richard Folwell. He related in 1797 after the affair became public that Maria had told him of *the "perfidy of Reynolds. Mr. Reynolds had frequently enjoined and insisted that she should insinuate herself on certain high and influential characters... and actually prostitute herself to gull money from them."* But Maria had hoped she would find her savior among these same persons of wealth and influence. This may in fact be the method of introduction to Hamilton who perhaps took pity on his revolutionary associates' sister. He would have likely offered his assistance, not his assignation to the child he had met at Washington's camp. He might have offered her a chance to free herself from the slavery described by Folwell.

If one can imagine in a little eight or nine year old girl's mind beaming with pride as she, under the supervision of her half brother, Henry, hands to the most important man of her generation a secret letter from her oldest half brother, Colonel of his own Fifth New York Regiment. Hamilton may have surely offered Maria another chance to serve her General now President of the new country which in her child's estimation in some small way she had helped form.

Legitimacy, honor, and plenty of honest money were Hamilton's offer. His proposal was a chance for Maria to serve her country and earn the respect of her leaders if not the country by carrying secret messages once again between her commander-in-chief in the person of Hamilton and her wealthy Patriot and Loyalist relatives. Were these the messages Folwell said were left in her entryway the contents of which caused her to fly off in the night to answer? Could Maria have been both a prostitute and a messenger; or solely the latter? Remember the Folwell affidavit, as you will, was nearly six years later, in August of 1797, after the fact and clearly after the public revelations of the Reynolds Affair of both Callender and Hamilton himself. What other conclusion could a suspicious mind like Folwell's have made: sex, surely, not patriotism?

Other notable ways for Hamilton to be currently familiar with the grown-up Maria Reynolds came in Hamilton's own words. Her brother-in-law, Gilbert Livingston, prominent lawyer in Dutchess County, was married to her sister Susannah Lewis. In the small fraternity of practicing lawyers in New York both Hamilton and Burr would surely have known Gilbert on rather intimate terms. Hamilton's co-councils in the *Rutgers vs. Waddington* case had been Morgan Lewis and {Henry} Brockholst Livingston. Although Morgan Lewis was not closely related to Maria's father he did marry Gertrude Livingston, sister of Robert R. Livingston, a King's College graduate and law student of William Smith. Morgan Lewis soundly beat Aaron Burr for governor of New York in 1804 with vocal support of George and DeWitt Clinton and Alexander Hamilton. George Clinton replaced Aaron Burr as Vice President in President Thomas Jefferson's second term. Morgan Lewis was also Quartermaster in both the Revolution and War of 1812. Brockholst Livingston was the son of Governor William Livingston of New Jersey and later Supreme Court Justice. Though these Livingstons were of different branches of a rather large and complicated family there is no doubt they were a clan of tremendous importance in the New York political landscape. A request for Hamilton's assistance to Maria from Gilbert Livingston especially would have sent Hamilton on a mission of mercy for the wayward sister-in-law of a colleague. Rather than take advantage of her situation, Hamilton would have been more inclined to mind his p's and q's as he had always done and try to be of service to her.

Gilbert James Livingston was third cousin once removed to Hamilton's wife, Elizabeth Schuyler and ancestor of the Presidents Bush's great grandmother, Flora Sheldon. The mention of Gilbert Livingston's name in the treatise published by Hamilton on the affair is similar to the selective publishing of Burr's letters by his proxy Matthew L. Davis. Both were intended to serve as hints to a posterity interested in the truth. Gilbert's name even out of context should raise suspicions as to the meaning of his significance in this whole affair. As he was the brother-in-law one should suspect his interest in Maria's well being which Hamilton must have respected.

At the time of the affair Tench Coxe had replaced soon to be disgraced Hamilton friend, William Duer, as assistant treasury secretary. The disgrace of Duer implicated in the discounted note scandal rubbed off on Hamilton. Coxe had espoused industrial espionage with Great Britain and sent Andrew Mitchell to England to steal British trade secrets. This included pirating and transferring patents to United States soil in violation of British law.

William Duer in his new position as head of the Society for Establishing Useful Manufactures picked the falls on the Passaic River at now Paterson, New Jersey, as the location of a new industrial town. Governor William Paterson, its namesake, encouraged the New Jersey legislature to grant the tax exempt state charter in November, 1791. Then Hamilton dropped the bombshell on Congress in December, 1791 with his *Report on Manufactures* at the same time as James Reynolds was demanding "hush" money from Hamilton for the Maria Reynolds Affair. The Jeffersonian agrarians chided Hamilton's work as dangerous and unconstitutional and the matter received no Congressional support. Had the opposition learned of the dealings of the Treasury Secretary in stolen British industrial secrets who knows how long Hamilton would have stayed in the Washington Administration. Hamilton had spent the previous summer collecting contracts from British textile defectors at the same time as Maria had *forced* herself on him. The coincidence begs the question were the two incidents related? Clearly for Hamilton to come out and admit that Maria was from a wealthy Dutchess County Dutch family would spill the beans. The very wealthy people Hamilton was trying to subscribe to his projects, both the Bank of the United States and the Society for Establishing Useful Manufactures, were related to his supposed amore.

As always the lie begot more lies. Hamilton was trapped in his own web of pretended vice from which there was no return. He could not deny his own contrived affair with Maria without accepting the charge of speculation in discounted notes of the government which he was insisting the government pay at face value. Telling the truth that Maria was related to the same people he was soliciting for his projects for a strong centralized federal government would result in an even stronger backlash against his pet projects even at such a late date as 1797. Hamilton as head of the emerging Federalist Party would bring down the politicians aligned with him, President John Adams and father-in-law Senator Philip Schuyler. If the story had broken before the two elections for president and congress neither would have succeeded in the close balloting. The threat of the leaking of the affair in the press as early as October 23, 1796 in the *Aurora* must thought to have favored the Jeffersonian Republicans which included Burr. The latter lost perhaps because Callender was late in publishing after the elections in 1797. What astonished all was that even in 1797 Hamilton continued to insist the affair with Maria had existed, but

29

to what end? Perhaps it was something of grave national importance in Hamilton's mind.

The subscription capital for the national bank of 10 million dollars (more than all the capital of the other existing banks in the United States combined of 2 million dollars) was taken up immediately upon offer. This was a feat not obtainable without foreign investors. Hamilton had arranged for the Banks of New York and Boston to offer subscriptions to the stock of the Bank of the United States. As agents of the stock offering they were in essence giving their own investors first crack. A majority of the stockholders of the Bank of New York at least were former Tories and foreign investors. Many southerners felt left out of the offering because there was no bank in the south to offer the subscriptions. This began the first division of the south and north into what would form the first political parties, Republican and Federalist.

Hamilton could not risk open public contact with foreign money sources. The charter of the First Bank of the United States was not renewed in 1811 because of too many foreign stockholders. This is proof that even in August 25, 1796 when hints of the scandal broke in the press; the subject of foreign investment in institutions of the United States was a hot topic. Hamilton had tried to soften this objection by making all trustees of the bank United States citizens. The actual pamphlets detailing the scandal were printed in Philadelphia in 1797 and have not survived intact today but their printing has led many to believe that the scandal was not made public until 1797 when it had in fact been leaked more than six months earlier.

This gives credence to additional theories on the timing and reason for the resurrection of the Reynold's Affair. The Affair was too hot a topic for exposure to the public then. It would be too much fodder for the Republican faction in the election of Hamilton's Federalist Party's Presidential candidate, John Adams in November, 1796 and Hamilton's father-in-law, Philip Schuyler for Aaron Burr's New York Senate seat. Hamilton's personal disclosure of the Reynold's affair on July 5, 1797 was a year later and well after the election. The political scenario would explain why Hamilton's wife seemed to quietly accept the tryst without demonstration or public comment, even after Alexander Hamilton's death. She stood by her man because he did not break her trust in him. The scandal was a political not sexual interlope. Sex covers and explains to the public a simple explanation to a deeper political intrigue.

Hamilton would later grow to despise President Adams and the feelings became mutual. This rift grew out of Adams' neutrality stance with all European powers despite the quasi war on the high seas where American shipping was harassed by French armed frigates with American sailors impressed into the French and British navies. Hamilton clearly favored renewed ties with England for both protection of American commerce and support for westward expansion into Spanish territories.

If Burr was involved with Clingman in some speculative scheme surely others were involved who had ties with considerable overseas money. That Burr interceded in the duel between Monroe and Hamilton might also suggest Burr's involvement in the scheme and the revelation of the Reynolds Affair. Hamilton challenged Monroe because he felt Monroe was responsible for exposing the Reynolds Affair to the public. Where there was smoke, there was surely Burr's fire for intrigue not far away. Burr lost his bid for the Senate seat of New York to Hamilton's father-in-law Philip Schuyler in 1796 in a hotly contested race spearheaded by Hamilton at the time of the revelation. Burr, a Republican also, might have been behind the earlier release of the scandal to help his campaign against Schuyler because of Hamilton's active involvement as opposition.

Chapter Six: The Political Assassination

Thus Aaron Burr was aware of Alexander Hamilton's penchant for the theatre of the duel. Had he wished any ill will of Hamilton then, he could have easily let Monroe dispense with Hamilton in his place. Hamilton came close to a physical duel it is said on eleven occasions before. Notable challenges from Alexander Hamilton were to General Charles Lee after the Battle of Monmouth and to Commodore Nicholson. Both were averted by friends further up the line of challengers or their direct intervention. From the frequent sparring over the years one can only surmise a growing enmity between the two. Was it sparked by any trivial event or was it being deliberately provoked? Although Alexander Hamilton considered Aaron Burr a man without scruples and not to be trusted with the reins of government, he otherwise considered Burr a friend socially and they met cordially.

In a letter to Governour Morris on December 24, 1800 Alexander Hamilton wrote of Aaron Burr, *"Jefferson or Burr? the former without doubt. The latter, in my judgement, has no principle, public or private; could be bound by no agreement; will listen to no monitor but his ambition, and for this purpose will use the worst part of the community as a ladder to climb to permanent power, and an instrument to crush the better part. He is bankrupt beyond redemption, except by the resources which grow out of war and disorder, or by a sale to a foreign power, or by great speculation. War with Great Britain would be an immediate instrument. He is sanguine enough to hope every thing, daring enough to attempt every thing, wicked enough to scruple nothing. From the elevation of such a man may heaven preserve the country."* Could Hamilton be predicting the War of 1812 with Great Britain with Burr as instrument of the Crown, and his own need to intercede? Clearly Alexander Hamilton had Aaron Burr's number. As we shall see he must have known or suspected more perfidy of Burr than he ever let on.

Equally puzzling is the incident related by John Church Hamilton that some time prior to Aaron Burr's challenge to Alexander Hamilton to the duel Burr had shown up at dawn at the home of Hamilton requesting urgent financial assistance. Hamilton in fact raised ten thousand dollars from none other than a former Burr dueler John Barker Church plus others to which Burr added his own seventeen hundred and fifty dollars to repay an unyielding anonymous creditor. One would think that Aaron might feel indebted to Alexander, rather than believe he would slander him in public as some would present as a reason for the challenge to duel. Instead following the disastrous duel Aaron Burr returned home to Richmond Hill where shortly thereafter a cousin, Ogden Edwards, visited finding him in high spirits on the same day without mentioning the duel. Much to his surprise the cousin found out about the duel on the streets upon leaving Burr's home.

Likewise Burr seemed to lack remorse at his presumed benefactor's demise and expressed astonishment at Alexander Hamilton's political enemies', the Republicans, shock and dismay at Hamilton's disposal by duel. This obviously shows the calculating self indulgence of Aaron Burr at the expense of others. A case could be made that Burr even used the funds enticed from Hamilton by deception of paying a debt instead for the grand scheme of western secession. Hamilton would not have otherwise approved funds for this use had he known the true use of the funds.

In support of this theory are the two transactions with John Jacob Astor on October 22 and November 18 of 1803 and recorded on June 1 and 4, 1804 (67/2,11) prior to the challenge to the duel with Hamilton and during the same time when he was supposedly raising money from Hamilton to pay off an impatient creditor. He surely raised more money from Astor than the $1750 he supposedly personally added to the pot of his unnamed creditor. Burr claimed to his daughter, Theodosia he received a handsome profit from Astor for the land lease around his home, Richmond Hill. In fact Astor paid Burr $62,500 for 345 lots excluding his home, Richmond Hill, and paid off debts of $41,783 encumbering the land to Manhattan Corporation (the water/bank corporation initiated by Aaron Burr and Joseph Browne) (7/20/1804, 67/411). This sum was in exchange for the yearly rent payable to Trinity Church for sixty nine years of $134.50 for three years increasing to $201.75 in the next 33 years and $269.00 for the last 33 years of the lease payable on the 25th of March of each year from the lease of May 1, 1797 (65/512). In essence the transfer of lease had cost Aaron Burr nothing but $1007 over the six years he held the lease for which he gained over $100,000 or several million dollars at today's valuation. That Burr did not retire at this point is testament to his egotistical attitude and megalomaniacal obsession with vainglory. Instead Burr died penniless, picking the pockets of a prostituted second wife.

At the time of the solicitation by Burr of funds from Hamilton Aaron Burr was running for Governor of New York. The High Federalists of New England known as the Essex Junto secretly supported Burr's candidacy in hopes that his position as Governor of New York would lend to a plan of secession of the New England states in conjunction with New York espoused by them and Senator Pickering. They hoped a return to the fold of Great Britain would improve their economic situation vis-a-vis world trade. The Essex Junto consisted of members of many wealthy families primarily located in the Boston north shore region of Essex County, Massachusetts. They were merchants and international traders and preferred the British protection of their commerce to the independence of their homeland.

The financial assistance Aaron Burr sought from Alexander Hamilton would be a profound roundabout way of getting even with Hamilton for his interference in this secession scheme with the Federalists of New England. We should note that Alexander Hamilton died in debt of some fifty five thousand dollars. Yet he was still a friend enough to help out Aaron Burr in time of presumed need. Burr's reaction smacks of scheming going as planned rather than accidental circumstances unrelated to one another and fits his personality rather than mere historical incongruity.

Angelica Hamilton, Alexander Hamilton's daughter and namesake of Angelica Schuyler Church, Alexander's sister- in-law and occasional liaison, had become quite insane following the duel and death of her brother, Philip. Hamilton felt guilty for suggesting to Philip the honorable thing to do was waste his shot and not try to kill his opponent. His opponent had not the same honor. It has been suggested that Alexander Hamilton was ill and penniless and at the end of his political influence in the Federalist party and thus suicidal. His last letter or will to his wife suggests this frame of mind. However Hamilton did law business on the morning of the duel and planned to finish the briefs following his presumed reconciliation with Aaron Burr. These facts do not support a suicidal ideation of Hamilton during the time of the duel. However, Alexander Hamilton did deed property to brother-in-law, John B. Church and others on July 6, 1804 just prior to the duel. Did Hamilton fear he would not survive the duel? Aaron Burr on the other hand might have had greater aspirations of which Hamilton had become an ever vigilant obstacle. Alexander Hamilton was willing to sacrifice his life to stop Aaron Burr's aspirations at the expense of the nation.

To that end on his deathbed Hamilton spoke, "If they break this union, they will break my heart." On the subject English utilitarian philosopher Jeremy Bentham wrote of his meeting with Burr, "He really meant to make himself emperor of Mexico." and of the duel with Hamilton. "He was sure of being able to kill him, so i thought it little better than murder."

Chapter Seven: Another plan of Secession

A few days before the challenge to the duel, which started as correspondence from June 18 and ended on June 27, 1804, and after the duel Aaron Burr had visited with a Charles Williamson, an ex-British army officer who was the principal in a Northern New York land scheme, the Pulteney Purchase on the Genesee River. Old friend and roommate in college, Robert Troup, had attempted unsuccessfully to persuade Alexander Hamilton to secretly join this undertaking which had been going on for ten years with the assistance of Aaron Burr. These associations of Burr's were just the reason why Hamilton knew Burr's victory for governor of New York in 1804 was to be feared. The secession scheme with Senator Pickering's New England was feasible if Burr won the governor's seat. Burr at the helm of the New England confederacy would be intolerable. Thus Alexander Hamilton had successfully done everything in his power to stop Aaron Burr's bid for governor.

Senator Timothy Pickering was descended from Sir Henry Pickering (born 1634) whose wife was Philadelphia Downing. Her father, Sir George Downing's (b. 1623) sister, Mary Downing (husband Anthony Stoddard) was ancestor of Aaron Burr's mother Esther Edwards.

Senator Timothy Pickering was a distant cousin of Aaron Burr's Downing ancestry. He was part of the Essex Junto of Essex County, Massachusetts, set on reestablishing ties with England. The Junto would later help Burr upon his return from Europe via Boston using an alias, M. Arnot in 1811. Arnot is coincidentally an archaic spelling for Arnold, as in Benedict Arnold. This entanglement with relatives establishes a pattern that rings true throughout Burr's life and helps unravel connections to other obscure events.

Williamson had visited Burr at Richmond Hill two days before Aaron Burr had challenged Alexander Hamilton to the duel about June 18. The Williamson family owned property next to Richmond Hill. This was possibly the location of one of the Montaltos Burr keeps referring to in reference to Celeste or Merry in writing to the Alstons. Williamson had assured Burr of British support for his plans for a new empire out of the Mexican territories. Two days after the duel Burr planned to meet Williamson in Philadelphia.

This meeting appears to have eluded the apologists of Aaron Burr who recently have attempted to expunge him of treasonous intensions to secession. Instead they currently attempt to elevate him because of his abolitionist views which probably caused his falling out with President Jefferson and the subsequent treason trial. Jefferson was an exponent of the agrarian culture and wished to see the newly acquired lands of the West stay agrarian which tacitly meant proliferation of slavery as the economic engine. Thus Burr could not succeed where Hamilton had failed because Jefferson sought to expand his Virginian lifestyle.

Williamson in turn reported to British ambassador Anthony Merry, an acquaintance from a transatlantic voyage together in 1803. Merry wrote to his superior, British foreign secretary, Dudley Ryder, Lord Harrowby in England at the same time about a further scheme to secede with British help the western American territories and add Mexico to a new British influenced empire with Aaron Burr at its head.

August 6, 1804

Most Secret

My Lord,

I have just received an offer from Mr. Burr the actual vice president of the United States (which Situation he is about to resign) to lend his assistance to His Majesty's Government in any Manner in which they may think fit to employ him, particularly in endeavoring to effect a Separation of the Western Part of the United States from that which lies between the Atlantick (sic) and the Mountains, in it's whole Extent. –His Proposition on this and other Subjects will be fully detailed to your Lordship by Col. Williamson who has been the Bearer of them to me, and who will embark for England in a few Days. – It is therefore only necessary for me to add that if, after what is generally known of

> *the Profligacy of Mr. Burr's Character, His Majesty's Ministers should think proper to listen to his offer, his present Situation in the Country where he is now cast off as much by the democratic as by the Federal Party, and where he still preserves Connections with some People of Influence, added to his great Ambition and Spirit of Revenge against the present Administration, may possibly induce him to exert the Talents and Activity which he possesses with Fidelity to his Employers-*

Matthew L. Davis defended Aaron Burr against the claim that he wished for secession of the western United States. June 10, 1835 in the presence of Dr. Hosack at Burr's death bed Davis asked the question of Burr at any time did he contemplate a separation of the Union? Burr replied indignantly *"No; I would as soon have thought of taking possession of the moon, and informing my friends that I intended to divide it among them."* This was not a flat out denial as some would have us believe, but rather a typical Burrian dodge of the question. He had tried twice in attempts at secession of different parts of the Union and failed, thus he had discovered it the impossibility as remote as the moon!

Indeed General Adair stated on March, 1807, *"So far as I know or believe of the intentions of Colonel Burr... they were to prepare and lead an expedition into Mexico, predicated on a war between the two governments; without a war he knew he could do nothing. On this war taking place he calculated with certainty, as well from the policy of the measure at this time as from the positive assurances of Wilkinson, who seemed to have the power to force it in his own hands. This continued to be the object of Colonel Burr until he heard of the venal and shameful bargain made by Wilkinson at the Sabine river;"* This bargain made by Wilkinson an agent of Spain was a sell out of Burr to the Mexican government for two hundred thousand dollars, never collected.

Burr had invested five thousand of a fifty thousand dollar interest in half of 720 thousand acres in the Bastrop Spanish land grant of Louisiana territory near Nachitoches (often reported as 400,000 acres) purchased from Colonel Charles Lynch. Many wealthy and important private citizens were interested in this project. One such person might have been Wade Hampton of South Carolina, one of the wealthiest land holders in the United States and grandfather of the Wade Hampton, famous Southern cavalry officer of the Civil War. Burr mentioned Hampton's name in his letters to Theodosia and Joseph Alston. Hampton eventually owned many plantations from South Carolina to Mississippi and Louisiana.

Burr's investment in the Bastrop grant of Washita in July, 1806 caused him to dislike Monroe, who helped change the sovereignty of this land from France formerly Spain to that of the United States. In effect no longer foreign territory for Burr to oppose the title of the United States in this instance would be treasonous. This area once settled by persons of *"worth and respectability"* would serve as a base for invasion of the Mexican territories further west predicated upon a war between the United States and Spain.

Burr misled Charles Williamson and Anthony Merry as to the extent of his intentions to *"liberate"* the western United States and conquer Mexico. Further he was deluded in his thinking about the extent of his support, garnered from those westerners in opposition to continued Spanish influence in the west, which was not predicated on a war with Spain. General Andrew Jackson promptly withdrew support for Burr when he learned President Jefferson was not behind Burr's aggression toward Mexico and might even involve Burr's claim to territory of the United States.

It is most likely that Burr molded the story of conquest to fit the ears of the listener. From his letters to his daughter it is no doubt that he intended to rule as monarch of his own country wrestled from the Spanish holdings of the west. He told Theodosia and her husband to expect to follow in his foot steps.

Chapter Eight: Burr, Hamilton, the Loyalists and Trinity Church

Alexander Hamilton and his roommate Robert Troup were two of a handful of the 236 graduates of King's College (now Columbia University) before the Revolution who did not remain loyal to the Crown. Most of his fellow alumni served in the British army and were greatly, literally, interrelated in New York Tory society, as for example was the founding De Lancey family.

The college got its initial grant of land for 13,000 pounds sterling in New York lottery money. It lies seven blocks north of Trinity Church (between Barclay and Murray Streets) in the northernmost 6 acre part of the former 32 acre Queen's Farm (now located north-south between Fulton and Charlton ((not Christopher Street by which Trinity tries to include Edwards land obtained by lease, not by grant of Queen Anne)) and the east-west Hudson to Broadway), now Park Place. Trinity gave the land with the understanding that only Anglican services be conducted at the college and all of its Presidents would be members of the Trinity Church Corporation. Should ever the college not adhere to these conditions the land would revert back to Trinity mimicking the quit rent feudal system of the Crown. Thus began the intentional control of the City pulse by the Loyalist Anglican Trinity Church. Columbia College deeded over the land on which Rockefeller Center is located in 1986. Thus both institutions played a pivotal role in the real estate of Manhattan.

It appears Alexander never profited from these associations. Aaron Burr on the other hand had many dealings with Trinity Church while Alexander Hamilton had not one, even though he had handled the Church's legal affairs. David A. Ogden and younger brother, Thomas

Ludlow Ogden were law associates of Alexander Hamilton and handled his practice in his absence in the latter half of the 1790s. Thomas Ludlow Ogden was the consul for the Trinity Church Corporation for 30 years and vestryman or warden in the early 1800s. Many of the Ogdens had been Loyalists and related to Aaron Burr through two aunts, wives of Pierpoint Edwards and Timothy Edwards, the surrogate parents of Aaron and sister, Sally. The Rebel and granduncle, Matthias Ogden, had found a position on Washington's staff for young Aaron Burr, just home from the trek through the Maine woods to Quebec. Alexander Hamilton was a member of Trinity Church and had three children baptized there. His wife, Elizabeth was a devout churchgoer, unlike her husband. The family had pew 92 from 1790 to long after Alexander Hamilton's death. Trinity Church recognizes some legal services by Hamilton, along with Robert Troup, and Richard Harrison, a Trinity vestryman and comptroller and first Attorney General of New York State. Alexander Hamilton is credited with legal counsel for the independent incorporation of St. Mark's Church-in-the-Bowery. He also defended Trinity Church in 1784 against the state of New York which wanted to assume the Annetje Jans or Queen's Farm land on Manhattan Island for the state. The Jans heirs claimed they rightfully owned it. Hamilton however found the deed to Trinity from the Crown of England. Yet Alexander Hamilton was not one of elite Loyalists, whereas Aaron Burr had been from the start.

During the War for Independence in 1775 Royal Governor William Tryon removed the old Dutch and English records of New York to his ship, *Duchess of Gordon*, anchored in the harbor. At the end of the war these records were removed to the Tower of London in England. Although subject to the elements and nearly lost in a fire upon their return from England, most of the records survived intact although some early Dutch records were lost. That Hamilton was able to find the records supporting the claim of Trinity Church to the King's Farm in 1784 must have been a coup. All the Dutch records and many of the English records were in Dutch such as were the Robert Edwards' leases. They were not translated into English until the 1970s, except that one copy in English has been found in Atlanta, Georgia prior to this translation. Alexander Hamilton, however, did not profit from this victory.

Burr's maternal great-grandfather was Timothy Edwards, Presbyterian minister; Burr's uncle, Timothy, his guardian, had been third President of Princeton. His maternal grandfather was the famous preacher Reverend Jonathan Edwards of later Yale and Princeton fame to its students; his father Reverend Aaron Burr was the second President of Princeton College. Orphaned at age 3, Aaron had been brought up in the strictly

41

religious family of his uncle Timothy and his six children, with 15 other orphaned relatives of uncle Jonathan Edwards. Aaron Burr's mother Esther Burr had boasted to a friend in a letter that his older sister, Sally not yet 10 months old cringed at the countenance of her mother, having been appropriately corrected by corporal reprimands at that early age.

It has been suggested that this austere childhood brought Aaron Burr to the brink of rebellion against authority from which he never recovered. One example of such rebellious nature was the confrontation with Benedict Arnold at Quebec over Burr's unauthorized leave (perhaps desertion) of the stagnated siege of Quebec. A second occurred when Washington at Newburgh discovered Burr reading at Washington's personal desk. Burr flew into a defensive tirade that surely ended Burr's career as aide-de-camp to Washington.

Both the Robert Edwards and Timothy Edwards families came from Hartford, Connecticut and were related back in England through Mary Downing Stoddard (husband Anthony), half sister of Sir George Downing of 10 Downing Street. This common Stoddard family ancestry might explain the connection of those named on the lease from Robert Edwards to Aaron Burr and the Crugers which was turned over to Trinity Church. The Stoddard family connects many of Burr's family and associates throughout his career (see Genealogical Chart in Appendix E). Trinity gave leases of some of this land back to Aaron Burr after the Revolution at the end of the century. This included 150 acres around his future residence in 1793, and Richmond Hill of 26 acres in 1797, which he subleased from Abraham Mortier's heirs, in the middle of Charlton Street and east of Varick (now bounded by Spring, Greenwich, West Houston, and Varick Streets). The original lease had a term of 99 years from May 1, 1767. General Abraham Mortier had been commissary to the King's Army. Another lease at Church and Partition (now Fulton) Streets became part of the World Trade Center site.

Colonel Aaron Burr, a Revolutionary, along with Colonel John Cruger, a Loyalist officer of Brigadier General Oliver De Lancey's battalion, both assigned a lease on May 28, 1778 before the Battle of Monmouth Courthouse in New Jersey raises many questions. First of all, it assures a winning side will hold the lease after the war. More importantly the British and Loyalists trusted Burr, a Rebel, with the land lease. How can one explain the assignment of the lease to Burr by a known Tory, Robert Edwards especially when a British officer is named with him as nominee during an active campaign of the war? Unless, the Loyalists considered Burr one of them.

The New York Legislature's Act of Attainder Law of 1779 which confiscated all lands held by the Crown of England as of July 9, 1776 as well as all lands of those who remained loyal to the Crown became the property of the state of New York. It could be said that those in the know saw this confiscation law coming (debated in the state legislature in early 1778) and acted to do something to secure their assets. One was to entrust the legal title of the lands to neutral or Rebel family members or trusted associates. Another was to deed the property to traditionally sacred sanctuaries such as churches (see appendix D). The understanding was either compensation for or eventual return of the property to the principal, his heirs or relatives would ensue following resolution of the hostilities. In any event a great majority of those named in the 1779 Attainder Law did not show up on the lists of Loyalist Property Confiscations of New York. For example Oliver De Lancey lost property in New Jersey but does not seem to have had the same treatment in New York. His home in Westchester County was fired at in retaliation for his army's depredations on the rebelling populace, but confiscation is not evident. His home in Manhattan on Broadway wound up in the hands of his relative, John Watts. However the estate of James De Lancey on the east side of Manhattan was divided among the wealthy and the commoner.

Burr began visiting his future wife, Theodosia Bartow Prevost, in the fall of 1777. She was still the wife of Swiss-born British Captain Jacques (James) Marc Prevost. Her home, the Hermitage, in Paramus, New Jersey, was situated between the fluid lines of the American and British Armies. James Prevost had a 5000 acre Royal Grant in Suffern, at the time Bergen County, New Jersey, which he sold to Robert Morris and John De Lancey, and John Zabriski. He held lands in New York with Ann Stillwell Bartow De Visme, his mother-in-law. Many British officers held Royal Grants and invested in land as did Robert Edwards, a British Naval officer. Theodosius Bartow, her father, was a wealthy lawyer in Shrewsbury, New Jersey, with connections to the Anglican Church. They were well connected by marriage to the landed Pell family of Westchester County. Her mother, Ann Stillwell was married a second time to a British Captain Philip De Visme at Trinity Church where Theodosia later married James Prevost.

It was Lt. Colonel Jacques Marc Prevost at this time along with his uncle, Major General Augustine Prevost and nephew who were setting the Revolutionary cause backwards in the South by taking Savannah, Georgia and Charleston, South Carolina in early 1779. It would be nephew General George Prevost who would invade New York State during the War of 1812. It might be assumed that it was Theodosia who arranged the lease and suggested Aaron Burr's name as insurance on the lease should the British lose. Further support for this is that a D.C. (DeWitt Clinton) Reynolds, cousin of James Prevost, a Stoddard also, witnessed the lease. A Stoddard married to Timothy Edwards was the grandmother of Aaron Burr. Also the lease was signed in the presence of Robert Nelson, Lemuel Nelson and David Jackson. The Stoddard name appears numerous times in the Burr family lineage. Robert Edwards owned 500 acres in New Jersey not too far away and could have been visiting his property behind British lines at the time. Theodosia Prevost had more than six months to entice Aaron Burr into participating in the leases. Colonel Aaron Burr did not have to be present at the assignment of the lease to have his name appear as assignee.

Aaron Burr had served with Benedict Arnold in the earlier Quebec attack. Benedict's new wife, Peggy Shippen, a British sympathizer and friend of British Major Andre, the British spy master who helped Arnold defect, had convinced him to turn traitor at West Point in 1780. Margaret (Peggy) Shippen was close socially to Theodosia Prevost. Peggy was the niece of Doctor William Shippen of Philadelphia, a Tory family, who had initially helped their mother raise the orphaned Aaron and Sally Burr after the death of their father from smallpox. With them at Quebec was a James Wilkinson, Hamilton's successor as head of the army, who would later in 1805 confess to Aaron Burr to be an agent of Spain and plotted with him to have the Louisiana Territory secede from the United States and seize most of the Mexican West. Treason was to be their common calling card. But when did each turn against their country?

The leases of May 28, 1778 between Aaron and known Tories before the Battle of Monmouth make Aaron suspect even then, long before his treason trial of 1807. Later in early 1779 Washington assigned Burr to Westchester County where Theodosia's grandfather, John Bartow, had been the first Anglican minister from England. She would presumably know the hierarchy still in this ministry and possibly that of Trinity Church in New York also. She even accompanied Burr to New York City in August 5-10, 1778. It was either here that Aaron Burr turned over the leases to Trinity or through its satellite church in White Plains, Westchester County on March 12, 1779 two days after he wrote to Washington resigning from the army.

This date can be inferred from a document found in the State Exchange Records once listed under Estates and Contracts in the Arcade Building, Peachtree St., Atlanta, Georgia, now moved. Attached to these leases for 77 acres and 80 acres both containing the Cruger brothers John and Robert, and John and George, respectively, as grantee with Aaron Burr also grantee of the latter, is another document for the 77 acres which amounts to an extension for another 99 years. (Copy of Lease page 3 shelf 11 #7 State of New York, N.Y. District, and another curious paper titled, Manhattan Island, City and State of New York July 4th, 1865). In the extension document *"we the undersigned decendents (sic) of Robert Edwards and his brothers and sisters and decendents (sic) of Thomas Hael on this day release the estate inherited by us and our decendants (sic) and all decendants of Robert Edwards, his Brothers Thomas, Leonard and Joshua and his sister Martha* (note John and Jacob are omitted). *We release to Trinity Church Corporation wardens and vestermen (sic) for a period of (50) fifty years... by the rules of the 99 years lease made to John and George Crugar (sic) and sold by them to Trinity Church March 12, 1779... a similar 49 years lease is pending making a total of 99 years lease rental to be paid in by them to the Edwards Estate for heirs and decendents (sic)."* Had this lease extension and renewal been known to the courts during the many suits brought by other descendants (many of Rebel Edwards branches) during the 19th and early 20th centuries, then the heirs had only to wait until approximately 1976 when the lease renewal expired to regain legal title to the Robert Edwards lands. Thus latches or adverse possession could not be the defense and conclusion of the courts as it had been universally applied. The fact that this lease extension was not brought to the courts' attention might infer fraud or disregard of the court in failing to expose all pertinent documents during the trials.

Incidentally, the Trinity Church did not exist in 1779 because its charter was revoked by the Continental Congress in 1775. The church then burned down in 1776 when the British occupied New York City. Copies of these leases were found in the exchange records of other states in the Arcade Building on Peachtree St., Atlanta, Georgia. Could these copies have been sent to Georgia for safekeeping in the hands of a military Lt Governor of Georgia, James Prevost? Colonel John Cruger was active in Georgia as far inland as Augusta and Ninety Six in South Carolina in 1780 with the British Army. The witness D.C. (Dewitt Clinton) Reynolds had a large tobacco plantation near Atlanta. Possibly even later daughter, Theodosia Burr Alston, wife of Joseph Alston, Governor of South Carolina, might have brought these leases south? Note also that George Edwards heir to brother of Robert Edwards lived in South Carolina.

Chapter Nine: Burr and Washington and the Beginning of Schemes of Power

Washington did several incriminating acts himself. He accepted the invitation of Theodosia Bartow Prevost, a profligate socialite of the British and American upper military crust, to station his headquarters in her home for four days in July, 1778 after the Battle of Monmouth. He obviously did not fear any secret conversations being overheard and forwarded to the enemy. Yet he well knew Theodosia was the wife of an important British officer. Then again he sent Aaron Burr (at the direction of the New York Council of Safety in Albany) on a barge down the Hudson River on several missions to escort Tories into the British lines in New York City in August and September, 1778. One such man was Tory William Smith, former attorney general of New York. Aaron Burr would study law under Robert Smith, his brother, in Haverstraw, New York in 1781 after retiring from the service. Washington had to know that Burr could be entrusted with the safety of the Tories where perhaps others could not.

After all these missions of Loyalist causes, Aaron Burr resigned his commission because of illness from which he recovered when the war concluded. Burr had fallen from a wounded horse and became prostrate from heat exhaustion at the Battle of Monmouth Courthouse.

In the many confiscation attempts by the New Jersey Committee of Confiscations to take the British officer, Prevost's residence, the Hermitage, Aaron Burr interceded. With the help of James Monroe, Charles Lee, William Paterson, William Livingston, Robert Morris, and Robert Troup former roommate of Alexander Hamilton at King's College, he succeeded in saving the residence in 1780, and then removed Theodosia, her mother and children to Connecticut to his sister Sally Reeve's home for the duration of the war. He would buy the Hermitage from the estate of James Prevost then later exchanged it in one of his many land schemes.

Did General Washington have Loyalist leanings himself, revealed by trusting Burr? There is no other indication that he did. General George Washington had served in the British army as an officer during the French and Indian Wars. He fought many battles with the British army but only succeeded in defeating them with the help of the French army and navy at Yorktown. Other victories at Saratoga under Generals Gage and Benedict Arnold, and in the South under General Green were not his doing. His only other significant victory for which he gained much favor was at Trenton, New Jersey, against the German mercenaries. Did he lack the will and stomach for beating the British or just lacked the resources? As we will see, Washington had to fight with his own officers to win his battles with the British. Did he suspect Aaron Burr was too compromised to be of further use in his army? He realized Burr had strayed too far towards the Loyalist cause with his interest in Theodosia Prevost.

Washington or rather Lord Stirling had used Burr to spy on the British in New York after the Monmouth campaign. It is possible Aaron Burr tipped off the British that the French were going to land in Rhode Island at Newport; he then reported to Washington that Sir Clinton had moved troops toward Rhode Island to check the landing of the French.

Washington accepted Burr's resignation possibly in lieu of some future harsher sentence for more overt disloyalty that he feared might become evident later. Washington tersely replied to Burr's resignation letter on April 3, 1779 with regrets for the resignation and *"its cause"* (unspecified). Would not illness have been remonstrated, had it been the true cause? Illness is mentioned in an earlier sentence, but not attached to the cause of his resignation. Similarly, no offer to return to the service of his new country is made should he recover in the future. Perhaps despite Burr's seemingly exemplary service to the Revolutionary cause even on his last assignment in Westchester, New York, he had become weary of the infliction of pain and suffering on his former, current, and future Tory associates that would not stand him well in the future. His future wife's grandparent Pell pro British family members had suffered wounds in Westchester County during Aaron Burr's service there. The Pell family was also related to his grandmother Ward's family. The bringing of order to the American camp in Westchester also served the benefit of the Tory residents in the vicinity who had been plundered by the rabble of the American army. Burr's sympathies toward the Tories are revealed in a letter to American General M'Dougall January 13, 1779 upon taking command at Westchester. *"I could gibbet* (hang) *half a dozen good whigs* (Rebels*), with all the venom of an inveterate tory* (British sympathizer).*"*

Just as would General Benedict Arnold a year later, Colonel Aaron Burr lost the will to fight his family and friends for the Revolution. Both defections from the war are further proof of the paradox of war among neighbor, family and friends that would reveal itself again years later in the American Civil War. To further solidify this supposition of empathy for the Pell family in 1790 Aaron Burr purchased as a summer residence "The Shrubbery", manor house of the Pell family since 1740 on the Boston Post Road in Pelham, New York for his bride, Theodosia Prevost married in 1782. Burr conveyed the home to his stepson Augustine Frederick Prevost in 1794.

Next he entered on a scheme to move the New York to Boston road (now the Boston Post Road) and form a toll road in the West Farms area of southern Westchester County and Connecticut near his Burr family ancestral home. Dr. Joseph Browne married Catherine (Caty) De Visme, Theodosia's half sister, in a joint wedding with the Burrs at the Hermitage. He owned some of the land on which the road was to be built. Dr. Brown had acquired it from the estate of John Embree in 1785. Road commissioners, engineered into the legislation for absolute control by Burr himself, were Dr. Joseph Browne, George Embree (the family of the city of Embree deeded to Trinity Church during the war and back to Effingham Embree on May 6, 1795) and John Bartow, Jr. Bartow was a brother of Theodosia Bartow Prevost Burr. The Lewis Morris family took all of the tolls from the new bridge over the Harlem River at their Manor of Morrisania.

Burr began speculating in land of Rebels caught in the no man's land between the armies in Westchester County. These poor farmers had been unable to sustain a living on their land because of constant predation by both sides during the War of Independence and after the war were unable to sustain the vast land holdings without slave labor. They were forced to sell their land at bargain prices. Burr was only too glad to oblige. With the new road Burr and Browne would have convenient access to their newly acquired lands from Manhattan making them more valuable to break up into smaller farms for new immigrants. The enterprise was unpopular with the local population because it required taking their land for the new road. Since Burr had been appointed Attorney General of the State of New York by Governor Clinton in March, 1790, he was forced to sell the Shrubbery Manor house, situated on the toll road, to his stepson Augustine Prevost, to prevent discovery of his connection to the tolls. Joseph Browne who had bought an Embree estate on the road continued to develop the Boston Road and subdivide the adjacent properties they had acquired until 1797. Aaron moved on to politics as Senator for New York in the new national Congress in 1791. Together with brother-in-law, Dr. Browne, they began buying the 99 year Manhattan subleases from Trinity Church of Abraham Mortier. Beginning in 1793 eventually 150 acres were acquired; this by 1797 included the eventual home of Aaron Burr, Richmond Hill with the profits they had obtained by selling the West Farms in Westchester County. Aaron Burr then borrowed more than forty thousand dollars from his Manhattan Bank (now Chase Manhattan Bank) against this land around his Richmond Hill home early in 1802 paid off by John Jacob Astor on November 20, 1803 (67/411). This obviously was an exorbitant sum for undeveloped land, the price for which John Jacob Astor more than doubled in one year.

There is some indication that he also used French money to buy land in Canada in 1797 perhaps in conjunction with this money from the Manhattan loans. This may explain some of the reason behind his interest in the British forts on the western frontier in Ohio in 1795. Then Secretary of State Jefferson denied him access to state department records. Whether this was in league with John Jacob Astor's fur trade is not definite. But the reference to visits to Canada by Joseph Alston and Theodosia in 1804 in a letter from Astor to Burr suggests a Canadian connection yet to be revealed. We do know that Aaron's protégé artist Vanderlyn had painted the Niagara Falls in 1801. The Burr in-laws had visited a relative of deceased wife Theodosia, Chief Joseph Brant, in Upper (now Grand River, Ontario) Canada on a visit to the Falls also related in Burr letters.

The Mohawk warrior and statesman, Joseph Brant, was seeking redress from the British government for freedom to sell or lease to white settlers Indian lands granted to the Six Nations along the Grand River in Ontario for their service in the American Revolution on the side of the British. Unsuccessful he threatened to seek the aide of the French who the British feared along with the Spanish would encroach on the Canadian territories from the Mississippi River. Brant visited British minister, Robert Liston, in Philadelphia in 1797. Brant mixed with the pro-French party in the American capital which was that of Jefferson and Burr, both Republicans. Did Burr plot an overthrow of the British Government in Canada with French assistance to the Six (Indian) Nations on the Grand River? Was he going to buy Indian land along the Grand River? While negotiating with British minister, Anthony Merry, in 1804 Burr admitted to courting both the French and Spanish at the same time as insurance. Obviously, Burr was short on loyalty and long on expediency.

Joseph Brant had attempted to consolidate the Indian tribes of Ohio in order to better resist the encroachment on their lands from the westward expansion of the new American nation of whites to the east. He was unsuccessful because the Indian policy of the United States was divide and conquer by dealing with individual tribes. These same tribes were also duped by the British into believing that the Treaty of Paris that ended the Revolution did not cede their lands to the United States which it did. This is why the British were slow to abandon the forts on the westward fringe of the United States and in the Ohio Valley, as well as retaliation for confiscation of loyalist properties against the terms of the treaty. Not until the Jay Treaty in 1795 did the British troops fully withdraw. The British considered the Indian nations a buffer between the United States and their Canadian provinces. This also may explain the interest of Burr in the occupation of these forts in the mid 1790s for the benefit of his Indian relatives.

Joseph Brant was married to the daughter of George Croghan, Indian agent under Sir William Johnson, Catherine, sister to Susannah, wife of Augustine Prevost, nephew to James Prevost, first husband of Theodosia Bartow Prevost Burr. He was also related to Burr himself through the Stoddard family as was Timothy Pickering, distant relative of Aaron Burr, his supporter in the 1800 Presidential election, a High Federalist of the Essex Junto, and Indian agent in 1790-94. Burr's theologian family was associated with Indian proselytizing in Connecticut and Stockbridge, Massachusetts. Burr by letter affectionately urged daughter Theodosia to visit Brant on a trip to Niagara.

Other Canadian connections of Burr include the portrait artist, William Berczy, who painted Joseph Brant, and architect of the Christ Church of Montreal in 1803. He was also European advertiser of the western New York land company, Genessee Association of 1791 funded by British investors headed by Charles Williamson, the same go between Burr and British minister Anthony Merry in 1804. Robert Troup, college roommate of Alexander Hamilton, was acting American agent for the British company and was supported by Aaron Burr and fellow Manhattan lawyer from Worcester, Massachusetts, Timothy Green. Mistakenly called Doctor by some historians, but rather son of Doctor John Green, Timothy would be sent to South Carolina to bring Theodosia to New York in December, 1812, when both were lost at sea in early January, 1813. Berczy would accompany the settlers from Germany to present day Canaseraga, New York where he reached an impasse with Williamson over promises of land for his charges. In 1794 he sought the help of prominent Republican New York politicians, Samuel Street and presumably, because of later involvement, Aaron Burr, a member of that group, for a new German Company which purchased three townships in Upper Canada for settlement for $60,000 along the Grand River. Governor Simcoe moved the settlement to York now Toronto in Markham Township. Failing to settle the full extent of the land grant in the allotted time Berczy was forced to forfeit the grant and ultimately returned to New York in 1812 before the outbreak of war between England and the United States and obtained a further $10,000 credit from none other than Aaron Burr and Timothy Green. One must remember that Burr was then just returned from exile in Europe and supposedly destitute himself. How his fortunes had quickly changed!

Associated with Brant, and Berczy and curiously Aaron Burr's name was an Asa Danforth who likewise had a Simcoe proprietor's grant to settle Upper Canada near Toronto. When Governor Simcoe decided to renege in 1796, Danforth eventually wound up in debtor's prison in 1800 in the United States. He then sought council with Presidential candidate, Aaron Burr, hoping that a Republican victory would *"afford something handsome to those who were dragged from home by fair promises of Genl. Simcoe... saw that our Americans had made choice of the best lands... plan*(ned) *to rescind and take away the lands..."* He assumed the British in Canada feared an eclipse of power in North America with a Republican Administration in the United States while *"three-fourths of the common people would be happy of a Change."* Was it true that Aaron Burr was plotting an overthrow of the British Government in Canada? Aaron Burr, a British agent, was plotting to oust the British administration of Canada behind their backs while on their payroll. This double agency was not uncommon as General Wilkinson while as agent number 13 for Spain would later scheme with Burr to seize the Louisiana Territory and as much of Spanish Mexico as they could in 1804-5.

This could be the source of friction between Aaron Burr and Great Britain in later years that led to the mysterious loss at sea of his daughter, Theodosia and co-conspirator Timothy Green in 1812 off Cape Hatteras. Perhaps Green not Theodosia was the object of assassination or was Theodosia carrying incriminating documents of both Burr and Green for inclusion in the proposed biography of Burr.

The Manhattan Company got its start in the yellow fever epidemic of 1798. Dr. Browne advocated a pure water source for the City of Manhattan from his property on the Bronx River draining the upper Westchester County. With the money collected from the water a Bank, The Manhattan Bank, now Chase Manhattan Bank, was formed in 1799 from which Burr and his friends tapped resources for their enterprises. Thus began the intricate schemes of Aaron Burr and his relatives.

Chapter Ten: Burr, John Jacob Astor and Trinity Church

Some of the founders of the new country were not especially religious. Several were termed Deists, believing in a God, but without the trappings of organized religion. Even Washington attended the Anglican Church later the Episcopalian Church without taking communion. Hamilton grew up religious, but strayed during his adult life, until his duel loomed. Aaron Burr was never the pious one. Yet during the Revolutionary War he and many other Loyalist turned over much valuable land in New York City and environs to Trinity Church far beyond a tithing. Even Burr's New York City home, Richmond Hill, reverted back to Trinity Church at the expiration of the lease that was assumed by John Jacob Astor upon his leaving New York City after the 1804 duel. In 1797 Aaron had assumed a sublease of Richmond Hill owned by Trinity until his departure in 1804. For some unknown reason he attempted to sell it in November of 1801 for one hundred forty thousand dollars, but the deal fell through at the last moment on November 20, 1801 Burr wrote his daughter, *"The sale of Richmond Hill is all off; blown up at the moment of counting the money, partly by whim and partly by accident; something else will be done to produce the effect* (of raising money)." In July of this same year he had leased land on Broadway jointly owned with John De Lancey to Henry Davis for $11,500 (114/500). It would be interesting to know when and how he had acquired this property with a member of the Tory De Lancey family. One could suspect this happened during the Revolutionary War period. This further supports the conclusion that Aaron Burr was deeply involved with Tory or High Federalist interests in Manhattan despite his

Republican political party affiliations with the Jeffersonians, as the Vice-President.

He sold most of the acreage around the home in November of 1803 to fur trader, John Jacob Astor *"all is sold, and well sold* (fancy price); *not all however. The house... four acres remain. Enough to keep up the appearance... are reserved with interest* (to be sold to Astor later, August 20, 1804, 222/43)*... This weighty business... a huge weight it has taken from the head and shoulders, and every other part, animal and intellectual, of A. B."* The animal is cunning as Burr is smart. This is not the words of a desperate man with creditors at his heels but a calculating man with a vision of HIS future. The money from the sale is not to settle old debts but to create new ones.

John Jacob Astor is implicated in Burr's first New England scheme as early as November 22, 1803. Burr wrote *"Mr. Astor left with me some days ago for Mr. Alston a very beautiful map of Lower Canada, price ten dollars, and two views of Montreal and its vicinity* (the Ohio Valley and the New England states, the first Federalist secession scheme), *two guineas* (British currency no longer used in the United States). *I am particularly charged by Mr. Astor that his landlord at Montreal* (the Crown of England) *paid to him* (Mr. Astor), *for the account of Joseph Alston, Esq., the sum of one half guinea; the said landlord having discovered, after the departure of the said Joseph Alston et ux., that they had not taken with them two bottles of Madeira wine which the said landlord had charged in the bill of the said Joseph Alston, and for which he had received payment. Thus I have discharged myself of a commission which has been enjoined upon me at least ten times."* Of itself, the letter seems petty and meaningless, after all, why should the loss of two wine bottles be such an issue tenfold. In the context of his other letters and the time frame written, the message conveyed by Burr seems to implicate Astor as agent of the Crown in his scheme. One can infer that the money that Astor gave Burr in the same month and year for his land in Manhattan around his Richmond Hill originated from the Crown of England *"well sold"* at a substantial profit. Burr may have added Alston to the list of conspirators due compensation by this time. Two bottles of Madeira or desert wine forgotten might refer to Theodosia and Joseph Alston left out of the deal with England. In flowing terms two of the sweetest persons to Burr deserved like payment from the Crown.

John Jacob Astor divided his purchase from Burr into lots and became extremely wealthy in his real estate dealings in Manhattan where Aaron Burr had failed. Some of these transactions of October 22 and November 18, 1803 are recorded on June 1 and 4, 1804 respectively (Book/Page: 67/2,

67/11), prior to the challenge to the duel and not subsequent to it as some have mistakenly reported. Other transactions with Burr occurred on May 1, 1804 prior to the challenge to Hamilton and November 17, 1800 about the time of the election for President which suggests that Burr was on the payroll of England then. These deeds were not recorded until August 24, 1819 (138/518, 138/521) suggesting a need to hide the transactions from public view for awhile. The final sale of Richmond Hill to Astor was on August 20, 1804 not recorded until May 25, 1827 (222/43), nearly twenty three years later.

John Jacob Astor rented some of these lots #198-200 (of the original 1797 Trinity Lease to Burr) to Moses Bedel for 41 years on King Street for $1300/ year on 1/20/1825 (307/568, 307/591).

At the time of the duel with Hamilton Aaron Burr also deeded property, his law office at Broadway and Trinity Church Cemetery, to Jacob Mark (the Jacob Mark Foundry at 5, 7 Worth Street, maker of manhole covers in the nineteenth century) on July 11, 1804 (69/23, recorded Jan. 26, 1805). Brother-in-law Joseph Browne, moving to St. Louis as Secretary to the new Louisiana Territory, also deeded property to Jacob Mark at Carmine and Bedford Streets (69/21, 12/26/1804 also recorded 1/26/1804). A little later on August 10, 1804 Matthew L. Davis, witness to the duel and author of Burr's *Memoirs,* and others by Power of Attorney received a deed from Burr (67/394, Aug. 21, 1804). It can be inferred the timely sale of both properties to Jacob Mark were prearranged convenience sales for liquidation reasons. Mark acted as intermediary for a more important source of funds. Remember, Joseph Browne was never implicated in the 1807 Treason of Aaron Burr involving the Louisiana Territory of which Browne was the Secretary. As presumed silent co-conspirator Burr had reasons to avoid implicating Browne in his *Memoirs.*

Astor would later retire to England in 1834 some say renouncing his American citizenship; although he is interred at Trinity Church graveyard! Burr himself had ended up in shame and in debt, then attempted to use his second wife, Eliza Bowen Jumel's fortune from her first husband, a wine merchant. This led to their divorce finalized on his deathbed. The irony is that Alexander Hamilton Jr. was Eliza Burr's lawyer in the divorce proceedings.

The family of Bowen, Eliza's maiden name, started Wall Street and Robert Bowen was one of the first directors of the Bank of New York. By coincidence Aaron Burr had corresponded with daughter Theodosia about purchasing or switching Richmond Hill for Roger Morris' estate a little north and east of Burr's home on Washington Heights. This home was acquired by Stephen Jumel in 1810 where his wife often stayed alone sometimes estranged from him while he was in Europe. It is another coincidence that Burr would be considering trading Richmond Hill for the Roger Morris estate in 1804, when he would later win it in marriage to Eliza. Her obituary suggested associations with George Washington, Benedict Arnold, Thomas Jefferson, Ben Franklin, Patrick Henry and young Aaron Burr. Although she was reportedly very beautiful, and a known prostitute, there are quite a lot of notches on her walking stick for the achievements of one woman, who is buried in Trinity Churchyard. She had an illegitimate son named George Washington Bowen. It was not uncommon for early Americans to name their children, legitimate or not, after the names of prominent American statesmen or ancestors.

Was there a hatred of Alexander Hamilton that came from a higher authority? Was Burr merely acting at the behest of the Crown? Hamilton was an upstart and an opportunist. He played both sides to his benefit. Yet he was an idealist, shunning those that he felt would use his position in the Government to their benefit. He had made himself conspicuous at Yorktown to the shame of the Army of the King of England. And what is one to make of that curious inscription on the headstone of Alexander Hamilton in Trinity Church Graveyard placed there by the Church itself? It is a glowing tribute to a man that aided the Loyalists from within the Government of the new United States without enriching himself in the process.

Chapter Eleven: Burr's Counselor, Theodosia

Aaron Burr was well known to use cipher with his daughter, Theodosia Alston. In fact he asked his wife once in a letter how their daughter's studies in cipher as an eight year old were progressing. The Burrs were grooming their daughter to be a spy at that early age. Cipher takes two major forms, substitution or transposition. The early cipher between friend Robert Troup and Burr used female names, often maiden names, for their husbands or boyfriends by substitution. Later correspondences with daughter Theodosia became more complicated, so much so that Theodosia once complained to Burr to send the new code key again because she could not decipher his meaning. These codes used writings of known philosophers, poets, and lyrics like Shakespeare's. Often Burr would tell about a switch in the code for the next letter by saying remember to read, or bring with you, or refer to such and such novel or writings of some individual known to them both. Then he might quote a passage in the novel often in French where one with the book could reference a page number, line and word placement perhaps to represent a number significant to the reader such as number of troops, date, money to be sent, or where to find another code within another source. It is highly possible that many of Burr's supposed "paramours" were merely covers for fellow plotters.

The letters themselves read alone seem meaningless, confusing and outright gibberish. They are meant to be so for after all they are coded messages. Anyone familiar with the people mentioned would be able to pick out tiny errors and discrepancies that alert the person meant to read the letter that a different meaning than the one seemingly written is meant to be inferred. After the duel Burr was on the lam. He really didn't have time to stop and resume an affair with Celeste with two indictments for his arrest in New York and New Jersey breathing down his neck! Taken in the context of the time frame of the letters and the sequence of letters themselves taken as a whole the picture becomes more understandable and the persons referenced become more obvious.

One such notable person, Celeste, probably represented Charles Williamson or British minister to the United States, Anthony Merry for in a letter from Philadelphia, August 2nd after the duel Burr writes *"Nothing can be done with Celeste. There is a strange indecision and timidity which I cannot fathom. The thing, however, is abandoned; and, for a few months, I believe, all such things."* It is not a woman he is concerned about being timid but the British Government being indecisive about his scheme. The original affair with Celeste in 1802 had reached ennui, thus the failed sale of his Richmond estate in that year. The resumption of which in 1804 might well be a cover for the affair of state simultaneously with Anthony Merry. Both Merry and Celeste resided in Philadelphia, a convenient conjunction of circumstance. *"If any male friend of yours should be dying of ennui; recommend to him to engage in a duel and a courtship* (not plural, only one, here England, not two, England and a woman) *at the same time-prob. est."* His letters before this refer to the on again, off again relationship with Celeste during this year leading up to the duel often in a sexual context. Celeste is known as an early Chinese Empire no doubt known to Burr and Theodosia, through the study of astrology and could here represent the Crown of England. The representation of Anthony Merry is a celestial match made in HEAVEN. He introduces on January 17th 1804 *"Mrs. Merry* (code for the husband, British Minister to the United States) *is tall, fair, fat- pas trop* (not their friend, Robert Troup, a plump man himself*), however... An amiable and interesting companion, with whose acquaintance you will, next summer, be much gratified... I want a French translation of the Constitution of the United States..."* Here Burr is referring to the scheme to secede the once *"French"* Louisiana Purchase now owned by the *"United States"* timed for the summer after the duel to come (not mentioned) with the help of the *"amiable"* British. Celeste appears on January 4th *"Celeste—(for this I begin a new line)"* (Burr now means to use Celeste's name in a coded context, i.e. for Anthony Merry) *"Celeste will be seen on the way home, but that La R.* (the King, Le Roi, or Austin Roe of the Long Island Culper Spy Chain of Major Tallmadge) *spoils everything in that place."* Here he either is saying the King of England is reluctant to buy his plots or more likely as we shall see further he is referring to a Revolutionary Spy Ring uncovered by him during the war. *"That place"* refers to the spying on Burr in Philadelphia. The analogy here is that he is cognizant of a current attempt to spy on his activities by his enemies who would report to President Jefferson just as Roe had passed on information to General Washington during the War. The implication is clear. Theodosia was privileged with the information about the spy ring of the Revolutionary War and would understand the significance of a Mr. (La) Roe (R.) carrying reports of Burr's secret rendezvous with British Minister Merry to President Jefferson. It also implies that Burr had a significant hand in revealing the Culper Ring to the British during the Revolutionary War. The Ring was supposedly successfully secret throughout the war. Or was it? There is evidence that the British knew of the Culper Ring and chose to let it remain intact in order to feed it misinformation and be cautious as to what sources it was exposed to in Manhattan. It would be easier to watch a known ring than to break it and have to uncover another that would surely spring up in its place.

In any event he courts other countries, France in the person of a Jerome Bonaparte and Spain's Marquis de Casa Yrujo in many of the same letters. *"The living languages, French and Spanish, may there be learned by association and habit. The French, the Spanish, the English (I mean the learners of those languages) are each in separate apartments."* He keeps each of his contacts in the dark about the others. He talks of the shawl or cloak, the rage of Paris and London, meant for Theodosia many times as too valuable to forward by sea or land. This represents the mantle of power he will bestow on his daughter when either France or England approves his scheme of secession. Meanwhile it is too dangerous for her to be implicated in the scheme for now. He tells her of the press' sniping at his character, *"Cath. C. (possibly referring to James Cheetham, Republican polemicist or trouble maker) la la."* (a tongue wager) November 7th, 1803. And again on July 1st · 1804 *"C.C. (Charles Cooper) says you are a good-for–nothing, lazy *****(I really cannot write her words; they are too dreadful, and must be left to your imagination to supply)"* Dr. Cooper is the one who wrote quoting Hamilton that *"Mr. Burr to be a dangerous man, and one who ought not to be trusted with the reins of government... I could detail to you a still more despicable opinion which General Hamilton has expressed of Mr. Burr."* This became the excuse for Burr to challenge Hamilton to the duel that ended Hamilton's life as it was being planned by Burr for several months before the statement attributed to Hamilton.

When in November 22nd Burr suggests trading Richmond Hill for Roger Morris' more spacious country estate of one hundred and thirty acres. *"Shall I exchange?"* Theodosia replied *"...and there is to me something stylish, elegant, respectable, and suitable to you in having a handsome country-seat. So that, upon the whole, I vote for Morris's."* By this is meant the exchange of Richmond Hill by way of John Jacob Astor and the Crown for a country of his own *"will be a principality* (the state of French Louisiana and Spanish Mexico, the scheme)."* This comes to fruition when on August 11, 1804 Burr writes Joseph Alston *"I have barely time to read them and transmit your orders to New-York about Montalto* (the code name for Richmond Hill)"*. Richmond Hill was just that, a prominent home on a prominent elevated part of Manhattan, thus the name Montalto or high promontory. Here he gives the order to sell the remainder of Richmond Hill and the four acres to John Jacob Astor as previously planned in late 1803. This is done on August 20, 1804 (recorded 222/43, May 25, 1827). Roger Morris was a Loyalist whose home was seized by the New York Committee of Attainder. Interestingly, John Jacob Astor bought out the children's legal rights to the reversionary interest in the property for L20,000. Probably Astor still owned the property in 1804 to which Burr makes a reference of exchange implying a gain obviously by way of John Jacob Astor.

"All strangers go to see Montalto as one of the curiosities or beauties of the island (Not Jefferson's Montalto which is not on an island such as Burr's Manhattan home, Richmond Hill made famous by his duel with Hamilton*)."* Montalto was known as the location for the home of President Jefferson, yet clearly writing from New York and Philadelphia he means some other place. From New York on June 9, 1803, *"We shall ride to Montalto this afternoon, and you shall know our reception."* In the guise of the affair with Celeste he reports from Philadelphia the next day *"I received a note from Celeste, advising me that she is in town for a few hours, and will be happy to see me. What in the name of love and matrimony can this mean? The conclusion was definitive, and a mutual promise that neither would ever renew the subject. I am all impatience, and I go to hear."* The same day, the tenth from New York he writes again *"in coachee to Montalto to-morrow afternoon."* On the eleventh he again writes from Philadelphia about the affair with Celeste.

One can conclude Montalto is in Philadelphia and has either to do with Celeste or her pseudonym, Anthony Merry, both of whom live in Philadelphia. One can not ride from Philadelphia to New York City in one day by coach as would be required by the sequence of letters. In this case Montalto must refer to the home of British minister Anthony Merry. Montalto is the Latin word for summit. Summit is both a lofty location and a meeting or discussion among the highest executives of government. Burr uses this term loosely for both a place and a meeting. By transference Burr later makes his home as lofty and important as that of the President of the United States. By saying people will flock to see his home then called Montalto when he succeeds in his scheme in Mexico, he is equating his home, Richmond Hill to the Monticello of Jefferson. He has attained parity with the man who beat him out of the Presidency in 1800. This is a small window into the mind of a grandiose schemer.

Alternately, is it the home of Roger Morris in New York, north and east of Richmond Hill? Some have supposed Montalto is the retreat of the Joseph Alstons on Manhattan north and east of Richmond Hill. This was most likely the location of the Rose Hill Farm owned by Nicholas Cruger now 23rd Street later owned by Bertram Peter Cruger, John C. Cruger and Alfred Pell. Clearly Montalto does not refer to the same location in each of his letters to Theodosia where Burr is to meet with others on some clandestine mission. The mention of swap of Richmond Hill for Roger Morris' brings up the possibility that Roger Morris had some dealings with Aaron Burr during these negotiations with the British Ambassador Merry. More likely it refers to the sale of Richmond Hill to Astor in order to pursue his scheme for grander things in Spanish Mexico. As shown later cipher codes evolved or rotated into new meanings and were not usually static references as clearly Montalto metamorphoses.

The competition of Burr with Jefferson for grandiosity of residence was matched by their interest in cipher, a popular method of sending secrets through an unreliable and less than private mail system of the time. Jefferson had invented a mechanical cipher drum machine not put into use until World War I. To Burr's credit he had a more lasting influence on the education of young females. He gave access to his residence to Madame de Senat, the mother of his unofficially adopted daughter, Natalie of whom he mentioned often to Theodosia in his letters. Madame de Senat ran a girl's school in Manhattan supported by Burr. Although not a rival to the University of Virginia founded by Jefferson within sight of his Monticello, Burr's interest in the education of females was visionary and revolutionary for its time, and based on the feminist book of Mary Wollstonecraft.

Likewise, Burr's interest in the arts in New York City and his patronage of John Vanderlyn especially, eclipsed Jefferson whose interest in the sciences and architecture were more self-centered than Burr's. However Jefferson did send his personal secretary, Meriwether Lewis, with William Clark on the Lewis and Clark Expedition into the Louisiana Territory in 1804-6 for scientific as well as national exploration. Burr also supported the education of author Washington Irving, and future U.S. President Martin Van Buren. Burr once referred to Washington Irving as Mrs. Irving recognized by author Thomas Fleming in an aborted attempt to decipher some of his letters. Fleming in *The Duel* came closest of all historians to discerning Aaron Burr. Some attribute Van Buren's parentage to Burr because he frequented the family Inn on his many trips from New York City to Albany, New York. However Mrs. Van Buren was a rather mousy woman and an unlikely attraction for Burr. Aaron Burr was said to have never denied an accusation of parentage. For if a young woman would honor him with the accolade; he was enough of a gentleman not to disavow it. This was the cocky nature of the self centered man.

As to that other rivalry in a letter by Aaron Burr to daughter Theodosia on July 20, 1804 after the duel Burr seemed to praise Hamilton's detachment from the enticements of public life. "*La G.* (Starts out as La Greque in earlier letters. Supposedly a woman but by substitution (just as Mrs. Irving was Washington Irving) in cipher becomes The Greek, Alexander the Great, or Alexander Hamilton.) *has, on a recent occasion, manifested a degree of sensibility and attachment which have their influence on gamp* (Burr). *Her* (his) *conduct is also highly honourable to the independence of her* (his) *mind, for all her* (his) *associations and connexions would lead to a different result."* Hamilton was above reproach in his political dealings which others might find tempting toward corruption. "*It was* (the duel*), indeed, a pretty ludicrous description which you received. On the other side you may add, real good-temper and cheerfulness; a good education, according to the estimation of the world."* Burr has no regrets and is happy of the result and hopes to increase his following, namely England in his scheme.

It seems from the letters to Theodosia, Burr has been considering the duel disguised as a match with a woman (La G.) for some time. On June 13, 1804, "*Another interview yesterday with La G. One more would be fatal and final. I shall seek it to-day; after which I will read Moore's fables* (fairy tales of a foolish and improbable story of his plans to secede the Western U.S. and conquer parts of Mexico*), you impudence* (surely not referring to Theodosia, but Hamilton's offensively bold, and brazen speech about Aaron Burr)." Surely his amours would not be considered *"fatal"* unless he refers to making the duel stick by design. He plans to proceed with his grand scheme after doing away with his nemesis, Hamilton. May 26 "*The matter there spoken of seemed to be in so precarious a state...but that day to this I have not seen La G., owing partly to accident and partly to apathy."* May 8th "*The affair of La G. is becoming serious. After due reflection, this does appear to me to be the most discreet thing-... I will offer homage* (referring to asking Hamilton for the $10,000 to settle a creditor?). *Are you content?* (With the decision to kill Hamilton?)" Burr is asking Theodosia to agree with the plan to remove Hamilton. How do we know? May 1st "*La G. may be forty-one* (code number for death?). *The* *election is lost by a great majority: tant mieux.... Even if La G. should not prevent it... What would you bet that La G. is not in a kind of quandary just now? Gods! What a pathetic love-scene it will make if it* (the duel) *shall go on."* Hamilton does not know what is in store for him. He imagines his reaction to the challenge to the duel, the predicament or *"quandary".* Burr anticipates the public reaction, or *"love-scene",* to the death of Hamilton at his hand in the duel to come.

Publicly Burr had later pretended that he had no knowledge of Hamilton's supposed scandalous descriptions of Burr until June about the time of his challenge when in fact we see here he has already in May begun the machinations of a plot to kill him for whatever reason. March 28 *"La G., of whom you inquire, is of the grave age of forty-six; about the age of the vice-president."* Burr plans Hamilton's demise, *"grave age".* There were six months difference in age between Burr and Hamilton. *"I would send you some new and amusing libels against the vice-president, but, as you did not send the speech, nor did even acknowledge the receipt of one of the many public documents which I took the trouble of forwarding..."* Clearly the die is cast well before the challenge on June 27th and without much indignation (*amusing* in the least). This even antedates the publication of Hamilton's scathing attack on Burr's unfitness for public office on April 24th. February 16th *"A critical knowledge of historical events may assist a statesman or form a pedant* (getting in the way). *For you, something less will do, and something more is necessary. La G. will not do... Hamilton is intriguing for any candidate who can have a chance of success against A. B.* (Aaron Burr)." The plan for Hamilton's removal as an impediment to Burr is hatched. February 8th *"Tomorrow I am to see La G. Pray for me".* And again February 9th *"Shall not see La G. to-day".* The most overt reference to the duel is made on January 3rd *"That General Jackson is my good friend* (Jackson, a notable combatant, could be the substitute for another supposed friend, Alexander Hamilton as the sequence of letters would imply.); *that I have had no duel nor quarrel with anybody, and have not been wounded or hurt"."* In the world of cipher the opposite is often meant from the text as written. Thus no duel or quarrel becomes the opposite; he intends to pick a quarrel and duel.

So we see that Burr has decided way before the challenge to the duel in June that Hamilton is in his way preventing Burr's schemes from reaching fruition. Burr has decided to remove him from the theatre. The next day, January 4th *"La G. is much better than I had heard...willing* (to supply the fodder, polemics, for Burr to pick the quarrel and the duel)." On December 27, Burr writes *"Madame G., whom you are pleased to term the rich widow."* If G. stands for Hamilton, Madame (not the same as La, although both feminine gender, Madame is the wife and La the husband) G. refers to Elizabeth Hamilton who Theodosia calls widow six months before the duel. Burr on December 4, 1803 says *"I rejoiced at what you tell me of La Grec."* Theodosia replies *"I must tell you that I have again heard from La Greque."* Thus we know La G. stands for La Greque, and La Grec., an evolution of cipher code perhaps to keep the reader on track. Is Aaron Burr implying that Theodosia has told him to remove La G., Hamilton? Hamilton is to be set up for the duel. Burr has only to wait for the right opportunity, Hamilton *"willing"*.

Chapter Twelve: Alexander Hamilton and his Gravestone by Trinity Church Corporation

Alexander requested last rites from the rector of Trinity Church, Reverend Benjamin Moore, an uncle of Aaron Burr, who initially refused on the basis of the impropriety of dueling and Hamilton's tardy churchgoing. Rev. Moore assented to a second request reluctantly. He received a state funeral in Trinity Church and was buried there in the presence of throngs of mourners from all political persuasions.

ALEXANDER HAMILTON
The corporation of TRINITY CHURCH has erected this monument
In Testimony of their Respect
FOR
The PATRIOT of Incorruptible INTEGRITY
The SOLDIER of approved VALOR
The STATESMAN of consummate WISDOM
Whose TALENTS and VIRTUES will be admired
By a
Grateful posterity
Long after this MARBLE shall have mouldered into
DUST
He died July 12th 1804 aged 47

It is a curious epitaph because it is placed there by the CORPORATION OF TRINITY CHURCH and not his family, wife or children or The Society of Cincinnati of which he was president. The Society of Cincinnati was made up of officers of Washington's Continental Army still in existence today by heredity exclusively of the first born descendant sons, surely a derivative of the British primogenitor system of heredity. There does not seem to be other such stones of the Corporation in the Trinity Church graveyard! He had publicly admitted to adultery in his own publication of the Reynolds affair, yet he is called VIRTUOUS by a church, no less, not unlike present political leaders. His TALENT was to take the model of the British system of banking and apply it in a new nation that had just repudiated that governmental system. With the help of the wealthy class of England he not only restored the world credit of the United States, but he in turn helped return lost property to that same group in New York City without seemingly benefiting personally. This was WISDOM not admired by the greater part of the populace of the United States newly separated from the oppression of this same group. The charter of the First Bank of the United States was not renewed by Congress in 1811 because the majority of the stockholders were British or European. Rather, this same group comprised the grateful ones since he WILL BE ADMIRED BY A GRATEFUL POSTERITY, even though the current population does not. He displayed VALOUR at Yorktown when in the final act of hostilities he led the attack that took the last redoubt. He resisted associations while Secretary of the Treasury with those that would seem to seek personal gain which displayed incorruptible INTEGRITY.

Is this epitaph an act of guilt or an expression of RESPECT and ADMIRATION by the Loyalists of Trinity Church? The guilt was perhaps for encouraging Burr's duel with Hamilton in order to eliminate too incorruptible and virtuous an opponent to the schemes of Burr for a new order in the Spanish Americas that included the British Crown. The RESPECT and ADMIRATION was because the Loyalist of New York City had been and were still the majority of the congregation of Trinity Church and direct benefactors of their relationship with the Crown of England.

Seven of the seventeen Presidents of the United States through Abraham Lincoln had been members of the Episcopalian Faith, a derivative of the Anglican Church of England.

Many of these Presidents including President Ronald Reagan, George Bush, Sr., and other prominent Americans, like Alan Greenspan, Mayor Rudy Giuliani of New York City, General Norman Schwarzkopf, Secretary of State Colin Powell, Bob Hope and interestingly, both Colonel Ollie North (What secrets did he withhold in his Iran-Contra Congressional hearings?) and General Tommy Franks have been knighted by Queen Elizabeth II of England. Is there a political and more importantly economic connection with these prominent Americans and Trinity Church Corporation or even the Crown of England beyond loyalty to the United States? Most recently Bill Gates in January, 2004 has been knighted KBE (Knight Commander of the British Empire) for his philanthropy and involvement in Great Britain. Wonder if he descends from General Horatio Gates?

This author a fan of all of the above means no disrespect or disloyalty, but purely with historical perspective is attempting to make sense and meaning to all these revelations. Why a mere colonel in the American army is deemed worthy of knighthood by a British monarch needs explanation. Colonel North has his own television program on Rupert Murdock's Fox News Channel concerning the history of World War II. The Franks family has a long lineage to the Crown of England.

Chapter Thirteen: Theodosia Burr Alston, God's Divine Gift; Her Portrait Artist and the Myths.

Even after death did Alexander Hamilton's path cross that of Aaron Burr's. While coming to the American colony of New York from St Croix as a young teenager, Alexander Hamilton's ship encountered a great storm and shipboard fire off Cape Hatteras, North Carolina. They were blown into Boston. Hamilton swore that a lighthouse there would have been very helpful and vowed if he ever had any power to, he would put one there. This he did as first Secretary of the Treasury under George Washington in 1790.

During the War of 1812 long after the death of Alexander Hamilton in 1804, Aaron Burr had already returned from Europe having fled there in disgrace following the duel and later, his trial for treason. He had been the guest of the British Banker Jacques Mallet du Pan, a French speaking British intelligence officer, of the Prevosts family, and of Jeremy Bentham. Bentham was the Geneva speech writer of French insurrection at the behest of East India Company chairman, the Earl of Shelburne who together would form the modern British Intelligence Service. Upon his return, Burr's very loving daughter Theodosia Alston yearned to meet him in New York City. By December, 1812 she had lost her only son to malaria in South Carolina and was in possible marital discord with her planter husband, Joseph Alston, Governor of South Carolina. She carried a portrait of herself dressed in white as a gift to her father and a letter of safe passage to the British Navy which blockaded the coast. The British did stop and let pass her ship, the privateer Patriot, but following a severe storm off the Nags Head, Cape Hatteras, North Carolina she was never seen again.

Gone with Theodosia were the papers of Burr's political and social career with which she was entrusted by her father for her husband, Joseph Alston to write his father-in-law's biography. Could it be that England wished for others not to know of their complicity in Burr's many grand schemes of conquest and secession in the Americas? True they let her pass, but into the clutches of their agents, Lafitte's pirates, who may have been there to execute the Crown's dirty work. Would they care what America would say about their enemy in time of War? Perhaps there were reasons other than political such as economic to maintain the status quo of ignorance. In any event the evidence was disposed of, surreptitiously or not.

With each myth there is a grain of truth. From the following myths there may be enough truth to paint a picture of reality. Among the myths are those literally about a painting by a talented artist, John Vanderlyn.

Some say the ship grounded on the beach under full sail without a trace of her crew. The locals were salvagers and found the portrait which an elderly lady in 1869 used to pay a medical debt to a physician, Dr. Poole, from Elizabeth City, North Carolina, who attended her. When the physician learned whose portrait it was he sold it to the Burr family who supposedly donated it to the Yale Museum of Art. Some have claimed the old lady was Theodosia herself who somehow had survived the wreck. The fate of Theodosia and her possessions at the time of her disappearance has fascinated many history buffs including some ghost busters on the outer banks of North Carolina for almost two centuries.

The Yale Museum of Art possesses two paintings of Theodosia. One attributed to Gilbert Stuart, circa 1797, as a young woman surrounded by books, and the other a supposed copy of a lost or damaged portrait of Theodosia dressed in white painted in 1802 or 1803 by John Vanderlyn (Leude), father, Nicholas. John Vanderlyn's first effort was a copy of a Gilbert Stuart painting of Burr which eventually led to their introduction to one another. Burr sponsored John's study with Gilbert Stuart, famous portrait painter, and then further study in Paris even as late as while Burr was there in exile. Burr also supported the education of author Washington Irving and future U.S. President Martin Van Buren.

John Vanderlyn painted James Monroe in Paris while he was negotiating the Louisiana Purchase. Perhaps with the news of the purchase he went to London to report the event to the British. He went to London under the pretense that he could not find an engraver in Paris worthy of his work. This was a specious argument because Vanderlyn was one of the first American artists to study in Paris as early as 1796 for four years. It was unlikely he could not find an engraver for his portraits there. Indeed, Burr himself wrote to Theodosia on December 16, 1802 that Vanderlyn *"is greatly occupied in finishing his Niagara views, which, indeed, will do him honour. They will be four in number, and he thinks of having them engraved in France."* Voila! Vanderlyn is caught in a lie!

The engravings of the painting of Monroe among others in London he claimed were lost in transit to Paris. It seems Burr was involved with the scheme of Spanish Mexican conquest before the run for governor of New York while still Vice President. John Vanderlyn could likely have been working for then Vice-President Burr and the British as a spy in this case on Monroe's negotiations with the French over Louisiana.

In the same letter Burr wrote *"He is run down with applications for portraits, all of which, without discrimination, he refuses"*. Vanderlyn was very much dependent on Burr for support, enough so that he didn't need to accept subscriptions from the public. Thus Vanderlyn was very likely in the service of Burr during the time of the portraiture of Monroe in Paris.

While in Paris in 1810 Burr mentioned in his private journal that he spent almost daily visits with John Vanderlyn often attending artistic events in the city even though Burr had claimed near destitution during this time. Vanderlyn spent much of the time of Burr's exile in Europe with Burr and is mentioned many times in his letters to Theodosia. Vanderlyn often said Burr never forgot anything. So likewise Burr's historians should not forget the details of Burr's life, as intricate as it was. It was the minutia that linked Burr activities.

"That the knowledge and use of men consisted in placing each in his appropriate position", and *"never negotiate in a hurry"*, Matthew L. Davis attributed to Burr's maxims. Davis felt to be one of Burr's *"most remarkable exhibitions of the force of his character, this bending every one who approached him to his use, and compelling their unremitted, though often unwilling, labours in his behalf."*

Vanderlyn, though married, remained in Paris until 1816. Vanderlyn's closest, some say sexual, friend in Paris in 1807 was Washington Allston, cousin of the husband of Burr's daughter, Theodosia. An eminently more successful but equally talented painter, Washington was the son of William Allston, younger brother of John whose wife, Esther was the elder sister of the famous Swamp Fox, Francis Marion. Burr mentions William in a letter to Theodosia on April 5, 1802 and again on May 3, 1802 although he may be referring to a cousin with Alston spelt with one "l".

The Allston family of South Carolina had two cousins by the same name who served under Marion. To reduce confusion one branch dropped one of the *l's* in Allston. Thus the name of Joseph Alston, husband of Theodosia had one letter *l*. William married Martha Dana as his second wife. She was the daughter of R. H. Dana who wrote the novel *Two Years Before the Mast.*

Burr on the eve of the duel with Hamilton wrote to Theodosia and told her to destroy letters from his lady friends among whom he mentioned those between *"Clara and Mentor"* sometimes labeled *"L"*. Burr obviously considered himself a mentor to Theodosia. Who else would apply? The young artist, John Vanderlyn would also be considered a student whom Burr had supported in studies with Gilbert Stuart and four years in Paris, France. Nearly a constant companion of Burr, younger Vanderlyn fits the accolade. *L* standing for Lyn as his ancestors had spelled Van der Lyn. We already know that in Burr's letters female names stood for male counterparts. Clara may be a pseudonym for clarity of the portraiture and artistry of Vanderlyn as was his style. If so, why destroy the letters to an artist unless this artist had a special relationship to the Mentor, either sexual or as a member of the Burr spy ring? In either event the reputation of a genius artist was protected.

What is evident was that Burr was capable of attracting many young men to his inner circle for prolonged periods of time. In such a case his *"aide-de-camp is Samuel Swartwout, the youngest brother of John, a very amiable young man of twenty or twenty-one"* during Burr's tour of St. Simons Island, Georgia on August 31, 1804 following the duel with Hamilton and during his flight from justice. Why a young man would tag along with Burr fleeing justice, discredited, grossly in debt, and politically demolished, is not entirely clear. Burr was still Vice President and definitely plotting grandiose schemes. There may be more to it as alluded to here.

A Reverend Benjamin Vanderlinde (Leude), relationship to the painter unknown, on July 4, 1782 married Aaron Burr and Theodosia Bartow Prevost at the Hermitage along with her half sister, Catherine De Visme to Dr. Joseph Browne. Browne as prisoner of the British had been put under house arrest at the Hermitage for the duration of the war. Rev. Benjamin was married to Elizabeth Schuyler, aunt of wife of Alexander Hamilton. Joseph Browne, son of Captain Jonathan Browne of Hampton, New Hampshire was perhaps married first to Martha Coffin, daughter of Amos of Newbury, Massachusetts, and niece of John Coffin who ambushed General Montgomery at the walls of Quebec in 1775 in the presence of Aaron Burr. Suppose Joseph Browne was a British spy planted at the Hermitage and not just under house arrest (a cover story)? During the American occupation of Paramus, New Jersey, the socializing at the Hermitage would be a perfect place for collection of intelligence for the British with the help of Theodosia Prevost.

Another version of daughter Theodosia's disappearance was told by two retired pirates, Jean Baptiste Callistre and Frank Burdick, in separate locations in Louisiana and Alabama. They had captured the ship and forced all the crew to walk the plank including Theodosia. One even stated he held the plank for them. They were on one of the pirate Jean Lafitte's ships, *Vengeance*, commanded by Captain Octave Chauvet far astray from the Gulf of Mexico the usual area of plunder.

Many other versions have appeared through the years. One suggested Theodosia was found chained inside a wreck of a pirate ship during the Great Storm of 1816 in Galveston, Texas. An Indian found her near death, the sole survivor, as a captive of the pirates. She gave the Indian who spoke a little English a gold locket with her name, Theodosia, on the back and containing the picture of a man and boy. She said she was the daughter of a great misunderstood man and made a captive of the pirates while trying to travel to meet her father. He should tell the first white man he sees the story to explain her fate. The *Vengeance* was found to be in Galveston, Texas in 1818 two years after the hurricane stripped and in a state of disrepair from recent privateering and later burned.

Theodosia was named for her beloved mother whom Aaron Burr had fallen in love with in 1777. The name Theodosia translates literally as God's Divine Gift. Her mother was the wife of a British officer, Colonel James Prevost and lived in Paramus, New Jersey while her husband was stationed in Jamaica. He became Lt. Governor of Georgia upon subduing the colony in 1779. Aaron Burr saved the family property from confiscation with the help of James Monroe and Robert Troup and married her in 1782 after the death of her first husband in 1781. It is strange that their daughter, Theodosia would marry a man to become another southern Governor of South Carolina. Aaron Burr's wife died in 1794 just before the Reynolds affair with Alexander Hamilton became public in 1796.

It is equally strange that Burr would never mention his first wife to his daughter in his letters after her death. In fact no letters between Aaron Burr and his wife during her last year of life were published in his *Memoirs*. He does mention her in his letters to his daughter during her illness and sends her different medicines to try. It is also possible that he did not attend to his wife during her prolonged illness with stomach cancer, but instead was politicking in Philadelphia or Albany as Senator from New York. Was she merely a stepping stone to the wealthy families of the Prevosts and Bartows? Was she a means to gain an accomplice in his daughter? Was she a cover up for same sex tendencies? In other words was she a convenience to his schemes?

Daughter Theodosia was to become the Empress of the new country, Burrania, with Aaron Burr as Emperor, forming it out of the Louisiana Territory and Mexico. Burr had raised his only child as a son of the times with all the education as befits a man, mastering five languages and all the topics of the day. Aaron Burr was heartbroken at the loss of his daughter. Just as Alexander Hamilton had been when his son died in a duel over the two men and his daughter gone mad because of her brother's death.

Did the British have a hand in the death of Theodosia? Was this one last encounter of Aaron Burr and Alexander Hamilton in a Greek Tragedy with the Cape Hatteras Light being the symbolic connection?

This author feels that the *Patriot* carrying Theodosia and escort, Timothy Green, to New York in December of 1812 was attacked by the pirate Captain Chauvet on the *Vengeance* for a specific reason.

Why would a southern planter and Governor give his wife a letter of safe passage through the British blockade during a war between his country and England? How would he expect it to be honored? Was Theodosia's husband, Joseph, a British agent? Theodosia was the daughter of the former wife of a prominent British military family, the Prevosts. Her husband, Joseph Alston, had land transactions with Trinity Church and Aaron Burr on March 16, 1811. Did the statement in the letter that Theodosia was the daughter of Aaron Burr enough to ensure her safety among the British? This would seem most likely and supports the theory that Aaron Burr was favored by the British for his dealings with them. Theodosia's husband had been an integral part of Burr's plots and in the line of succession. He had financed Burr's purchase of one million acres of land in Orleans, Louisiana Territory during the planning for the secession of the western states and conquering Mexico. Was this act made to silence the truth? We have no personal writings of vindication from the man who lived many decades more. Although his papers were gone, his mind did not recall the facts for recording in his waning years. Curiously, there were only selected letters between Aaron Burr and Theodosia Prevost published by his close friend of forty years, Matthew L. Davis.

Chapter Fourteen: Aaron Burr's Spy Ring

Aaron Burr remained strangely silent about his political beliefs. He never publicly spoke or published any thing, unlike his peer Alexander Hamilton. It would appear that Aaron Burr was only about Aaron Burr and had no higher moral code. Everything he did to benefit others was ultimately done to benefit himself. To think like Burr, a lawyer and a good one at that, perhaps it is not strange at all that Burr did not personally publish his memoirs or write down his political beliefs and activities. At first he desired his son-in-law, Joseph Alston, then Theodosia, and finally his close friend Matthew L. Davis to do this for him, because his enemies could not use any statements or evidence revealed in these memoirs against him or his friends and accomplices. Why? Because, they would be second hand revelations and therefore hearsay, inadmissible in court. If he were to write something that would implicate another it could be used against them. If anyone else wrote the same thing it would be hearsay and inadmissible.

Davis states Burr had "an *unwillingness, on all important questions, to commit himself in writing.*" He wrote to Mrs. Burr on November 14, 1791, *"To the subject of politics I can at present make no reply. The mode of communication would not permit, did no other reason oppose."*

He did have his long time friend and third at the duel with Hamilton, Matthew L. Davis, publish his memoirs posthumously. In it Davis admitted to destroying correspondence of Burr with his many female acquaintances supposedly out of delicacy to their reputation. But we have already seen these ladies always figured significantly in his schemes. His *Memoirs* are woefully deficient in the areas of his two wives and Peggy Shippen.

For instance he fondly remembers the Shippen family that sheltered both him and his sister, Sally upon the death of their parents for three years. A Shippen girl, Sulky, had been hired by their mother, Esther Burr, to care for the children in Princeton. Yet he neglects to remember the good Doctor Shippen's niece, Peggy, who later married Benedict Arnold and self professed to Theodosia Prevost, Burr's future wife, to be instrumental in her husband's desertion from the American Army at West Point. British General Henry Clinton's papers reveal Peggy was most definitely a British spy. Theodosia wrote to her husband Joseph Alston on August 6, 1805 when she feared an illness would take her life, that *"I beg, also, you will write immediately to New-York, forwarding some money for the comfortable support of Peggy until my father can provide for her."* Peggy Arnold had already died in August, 1804 in New Brunswick, Canada, three years after Benedict and in financial need. If Theodosia had known that fact, then Peggy was the loyal servant, Peggy Gallatin, in Aaron's household. More likely Peggy is a code word for Burr himself in need of money as usual for his scheme. Peggy was a favored slave, educated, and able to transact business on behalf of Aaron Burr. Burr even transferred a deed to her name "Peggy Slave" on December 24, 1801. To send money to Peggy was the equivalent of sending it to Burr himself.

The *Memoirs* likewise leave out the initial introduction of Theodosia to her husband while she was staying with her sister in Westchester in 1777. The period preceding her death from cancer from 1794 to 1796 is also absent. It alludes to the use of Burr by Washington to transport Tories down the Hudson River from Fishkill to Manhattan, but without mention that Theodosia accompanied him on the first trip in August, 1778. No mention is made of Aaron Burr's second wife, Eliza Jumel, who divorced him on his deathbed because he had absconded with her inheritance from her first husband. The fact that by the author's own admission all references to female encounters of Aaron Burr had been deleted or omitted from his *Memoirs* makes them suspicious and decidedly tainted by inaccuracy and deceit. Aaron Burr had instructed daughter, Theodosia to destroy many personal letters from his amours in her safekeeping prior to the duel with Hamilton, including a stack tied with red string and another in a handkerchief which maybe implicated others in his schemes, including his artist protégé, Vanderlyne. Likewise the absence of mention of the land transactions between Trinity Church and Burr, and Burr and John Jacob Astor, is not surprising should they then be compromising in their revelation.

Again when in 1778 while an officer in the American army he accepted along with Tories John and George Cruger land leases from a Loyalist naval officer, Robert Edwards, a favorite of the Crown. He turned them over to Trinity Church in 1779. His *Memoirs* hold another clue without relinquishing acknowledgement for this deed. A letter therein from Theodore Sedgwick at Kinderhook, August 7th, 1778, *"... I believe I shall visit the (your) camp soon, in which case you will have the pleasure to see Mr. Edwards in company."* (Not referring to a relative of Burr's he might be referencing a Uriah, son of William Edwards of Kinderhook and nephew of Robert Edwards or even Robert himself. Uriah Edwards' son, George W. Edwards was in possession of a copy of the lease in South Carolina and may have deposited it in the Peachtree Street Arcade Building in Atlanta, Georgia containing exchange records from other states.)

In the same paragraph Theodore Sedgwick, Loyalist, writes, *"I most sincerely congratulate you on the happy prospect of a speedy termination to the war."* In 1778 neither side could foresee a successful end to the war that actually continued for five more years, leastwise the American army. Then this must reference an act of treason of Burr's to win the war for the British or more likely that Burr had already decided to resign his participation in it. Thus this would be the speedy termination for him personally. Not until October 24, 1778 did Burr write Washington for a leave of absence without pay for reasons of health. Yet there is no mention in August of ill health as the reason for the speedy termination of the war. In fact, the happy prospect could entail the manipulation of the Loyalist Robert Edwards' lease for some future personal gain. Aaron Burr did gain control of much of this land from Trinity Church throughout his life.

Curiously, on June 20th, 1780 friend Robert Troup wrote Burr *"I have obtained a few particulars of ____ (blank), which I was before unacquainted with.... The girls here think him handsome, genteel, and sensible, and say positively he is no longer engaged to Miss Shippen."* In an earlier letter Troup had mentioned an important piece of information unrelated to their studies of law that he could not reveal in the letter, but only in person. This letter was alluding to a Major John Andre, head of Sir Henry Clinton's espionage ring who was intimate with Miss Shippen just prior to her marrying General Benedict Arnold. Troup had served with Arnold as Major at the Battle of Saratoga along with Colonel Wilkinson, and Major General Philip Schuyler. Of note is that Miss Shippen was already Mrs. Arnold as of April, 1779, one year previous to this letter. Major Andre was not of a Philadelphia family as noted in the letter.

Benedict started correspondence on May 10, 1779 with Sir Clinton a month after his marriage. The first letter came via Joseph Stansbury, a Loyalist spy and courier for Major Andre's (code names John Anderson or Mr. Moore; Monk was Benedict Arnold) spy network. The letters in cipher code used the *Commentaries on the Laws of England* by William Blackstone. The page number, line and word placement on the line represented haggling points over payment to Arnold for his information and defection. Benedict Arnold later tried to turn over West Point to the British for money at the urging of Peggy Shippen Arnold a mere three months after the Troup letter in September, 1780. Major Andre was the British contact in this affair arranged by Peggy Shippen Arnold for her husband. What Troup and thus Burr knew of this event prior to its happening is open to inference. The mere fact that his name was presented as newsworthy in their letters is noticeably timely. Major Andre ceased corresponding with General Arnold in late 1779 and early 1780 when he went with General Clinton's forces to capture Charleston, South Carolina. In their stead William Tryon was left in military command of Manhattan during the winter of 1779-1780. In early 1780 Tryon became ill with gout and returned to England where he died.

Upon Andre's return to New York City he was surprised that the plan to turn over West Point under Arnold's command to the British was already well formulated. It is in this hiatus of correspondence between Andre and Arnold that Troup, Burr and Colt took up the mantle of perfidy. History has not yet been able to fill that void herein revealed. But it was with William Tryon that the negotiations with Benedict Arnold reached a peak.

In nearly all the correspondence between Troup, Theodosia, Burr and others, health is constantly inquired of and stated. The means of correspondence between Benedict Arnold and the British was cipher and invisible ink amongst the innocent conversations of an old woman's health. Likewise Burr would quote various French authors and cite reference to publications of esoteric philosophers. Since Burr was known by his biographers (i.e. Fleming) to use cipher with his daughter Theodosia and others, these quotations when found in the publication referenced would locate a page number, line and word placement corresponding to the locations of the information contained in the letter or the number would represent a date or number of troops or money requested. Peggy Shippen Arnold herself described this technique and the use of invisible ink in educating her husband Benedict Arnold. On June 27th, 1780 Troup's description of a man whose name is deleted from the printed letter by the editor Davis as the son of a vice-president of Pennsylvania is a non sequitur, since there is no such title. The code is referencing Benedict Arnold himself, the military governor of Philadelphia appointed by Washington, thus second in command in Philadelphia or a vice-president.

Other errors of title in the letter further represent obvious pseudonyms for related persons. *"...say positively he is no longer engaged to Miss Shippen."* Miss Shippen was then Mrs. Benedict Arnold by a year at this date. An obvious error in reference designed to make the knowledgeable reader realize the mistake refers to Major Andre who was intimately involved with Miss Shippen before her marriage. *"He has frequently spoken to them in raptures, latterly of Miss De Visme,* (half sister Catherine (Caty) DeVisme, later to marry Dr. Joseph Browne under house arrest by the British at the Hermitage for the duration of the war). Theodosia had unsuccessfully sought Washington's influence to promote the exchange of half brother, Peter DeVisme, a British marine officer and prisoner of war in American hands. Mother and widow Ann Stillwell Bartow DeVisme had been married to a British officer, Philip. Her two Stillwell sisters were also married to British officers. This references by transference Sir Henry Clinton, or more likely William Tryon, as the British officer and temporary head of the British espionage operations, *"and once declared he was half in love with her."* *"Half in love"* refers to espionage or defection. This represents a request from Benedict Arnold via Robert Troup to Aaron Burr to come over to the British side. The word *"latterly"* reveals a recent wish to defect.

Finally Troup closes his letter to Burr with *"Miss Susan Governor Livingston desires her compliments to you and the two families."* The error here is Miss Susannah French Livingston is currently the wife of William G. Livingston, Governor of New Jersey, and not a Miss. Miss Susan is the cipher word for West Point in this letter which Arnold is offering for his defection. The Livingston families were from Poughkeepsie, New York, the closest large city to West Point, New York on the Hudson River. In other letters Troup says the Livingston girls ask about you. The daughter Sarah had just married in 1774 John Jay, then president of the Continental Congress from December, 1778 to September, 1779. This is obviously a warning to watch out for the Continental Congress might suspect them. Another sister, Judith married in 1780 a cousin of Theodosia Prevost, John Watkins, Jr., son of John Watkins and Lydia Stillwell, officer in Burr's regiment who had introduced Theodosia Prevost to Aaron Burr.

Alternately Burr had first met Alexander Hamilton at the Elizabethtown Academy founded by William Livingston with whom Hamilton had stayed upon arriving in the colonies from St. Croix. The beautiful Livingston girls had made an early impression on young Alexander who had been smitten by one Catherine, Kitty. William Livingston, Rebel and first governor of an independent New Jersey in 1776, had opposed the De Lancey's formation of King's College in Manhattan in 1754 because it would become an instrument of royal power. He founded an alternate New York Society Library for safe alternate reading matter for students which Alexander Hamilton made use of while at King's College.

Another close friend of Hamilton's during this period was William Alexander, known as Lord Stirling of Basking Ridge. Lord Stirling, a brigadier general, distinguished himself at the Battle of Brooklyn. He was a cofounder of the New York Society Library with Livingston. His aide-de-camp was James Monroe. His daughter Catharine, Lady Kitty, married Hamilton's notable friend, William Duer, caught profiteering on discounted notes of the government in 1792. Troup's reminding Burr about Baskenridge or the Baskenridges and alternately the Livingston daughters are asking about you meant reference to the Rebels notably, Governor William Livingston, Brigadier General William Alexander, and President John Jay, as well as Colonel Alexander Hamilton. In essence Troup was warning Burr to watch his back.

Thus Robert Troup and Aaron Burr were intimately involved in Peggy Shippen's and Sir Henry Clinton's British espionage ring. In fact from the following letters they were instrumental in arranging the negotiations for the payment of money to Benedict Arnold for the surrender of West Point to the British.

Aaron Burr had given Matthew L. Davis a select group of letters for him to publish in the *Memoirs* of Aaron Burr. The letters of this critical time are sequentially complete, and uninterrupted in timeline more so than any other time frame of his life. Thus one could conclude that Burr hoped and expected that someday someone (perhaps yours truly) would decipher these letters and connect him as one of the masterminds of the treason of Benedict Arnold. Aaron Burr much more the rogue than had previously been thought would have his place in history, if not as the Emperor of Spanish Americas denied him by Alexander Hamilton. On the eve of the two hundredth anniversary of his Treason Trial and 225th year of his second treason with Benedict Arnold, Robert Troup, Peter Colt, and Peggy Shippen Arnold, and lastly the 225th anniversary of his initial treason of accepting in conjunction with other Tories, John and Robert Cruger, land from Loyalist Robert Edwards while an officer under Washington's command at the behest of Theodosia Prevost, it has taken this long for the cipher code to be broken and revealed to the world.

In the same letter Troup writes something curious "*Since I have been here, I have had an opportunity of removing entirely the suspicion they had of your courting Miss De Visme* (Caty, half-sister of Mrs. Prevost the future wife of Aaron Burr to marry Dr. Joseph Browne. The De Visme women were universally married to British officers. Thus courting Miss

De Visme meant the British army.).".'" Obviously, someone such as Robert Morris mentioned American suspicions on Burr's loyalty to the patriotic cause since his resignation from the army. *"They believe nothing of it now, and attribute your visits at Paramus to motives of friendship for Mrs. Prevost and the family. Wherever I am, and can with propriety, you may be assured I shall represent this matter in its true light."*

To further assuage suspicions on Burr's loyalties a ruse was devised to put off the track those that would disparage him. While Burr was in New Haven, Connecticut (home of sister Sally Reeves and visitor Theodosia Burr and mother Edwards family) on July 5, 1779 a British attack on the city threatened. Burr supposedly roused himself from a sick bed and entreated the students of Yale College to form a militia to repel the invaders at a key bridge. The British contingent of crack regulars commanded by none other than hardened former British Governor of New York, General William Tryon, (once again!) quickly retired for a while upon seeing the resistance organized by our heroic Burr. (Tryon had been implicated in the plot to kidnap or assassinate General Washington in Manhattan in 1776, and retired as British Governor of New York in March, 1778.) Burr never lost the advantage in the future to refer to this same military fete to his aggrandizement. One could suppose this was a set up to make him look still loyal to the patriotic cause all the while he was passing information between Benedict Arnold and British William Tryon, interim commander at New York City in place of the absent Sir Henry Clinton. It is hard to believe the seasoned troops of His Majesty would blanch at the sight of Yale students arrayed in their front. The British commander was known for his ruthless pursuit of the War with the Rebels recently in the Carolinas.

General Tryon's own account to General Clinton of the raid on New Haven, Connecticut on July 20th, 1779 tersely reports his second in command General Garth *"he should begin the Conflagration, which he thought it merited, as soon as he had secured the Bridge between us over the Neck Creek* (with General Tryon's contingent on the other side). *The Collection of the Enemy in Force on Advantage Ground, and with heavier Cannon than his own, diverted the General from that Passage...I went over to him; and the Result of our Conference, was a Resolution that with the first Division he should cover the North Part of the Town that night while with the second I should keep the Heights above the Rock Fort."* The resistance the next morning had evaporated. There is no mention of retired Colonel Aaron Burr. The British left New Haven virtually unscathed, *"General Garth changed his Design; and destroyed only the public stores..."* However in the same report of the next raid on

Fairfield, Connecticut, *"driving the Enemy, with great Alacrity and Spirit, dispossessed them of Drummond Hill and the <u>heights</u> at the End of the Village, East from and commanding the Bridge... pushing the main Body and a Hundred Cavalry from the Northern Heights, and taking one Piece of their Cannon... The Rebels in Arms at New Haven were considerable more numerous at Fairfield and still more so at Norwalk...upwards of two Thousand"* The timidity of the British at New Haven gave way to vengeful retribution at Fairfield and Norwalk, *"I should be very sorry if the Destruction of these two Villages would be thought less reconcilable with Humanity..."* Although Tryon does not outwardly admit preferential treatment of New Haven it is evident from the vigor of his execution of the war at Fairfield and Norwalk against a superior force which should have caused more caution than he exhibited at New Haven, to be consistent.

Not for more than another hundred years would the Crimson Line in actuality shrink before the formidable Blue Line of the Bulldogs at the Yale Bowl in New Haven, Connecticut. This time the Crimson color would be worn by the Harvard University football team and not the Red Coats of the Regular Army of Great Britain. Back in 1779 many of those present at Yale were still in fact divinity students. Although probably skilled marksmen, yet untrained, undisciplined, and most likely unarmed these students would hardly make the Harvard football team squirm, let alone the crack veterans of the British army.

We do know that in 1780 negotiations between Arnold and Clinton or more correctly Tryon reached a lofty sum for the times. On February 29th, 1780 *"ten thousand dollars per annum"* is rejected ostensibly as a salary for Troup *"I cursed and quit them."* However such an amount for an officer's salary in the army would never have been given by the cash strapped Continental Congress. This sum might be the opening offer of the British to Benedict Arnold which he rejects through Troup. On May 23, 1780 Colonel Troup writes to Burr *"Daddy Plumb* (Benedict Arnold, he who divides (a plumb line) the colonies by giving up West Point to the British) *informs me the* (post) *riders are ordered to ride forty miles* (Benedict asks the British for forty thousand pounds for his defection) *a day during the season. Must I attribute it to the fatality which has already separated us, and, I fear, is determined to put an eternal bar to our junction* (the treason, Troup fears this is too much for the British to accept)? *Such an event would blast all my hopes of future happiness. Besides the time we lose by postponing our settlement, I have a matter of great importance to us both to communicate to you, that has no connexion with our studying, and which makes it necessary for me to see you immediately."* This may represent an impasse in the negotiations.

A Peter Colt of Weathersfield, Connecticut, a close friend of Aaron Burr who congratulated Burr on his appointment in the army in another letter, was Deputy quartermaster-general; subsequently commissary for the French army, and treasurer of the State of Connecticut on July 7, 1780 wrote *"...who have so long neglected to inform you of the situation of your affairs left in my hands?....Of course, about L20,000, the amount of her last outfits, were thrown away. ...I am advised to sell every thing for continental money, at the present going prices, and exchange it for hard... Let me know what I am to do with your money when I get it into my hands. I have not settled any of your accounts but Stanley's* (Benedict Arnold's)*... Miss H___* (Henry Clinton?) *has been quite unwell since you left us, as she tells me she hears you are."* This is supposedly reporting on the loss of the ship *Hawk* on Long Island. Yet at this time Aaron Burr would not be engaging in commerce nor investing in blockade running. So this account seems a little out of place. The British offer to Arnold of L20,000 is supposedly the final agreed upon amount. On July 16, 1780 Peter Colt writes to Burr *"I have to acknowledge the receipt of your polite and friendly letter of the 1st inst. My little family would have been too much elated with your attention to them had you not dashed the pleasure with the account of your ill state of health.... It is vain for them to attempt copying Rivington* (Printer to the King in New York City, and is a reference to a known but secret American Long Island Spy Chain. Copying refers to being able to keep it from the American spies. The opposite is true of vain to attempt. Rather it is desirous to keep this information from Rivington and his spy chain.)*."* Thus Peter Colt as the agent for the British connection between Burr and William Tryon and Sir Henry Clinton acknowledges the deal is finalized or published as in the paper or worse has been passed on to the Americans through the Long Island Spy Chain starting at Rivington's press.

James Rivington was a supposed supporter of the Loyalist cause during the War of Independence. Before the war he had tried to publish both sides of the issues between England and its colonies. But Rivington was trapped by the British occupation of Manhattan and printed British propaganda during that time. Even after the war was concluded and the British and Loyalists had evacuated Manhattan, Rivington never admitted to helping the Long Island Spy Ring of which he was an integral member because he had two sons in the British army whom he wished to protect from any repercussions. Washington reportedly left a bag of gold, the spy's usual payment, with Rivington when Washington reentered the city. Rivington reportedly gave to Washington's agent, Allan McLane, the

British flag code book which gave French Admiral de Grasse the edge on the British fleet in the Chesapeake Bay off Yorktown.

The Long Island Spy Ring supposedly remained a secret even after the war. Washington had cautioned *"There can be scarcely any need of recommending the greatest caution and secrecy in a business so critical and dangerous."* But we see both Rivington and his part in the Long Island Culper Ring were known to the British and Burr and Troup, for that matter, during the war. Indeed one four-month pregnant female spy member was caught, imprisoned, gave birth to her son and died soon after, in the odious British prison ship *Jersey.* She was the wife of Robert Townsend, code name Culper Jr. Her own name has never been revealed. In the battle of misinformation Washington won what he couldn't win on the battlefields. The head of British intelligence in America at the end of the war, Major George Beckwith wrote *"Washington did not really outfight the British, he simply outspied us!"* Although the British knew more than Washington realized, he was able to outwit them with misinformation and better gamesmanship.

On July 18, 1780 from Troup to Burr, he writes *"I am charmed with my present situation in every respect. It could not be more agreeable to my wishes. I shall have reason to thank you, as long as I live, for my change."* Arnold is pleased with the agreement and looks forward to the change of sides. Then Troup relays the time and date of the surrender of West Point. *"I am reading Wood at present. I have almost done with his 4th chapter, and am looking over his chapter on courts. I confine my whole attention to the practice, for reasons I will tell you when we meet. I am translating Burlamaqui's Politic Law. Reading Robertson's Charles V., Dalrymple on Feudal Property, and Swift's Works. The morning I devote to the law. I am up sometimes before, generally at sunrise. From two to half after three in the afternoon, and from nine to eleven in the evening, I apply to other matters. I am in a fair way, if public affairs will suffer me, to be retired."* The latter nine to eleven may be the eleventh day in September proposed when the 23rd was the actual date Andre was captured. The former date two to half after three or 23 (fourth chapter of Wood might mean every fourth word is pertinent, the chapter on courts being chapter three reveals a reverse order to the sequence of numbers by taking chapter four before chapter three) is more likely the day and the nine to eleven is the time of day in the evening or before sunrise, or alternatively the ninth month, September at eleven in the evening. *"The morning I devote to the law"* refers to the following time table that is to apply to the handover of West Point to the British. *"I am up sometimes before"* alerts the reader that in the next sequence the date comes *"before"* the month which comes *"before"* the time of day. Thus 11 PM (*"before, generally at sunrise"*), September 23rd is the translation of numbers, 23, 9, 11, in reverse sequence. *"Feudal Property"* refers to West Point on the river Hudson designated by *"Swift's Works"*. *"Feudal"* means soon to become the King's property. *"Charles V"* refers to the King's men. *"Translating Burlamaqui's Politic Law"* is instructions for Burr to read into the following book titles what will transpire. *"Reading Wood"* could refer to the woods on the Hudson near West Point where the British are to land.

    "Paterson (Washington) *is the very man we want. I have heard him examine Noel* (Benedict Arnold in the guise of Santa Claus) *yesterday on the practice* (West Point posting for Arnold) *and I find his examinations are critical. In a couple of months I expect to be as far advanced in the practice as Noel. I cannot bear that he should be before me. It must not, it shall not be."* Troup is implying he will likewise go over to the British side soon after taking with him secrets from the Americans later described.

    We know that prior to Benedict Arnold's assignment to West Point Washington had attempted to post him elsewhere whereupon in the presence of Robert Morris and family Peggy Shippen Arnold pitched a fit and insisted upon West Point as the post for her husband. The Morris' remarked after Arnold defected that her performance made them now suspect of her duplicity. This incident is related to Burr by Troup in the letter dated Morristown, October 23, 1780 *"I must communicate to you a disagreeable piece of news respecting myself. It shows how rare it is to find a man of real disinterested benevolence. Sears and Broome* (shears and broom means woman or Peggy) (alternately Isaac Sears and Samuel Broome were notable rioters and Sons of Liberty in New York; this could represent Washington reneging on his pledge to assign Arnold to command of West Point), *I understand by Mr. Noel* (Santa Claus, the giver of West Point to the British, i.e. Benedict Arnold) *who returned from Philadelphia a few days ago, have protested the bill* (scheme) *I drew upon them last summer. Colonel Palfrey* (former aide-de-camp to Washington and then paymaster of the American army, the alternate post offered to Arnold in place of West Point; the scheme for West Point has been halted) *bought it, and has it returned to him, for what reasons I cannot say positively, but I suspect they are determined not to assist me, although they were lavish of their offers when they supposed I never would be reduced to the necessity of accepting them. Such conduct is characteristic of excessive meanness of spirit, and I confess I am deceived in my opinion of them most egregiously. True it is, that instances of this kind of behaviours often occur in our intercourse with mankind; but, from the fortunes these men have made since the war, and the frequent reports of their generosity, I was led to imagine there was something more than mere idle compliment and ostentatious parade in their offers. I was deceived, and I hope it will be the last time. This affair has wounded my pride so sensibly, that I shall be extremely cautious in future."* This refers to the scene of protest by Peggy to Washington on the re-assignment of her husband, Benedict Arnold to a post as paymaster other than as West Point commander, or the protest of her innocence to Washington in the scheme of her husband's. The letter reaffirming the resumption of the plan and the assignment of Arnold to West Point command is not available. History tells us it did happen as planned up to the capture of Andre and his hanging as a spy, the flight of Benedict to the British to escape a similar fate and another theatrical scene by Peggy before Washington at West Point to dissuade him of her culpability in the plot. This letter written after the capture of Andre must reference the foiled plot at West Point and the lack of assistance by the British in the prisoner exchange of Arnold for Major Andre.

From the Clement Library at the University of Michigan's collection of Clinton letters we know that Arnold had been suspicious of his first communicators with General Clinton, Joseph Stansbury and Jonathan Odell, and switched to Samuel Wallis of Lycoming, Pennsylvania. Much of the earlier correspondence to Clinton seemed to have not reached its destination. At the time of mid July, 1780 the communication must have been changed to Troup and Burr and Colt. Wallis must have been part of the loop either in Philadelphia or most likely New York City which Clinton admits to.

Far fetched as this might seem another letter illustrates the seriousness of this treasonous espionage between Troup, Burr and others. Troup, now a civilian, spent time at the home of Robert Morris the American financier of the Revolution in Princeton ostensibly studying law from whom Troup could learn the following details. On August 21st, 1780 Troup wrote to Burr *"the second division of the French fleet has arrived, with a re-enforcement of 4000 troops. This event will render it necessary for me to be ready to move at a moment's warning; and, presuming there will be no delay in commencing our operations, I think in the course of a fortnight, or three weeks at most, I shall be at Paramus (in New Jersey)."* He is here describing the movements of Rochambeau's Army against New York from Newport, Rhode Island. He goes on *"Will your health permit you to join the army? I fear not. Fatigue and bad weather may ruin it."* This means that this is a feint toward New York but not an earnest attack. *"I am disappointed in my opinion of the mineral waters... the stock of health you have gained since I left you is scarcely perceptible. Something else must be tried."* An alternative plan is afoot. An attack will be by sea. The Chesapeake could be the mineral waters. *"Mr.Paterson* (attorney general of New Jersey stands for General Washington) *and I have often spoken together on this subject, and we both agree that a ride to the southward next winter, and a trip to the West Indies in the spring, would be of infinite service to you."* This refers to the movement south of Washington's and Rochambeau's forces in early 1781 into Virginia and the use of the French fleet of Admiral de Grasse located in the West Indies. *"This might be done with ease in five or six months* (from August, 1780*). Mrs. Paterson* (Washington's army) *is perfectly recovered, and her little girl grows finely, and promises to be handsome."* This could mean the American army in which Mr. Paterson is an officer has recovered its strength and joined with the French army poses a threat. Thus Troup is forewarning the movements of the American and French armies with the help of the French fleet now located in the West Indies, towards the south, eventually Yorktown and the British army there under General Cornwallis in 1781.

Some historians have fixated on the belief that the plan of attack on Cornwallis was formulated in early 1781 and that Washington was stubbornly holding onto the idea of recouping his loss of face four years earlier at the disastrous retreat from Manhattan Island by retaking New York City back from the British with the help of the French army and navy. Despite the reference to Washington's own admission that the *"idea was broached at a meeting with Rochambeau in September, 1780"* after the Troup letter to Burr outlining the revelation from financier Robert Morris himself, historians (including the most recent) insist on promulgating the belief that *His Excellency,* George Washington was headstrong and foolhardy in his persistence on attacking New York City up to July 30, 1781. When in fact these same historians are today the victims of the same misinformation that kept General Clinton holed up in New York City awaiting the attack that never came. In other words the old *Spy Master* himself, George Washington, has successfully outwitted his own biographer, two hundred and twenty three years after the British had fallen for his deception.

Why Sir Clinton with this information one year in advance did not act on it is confusing.

Another spy story perhaps explains why Clinton was reluctant to leave New York City to come to the aid of Cornwallis. In a letter to Sir Henry Clinton by Baron Ottendorf on August 15, 1781 he mentions a spy woman named Miss Jenny who he had sent to the French lines to find out what they were planning. Ottendorf, a German mercenary, had been dismissed from the American army by Washington in 1777 and promptly joined the British side. Jenny reported back that she believed Washington and Rochambeau were planning a two pronged attack on New York City soon. She had been discovered however and her hair had been shaved to humiliate her. Thus it is possible that the Americans and French had purposely planted the seeds of this idea in her head to deceive Clinton while Washington intended to join General LaFayette on the Yorktown Peninsula against Cornwallis with other French troops while Rochambeau entertained Clinton in New York with ideas of imminent attack. Washington had planted the same seed in the minds of his own soldiers by making them prepare roads in the direction of Staten Island from which to launch an attack on Manhattan. He even sought the advice of local Tory farmers as to the best routes. This information convincing enough for Washington's own troops got to General Clinton. Thus Clinton was unsure whether to believe year old information about Virginia ultimately Yorktown plans or fresh information about an army now camped on his doorstep and making preparations in his direction. He chose the present threat as more real and plausible.

Again the reference to a publication *"When you come, remember to bring with you the book you took with you on our way to Paramus. I believe it is an essay on health. Mrs. Paterson wants it."* Reference is made to Aaron's health and Mr. Morris. *"Mr. Morris's family is exceedingly particular in their inquiries concerning your health."* This means the information comes from Robert Morris himself who would finance the movement of the American army against Corwallis. Usually the next cipher code will use the book noted above. Without a title most likely this *book* reference has a different meaning. Here the reference to *Mrs. Paterson* means the American army's *health* to which Robert Morris was attending by raising funds for its support. The likely interpretation is a little more direct. *Mr. Morris* told me (*exceedingly particular*), Robert Troup, that the American army (*Mrs. Paterson,* as in other letters) *wants* the *health* (or lack thereof and plans to attack) of the British army of the South (*Paramus,* the location of the home of Theodosia Prevost, wife of the British Officer fighting the American army in the South). Until now how Clinton got the plans to the Virginia movement south ultimately to the Yorktown campaign was not known, even though it was known he did have that information in his possession and chose to ignore it or think it false because of Washington's masterful counter espionage. We now know Troup and Burr were the source of this information.

Then Troup warns the British not to engage the French army *"They insist on paying you a visit as soon as you are settled here... Let me entreat you to avoid engaging any of your French books in Connecticut, especially Chambaud's Exercises..."* is a direct reference to maneuvers of

Rochambeau's army in Rhode Island and Connecticut. Chambaud is a play on Rochambeau. *"I, and perhaps you, will stand in need of them all."* The word *you* refers to the British army and directs them to save their strength for a bigger engagement to come. *"Assure Dom. Tetard* (French translator of the American army during the Quebec campaign, French tutor to Prevost children employed by Burr) *of my friendship for him, and fixed determination to use all endeavours to metamorphose him into a Crassus after the war is ended."* Tetard is Major Andre, both names being French. General Benedict Arnold is Crassus the Roman who put down the Spartacus slave revolt (the American Revolution). Without due recognition for his accomplishments Crassus formed a political partnership with Pompey who got the credit. Arnold is agreeing to use Andre as his go between. *"I* (Benedict Arnold) *am greatly indebted to the good family* (British Crown) *for their favourable sentiments* (agreeable sum of money*), which, as I said once before, must proceed* (it's a go) *more from affection to you than what they find meritorious in me."* Arnold has agreed to turn over West Point to the British. *"I am certain, however, that their esteem for me cannot exceed mine for them, and this you will be kind enough to hint to them when you present my respectful compliments."*

Aaron Burr was ultimately rewarded with leases from Trinity of some of the same property as in the Robert Edwards lease of 1778 in 1796, 1800, 1804, for his services as a spy and traitor to the American cause. This does not appear to be the case with Alexander Hamilton who had no dealings with Trinity Church, while even being their attorney on occasion. Then could one conclude that the date of the lease of May 28, 1778 antedating the Battle of Monmouth, New Jersey could have been a payoff to Burr to help the British by somehow throwing the battle in their favor? Or at the very least, Burr thought he could increase his worth to the British if he did something stupid militarily to throw the battle in their favor. He could do that as he assumed the position of a Brigadier General (commander of a large section of an army) even while still a Lieutenant Colonel.

Chapter Fifteen: Colonel Burr the Revolutionary War Hero or Traitor

The talk of illness throughout these letters is not factual. Heat prostration comes from potassium deficiency caused by sweating during exertion. This does not become a lifetime illness as presumed by all that speak of it in these letters. Aaron Burr, while in command of a wing of the American lines as a diminutive (in Burr's eyes) lieutenant colonel without the trappings of a Brigadier General Malcolm whose brigade he commanded at the Battle of Monmouth, was knocked off his horse by a cannon ball without injury to himself. The often truncated rendition is he became prostrate and fell asleep under a tree during the finale of the battle. But this now has to be viewed with suspect in light of the other revelations of his subsequent actions in regards the loyalist cause and British involvement in his schemes.

In Malcolm's regiment was John Watkins Jr., son of John Watkins and Lydia Stillwell, Theodosia's aunt, her mother, Ann's youngest sister. The Watkins lived near Theodosia in Paramus, New Jersey, and it was their home Washington passed up in July, 1778 for the Prevost home as his headquarters after the Battle of Monmouth.

Battlefield accounts state Burr advanced the left wing of the army without orders across a bridge to attack an unsupported British grouping in his front, only to be enfiladed with destructive artillery fire upon advancing. The result was loss of two thirds of his force and surely near destruction of the American army as it exposed the flank of the army to a strong British force. Only countermanding order from General Washington recalling his force to their former positions prevented a complete route. It was only after this that Burr became ill with heat stroke during the evening.

In this time of European battle formations used up to the American Civil War this author, a Civil War re-enactor, recognizes the strategic blunder of Colonel Burr's maneuver as commander of the left wing of Washington's army at the Battle of Monmouth. Namely, that exposure of the wing of a linearly arranged battle formation to destruction meant certain collapse of the whole army. By advancing his command on the left wing especially across a narrow bridge without orders Burr purposely brought the army to its death only to be timely halted by Washington's countermanding order. The purpose of many battlefield maneuvers is to turn or outflank the wing of the opposing army. Burr graciously handed the British that opportunity gratis.

Many would relegate this error to inexperience on Burr's part. Washington obviously recognized the seriousness of the error and removed Burr from command of this part of his army, and detached him to spy on the British retreat to Manhattan. Taken in context of other actions during the war and his pride in the knowledge of warfare as Davis reveals in Burr's *"Memoirs"* I believe that Burr purposely exposed his command to destruction in order to help the British destroy Washington's whole army.

While Burr slept from heat exhaustion, the British retired in the American's front during the night when Burr would have been otherwise vigilant. Burr had been known to harass the picket posts throughout the evening watch in prior and subsequent commands, notably his last at Westchester, New York.

In December, 1813 to January, 1814 two affidavits of Judge George Gardner and Lieutenant Robert Hunter to Gabriel Furman of the New York Assembly regarding the pension application of Aaron Burr relate just such an instance of night stalking by Burr. Again disobeying a direct order to retire Burr advanced toward the enemy at Hackensack in September, 1777. *"Colonel Burr then went alone to discover the position of the enemy. .....But the enemy, probably alarmed by these threatening appearances* (or Burr) *retreated the next day,"* Sound familiar?

While Burr was commanding at Westchester in 1779, his disciplined and reorganized units did not come under a concerted attack by the British. Upon his retirement from the service in the American Army Burr's successor was Colonel Thompson. According to Davis, *"the enemy in open day, advanced to his headquarters, took Colonel Thompson, and took or killed all his men."* And again a year later Colonel Green was surprised and he and many of his officers killed, *"yet these officers had the full benefit of Colonel Burr's system."* And might so have had the enemy, compliments of Burr? A little suspicion of the happy circumstance of Burr's luck goes a long way to explain the outcome of these individual events.

That winter of 1779 at Westchester Burr had even chased former New York Governor then General William Tryon through Connecticut but *"information, which unfortunately was not correct, altered Colonel Burr's route towards Mamaroneck, which enabled Tryon to get the start on him."* Remember Tryon was not accustomed to being chased off the field by the American *rabble* without a fight despite Burr's reputation or rather to the aggrandizement of same. Would this then not be another instance of a staged victory of sorts to increase Burr's esteem with his superiors and deflect suspicion of his loyalties? Burr chased the British commanded by an aggressive officer out of Connecticut without a fight. How convenient and artificial!

What of the many instances of detached service by Burr at Quebec, after Monmouth, the Tory escort into New York City, and his infamous solo night tours of the front lines at Valley Forge, Hackensack and Westchester county? Here it could also be surmised Burr at the limits of the American army in the dead of night could have passed secrets to the British without suspicion and without the aide of an entrusted courier.

General Lee whom Burr supported received the court martial for retreating during the battle at Monmouth without orders from Washington, while Burr more culpable undeservedly came off unscathed. Hamilton was instrumental in the conviction of Lee. This court-martial may have been directed at Lee not so much for his performance at Monmouth, but in addition to his participation as principal in the Conway Cabal just prior to the battle to remove Washington as head of the American army. Hamilton had checkmated Burr once again.

This is the third time Burr had avoided the court martial. The second time he nearly severed the arm of a soldier he suspected of mutiny to murder himself at Valley Forge. The first time he deserted the army at Quebec under Arnold's command, *"You have the power of stopping me, but nothing short of force shall do it."* His friend from Princeton, Matthias Ogden, was brother of his two aunts, wives of Pierpoint and foster father, Timothy Edwards. Ogden, still a presumed staunch Revolutionary brigadier general later imprisoned by the British in 1780, went to Quebec with Burr. He subsequently obtained a post for Burr on Washington's staff. This insubordination of Burr toward Arnold may have soured Washington's opinion of Burr from the beginning. Not long on Washington's staff Burr forever sneered at Washington's *"defective grammar and even in spelling, owing to the insufficiency of his early education."* Both men were on less than friendly terms from then on. Burr would likewise complain that he could not ascertain the deliberations of Continental Congress from this post as aide to Washington. For what reason would he need to know these things at all?

It is then somewhat strange that Washington would entrust Burr with important matters or listen to his counsel. Burr proposed an attack against the British on Staten Island which Washington did not accept. This same plan was soon attempted in January, 1779 by Lord Stirling, General Alexander, with disastrous results. Again the Burr advice had led to disaster outside the control of Burr. But was it without enemy knowledge of his plan? Burr had said at a Federalist dinner honoring the departed Washington's Birthday a toast to the *"union of all honest men"*, as if Washington was not one of them. The slight was not lost on the High Federalists in attendance some of whom also interpreted Burr's enlisting their support. Burr had supported General Charles Lee at his court-martial instituted by Washington after Monmouth and as an alternative to commander-in-chief of the army in place of Washington in the unsuccessful Conway Cabal prior to the Battle of Monmouth.

During his next assignment as aide to General Putnam following the fall out with Washington in New York he may have smitten a thirteen year old named Margaret, the daughter of British Major Moncrieffe, who was left behind the American lines at Elizabethtown. She became the guest of the Putnams where Aaron Burr frequented. Margaret became suspect when noted to spend much time at her telescope. Burr alerted Washington that she might be spying while painting flowers to represent the American fortifications on Manhattan *"in the language of flowers"*. Margaret was sent packing to the British fleet. Perhaps she had important information to reveal in her head. Was this espionage abetted by Burr and acquiesced by Washington? Who better to be the courier than the agent herself? Aaron Burr was also betting that Washington would not harm a spy child for the good of the country. Margaret espoused her affection for the one who first aroused her virgin heart in her memoirs many years later. Obviously, this supposed betrayal of Burr's was not a source of concern to Margaret. Margaret never mentioned Burr's betrayal in her diary, or that she took information to the British after she left the Putnam's care.

Chapter Sixteen: Guilt by Association

Any correspondents with Burr during these periods must be closely scrutinized and carefully evaluated as to their complicity as spy and co-conspirator especially where reference is made to each others health ad nauseam. William Paterson, Princeton college friend of Burr, then attorney general of New Jersey, wrote from Morristown to Burr on August 31, 1780 *"My life is quite in the militant style-one continued scene of warfare. From this place I go down to the Supreme Court at Trenton, which will be on Tuesday next, and the Tuesday after that I shall return once more to Morristown, and when I shall leave it will be uncertain... Mrs. Paterson, who is well. Our little girl, who was indisposed when I left Home, is not worse. I flatter myself I shall find her better when I return. ...A husband and a parent have a thousand tendernesses that you know nothing of."* Here Paterson is telling of troop movements in the vicinity of Trenton and Morristown of one thousand men of the American (*Mrs. Paterson*) and French army (*our little girl*) on next Tuesday. Other vital information was relayed by Troup to Burr from Philadelphia on February 29, 1780 *"That the combined fleets have a decided superiority; and that it would have been highly dangerous for the English fleet to have fought them last fall. The bills on Spain and Holland sell very fast* (loans from these countries to America*). They will all be disposed of in a very short time. There are large arrivals in Virginia and Maryland; and there are several vessels below, waiting for the river to be cleared of ice, which will be in three or four days. Poor continental is still going down hill. Fifty eight was refused yesterday; and I have no doubt it will be seventy for one before ten days hence."* He is reporting that financial assistance has been offered the Americans by Holland and Spain. And that troop strength is 5,800 today growing to 7,100 in ten days in Virginia. 71 before 10 (days) is 7110.

Even more amazing is the letter from James Monroe to Mrs. Prevost from Philadelphia on November 8, 1778 reporting on attempts for getting France into the war on the side of the Americans *"...turn the conversation to a different object, and plead for permission to go to France....The personal improvement, the connexions I should make...I was unfortunate in not being able to meet with the governor* (Reference is to William Livingston, Governor of New Jersey, by analogy his son-in-law, John Jay, newly elected President of the Continental Congress; by inference the *"connexions"* between France and Continental Congress.). *He was neither at Elizabethtown, B. Ridge, Princeton, nor Trenton* (places in New Jersey, thus making *governor* reference that state and ultimately the Livingstons). *I have consulted with several members of Congress on the occasion. They own the injustice, but cannot interfere. The laws of each state must govern itself. They cannot conceive the possibility of its taking place. General Lee says it must not take place; and if he was an absolute monarch, he would issue an order to prevent it. I am introduced to the gentleman I wished by General Lee in a very particular manner..."* Monroe is talking of some unknown intrigue, perhaps the Conway Cabal to replace Washington with General Charles Lee as head of the American army supported by Burr and Wilkinson. However the Conway Cabal had already fizzled earlier in 1778 before this letter. Or had it? The other gentleman introduced to Monroe by Lee might even refer to another traitor, Benedict Arnold. Arnold is to take up the cause to derail the war effort (*prevent it*) where Lee had failed. *"Absolute monarch"* suggests the King of England, the aspirations to serve are Lee's and of the *"gentleman"* (perhaps Arnold). Of this we can not be certain, but clearly the unnamed gentleman is known to both Monroe and Prevost at this point in time.

Is it also possible that Monroe was referring to the lack of support by Continental Congress for Benedict Arnold in his court-martial (*the injustice*) for profiteering in monopolizing trade in Philadelphia as military governor there (*the laws of each state must govern itself*)? As the direct result of this insult to Arnold, he became the substitute for General Charles Lee who we now know was planning to subdue the Revolution in short order after his release from British capture in Rhode Island just prior to the Battle of Monmouth. In other words Monroe was then privy to the intrigues of both Lee and Arnold against the Revolution and did nothing to interfere! In the guise of Lee championing the cause to save Theodosia Prevost's home, the Hermitage in Paramus, New Jersey Monroe was revealing the treason of Benedict Arnold (*absolute monarch...prevent it*). If this is true, then the anonymous letter to President Jefferson in December, 1805 warning him about the British *pensioner* Aaron Burr could well have been penned by James Monroe, then ambassador to England. Monroe's timidity about whose side to take in the war and his knowledge of the intrigues and connection to the Paramus cabal makes him the likely author and gives the reason for the later anonymity.

On September 14, 1778 Congress decided to replace the three commissioners to France, Benjamin Franklin, John Adams and Arthur Lee by one minister plenipotentiary to the Court of Louis XVI, Benjamin Franklin. This was done because Franklin had shown the most effect with the Court. Already the French Navy under Admiral Charles-Henri d'Estaing had failed to take Newport, Rhode Island from the British that summer. Franklin was to plead for more ships to secure naval "*superiority... acting in concert with the armies of the United States.... destroy the whole British power...*" It is possible Monroe was referring to this decision of Congress to effect a mutual alliance through Franklin's efforts, "*connexions*" in Paris. If so he was revealing this information to the wife of a British officer.

"*I cannot determine with certainty what I shall do till my arrival in Virginia.*" Here Monroe is talking about the confiscation of the Prevost property by the New Jersey Committee of Confiscations and his and General Lee's attempts to intercede on her behalf. At the same time he interposes references to some intrigue of Lee against Washington about which he is himself not yet decided. This letter seems innocent enough but for the vital information on the attempts of the Americans to entreat the assistance of the French given to the wife of a known British officer. The paragraph on the health of Mrs. Duvall recovering, Kitty's indisposition (Hamilton first flame, Kitty Livingston, perhaps referring to Hamilton's rage at General Charles Lee at Monmouth and Lee's subsequent court-martial), "*Mrs. De Visme* (wife of British General, thus the British army's health) *delicate nerves, her children are well for her health depends entirely on theirs*" (children of Mrs. De Visme are the Prevosts and her British married half siblings and thus by inference, those associated with her at the Hermitage, including Burr making up a spy ring), demands more inspection for the format of an espionage letter. This must be left to other scholars for this is the only letter of Monroe's published in conjunction with Aaron Burr or the Prevosts during this important period of the war.

In the letter Monroe referred to an amour left blank and a "*Lady C*". Lady C--- could refer to Theodosia's aunt, Mary (Molly) Clarke, widowed in 1776. Theodosia's mother's sister Mary Stillwell married Captain

Thomas Clarke 22 years her senior. He had an estate north of Manhattan called Chelsea. They had three daughters and a son. The oldest, Mary married in 1770 to Richard Vassel. Charity Clarke married in 1778 Reverend Benjamin Moore, later pastor at Trinity Church. Moore would administer last rights to Hamilton. Grandson Clement Clarke Moore at the family home, Chelsea, would later write *A Visit from St. Nicholas*, *"Twas the night before Christmas when all through the house..."* Maria Theresa married Captain William Barrington of the 70th British Regiment in 1778 also. Either of these daughters may have been the unnamed love of Monroe at the Hermitage. *"She and Lady C--- promise to come to the Hermitage to spend a week or two"*. Mary Clarke welcomed officers of the Continental Army while billeted in New York City, including Major Aaron Burr. She would later become friendly with the commanding officer of the Hessian mercenaries stationed in New York.

The connections between Lady C--, Mary Clarke and Theodosia Prevost, and Mary Clarke and the British and Hessian officers may be the reason Burr included this letter in his Memoirs. Mary Clarke may well have introduced them all to Burr through her daughters at one time or another. Further proof is a letter to Mrs. Clarke from Aaron Burr recently auctioned on the internet. In it he mentioned sending L14 by way of his slave, Carlo, to the aunt of Theodosia Prevost.

The revelation of this single letter of Monroe to Theodosia is further proof that Burr had purposely selected entries for inclusion in his *Memoirs* written by Davis. In this case Burr wished to expose Monroe's early inclusion in his group of Loyalist conspirators at the Hermitage. The ever calculating Burr left nothing to chance. This exposure was a pay back for Monroe's Purchase of the Louisiana Territory which changed if not eventually stymied Burr's chances for his own takeover of Spanish territories in the West. He wanted to make sure that history would not completely revere Monroe as an American patriot without some reservation supplied by Burr himself.

Later in correspondence between Aaron Burr and daughter Theodosia in 1809-1811 while Burr was in exile in England and France, the subject of Monroe as co-conspirator resurrects itself. The cipher code of 85-87 was used in reference to seeking assistance for Burr either in finances or in furthering his scheme of *"X"* which referred to conquest of Mexico. In these letters repetition appeared because many letters referred to were lost in transit between the United States and Europe. Many were received opened and thus feared read by others.

In particular Theodosia wrote to Mrs. M. whom she hinted might not be sympathetic to their cause. *"My letter to Mrs. M. has been sent long since; but no answer has reached me, and this delay strengthens my apprehensions as to success. The gazettes under that influence continue every now and then to propagate calumnies and make use of expressions calculated to enliven every spark of animosity which exists in the country. This looks ill. Our best and most numerous collection of friends is in New York. There are many there who wish to see you once more established at home."* Mrs. M. referred to the wife of Monroe, Elizabeth Kortright. The Kortrights were a very wealthy Dutch family of Westchester County and Baskenridge, New Jersey. Although very young in 1778, age ten, Elizabeth may be the lovely young woman referred to at the Baskenridge in the letter of Monroe to Theodosia Prevost. They most probably had been introduced to each other at the Hermitage by Theodosia Prevost. This fact made daughter Theodosia hope that they could call in a favor from Mrs. M. to intercede with her husband for Burr. In fact a reference to *"Judas"* in hopes of becoming a *"Peter"* was made to indicate the long shot wish that perhaps Monroe could be persuaded to return to their side. On May 10, 1811 Theodosia referred to *"Munroe"* (sic) becoming Secretary of State in 1811, replacing Robert Smith in the administration of President James Madison. Prior on August 1, 1809, *"My letter to Mrs. M. has been sent long since; but no answer has reached me, and this delay strengthens my apprehensions as to success."* Followed by one on August 10, 1809, *"I have written a second time to Judas. My letter cannot fail to reach him. It is written openly, in my own name... M. (*Mari or Joseph Alston, Theodosia's husband*), of course, has no part in my correspondence with Judas. Oh that he could prove to be a Peter, and repent of his sins!"* The biblical story of Peter denying Christ three times followed by repentance and acknowledgement is here the symbolism of Monroe returning to the side of the Burrs. The Judas reference must mean that the Burrs felt that Monroe had turned them in as spies for England either during the War of Independence or later to President Jefferson. This would explain the dislike of Jefferson for Burr and his vehement insistence on Burr's guilt of Treason before his trial.

There is a possibility that Mrs. M. referred to Dolly Dandridge Payne Todd (Madison) whom Aaron Burr had introduced to James Madison when Burr resided at the boarding home run by her parents. Sarah Todd was the wife of John Jacob Astor and possibly sister-in-law to Dolly Payne. Dolly's mother, Martha Dandridge was related to Martha Dandridge Custis, wife of General George Washington and through her child with first husband Custis ancestor to General Robert Edward Lee of the American Civil War (Appendix E). Dolly Madison made Burr her son's guardian. Madison had graduated in 1771 from Princeton, the year before Burr. But though the circumstances are similar to the Monroe's in that both were introduced to their wives by the Burrs there is no evidence that Burr and Madison had a mutual dislike or that Madison had betrayed Burr. Reference to Baron de Montesquieu in the correspondence of the Burrs is surely that of Baron Charles de Secondat, the famous French political philosopher and author of the separation of powers of government adopted by James Madison in his Federalist Papers and his influence on the formation of the Constitution of the United States. Other connections of Burr made at Princeton included William Paterson, future Governor of New Jersey, Brockholst Livingston, future lawyer and associate of Alexander Hamilton, future ministers Allen Moses of Georgia and Samuel Spring of Newburyport, Massachusetts, and Henry Lee (Lighthorse Harry of the Revolution).

Further support to this latter theory is the reference by Theodosia on March 8, 1809 to, *"The inaugural speech of Mr. Madison... It is said that, so far from being influenced, as was generally supposed, he will act a most independent part. Even Mr. Jefferson professes not to know by whom (sic) any office is to be filled. When questioned, he declares his ignorance and the reserve of Mr. Madison... I have thought it a piece of policy to conceal a determination of being guided. But it may be otherwise."* Theodosia is hoping friend Madison will not take the stance of the government toward Aaron Burr as that of his predecessor, President Jefferson.

Burr before the duel with Hamilton had referred Theodosia to Madison on April 3, 1804, *"You will read Montesquieu with interest and instruction. Yet he has a character..."*

In conclusion Theodosia stated that 85-87 refused to intercede for Aaron Burr. *"I have frequently mentioned the fate of my letter to 85-87. There is no hope from that quarter."* On February 14, 1811 she wrote, *"85 expressly said that nothing was in the power of 87."* And on January 8, 1811 Theodosia wrote, *"I told you that I wrote to 85-87 shortly after my return from New-York. Her answer was full of friendship, but nothing more. She says that nothing is in his power, and that he regrets it. I will obtain the opinion of Luther Martin, and send it to you."* Thus 85-87 was cipher for Elizabeth and James Monroe or possibly Dolly and James Madison. James Monroe was born in 1758 (number reversed 85) and he met his younger wife at the Hermitage in 1778 (87). Thus 85-87 represents the Monroes.

The mention of Charles Lee raises another point. He refused to swear the oath of allegiance with his hand on a bible (a devoted Christian) to the American Confederation at Valley Forge on May 12, 1778. When asked to replace his hand on the bible Lee replied *"As to King George, I am ready enough to absolve myself from all allegiance to him; but I have some scruples about the Prince of Wales* (a reference to Washington)." This sets the tone of suspicion about Lee's loyalty. Recently a letter from Lee to General Howe while a prisoner of the British early in the war has come to light by Charles H. Moore, LL.D. which showed a plan of speedy subjugation of the colonies. His involvement in the Conway Cabal with the support of Monroe, Burr and Wilkinson makes all suspects. They all were also intimate friends of Theodosia Prevost. The Cabal planned to replace Washington and install General Horatio Gates, if not General Charles Lee, in his place. Lafayette among others refused to acquiesce and the plot fizzled. General Lee was court-martialed because his loyalty had already been suspect and his performance on the field of battle confirmed it. Lee was removed from the army for one year and during that time Congress made it permanent. That Burr escaped a similar fate is amazing considering his performance on the field also.

Perhaps Washington's acceptance of the invitation from Theodosia Prevost to use her home as his headquarters for four days in July after the battle of Monmouth was not a sign of weakness or indiscretion among pro-British hosts, the wife of an important British officer in the Southern theatre. But rather it was a means to observe the interaction of the host and his junior officers; a test of their loyalties in a more relaxed atmosphere to cause a possible compromising situation by which to evaluate the rest of his staff. Immediately, Washington sent Burr on a "spy" mission toward Sandy Hook to determine the direction or intentions of the British Army retreating from Monmouth. Washington did not pursue the retreating British because he did not trust all his staff after what had just occurred during the battle. He had to devise a way to evaluate their loyalties and what better place to do that than at the home of a known British officer's wife and entertainer of both sides. Washington already suspected Burr's compromising situation as close friend of Theodosia consequently he sent him away to observe if any of the others would relax their guard in her presence.

Aaron Burr did however ask his son-in-law Joseph Alston, Governor of South Carolina to intercede in the nomination of James Monroe for President of the United States preferring Andrew Jackson. Several reasons may have soured Burr on Monroe. First James Monroe had supported Thomas Jefferson for President over Aaron Burr in the 1800 election, which was tied for a considerable number (36) of votes in the House of Representatives. During Washington's administration Monroe was chosen over Burr for the post of minister to France. John Bartow Prevost, Aaron's first wife's son, went as Monroe's secretary to Paris also, an odd coincidence. This could be a payback to Theodosia Prevost or consolation prize for Burr. It was surmised by James Monroe that Burr was passed over because of Hamilton's invectives against Burr and Washington's own experience during the Revolution when he caught Burr reading papers on his desk at Newburgh after the evacuation of Manhattan plus the *"circumstances"* of Burr's resignation from military service. Just as has been thought all along Burr's short stay as Washington's aide-de-camp was for reasons other than Burr's boredom with Washington. Burr had said that he was unable to discern the workings of the Continental Congress from this position in the army. He was caught red handed looking for secret information among Washington's belongings which led to a blow up between them and Burr's short lived stay as aide to Washington.

Another interesting reference on August 31, 1809 is made to *"Z. is good, but meek and timid, rest assured. It is astonishing how our enemies strive to keep alive the flames. Paragraphs to that intent are constantly appearing in the newspapers; but we have many friends."* This is preceded by, *"A.B.A.* (grandson, Aaron Burr Alston) *shall read history as you approve. It is best, because fragments may be selected to suit his present capacity, to excite his taste, to form and elicit his character."* Z. most probably refers to a British Tory spy in Paramus, and Hopperstown, New Jersey, Albert Zabriskie, who from Loyalist informants passed on to British Generals Tryon and Clinton in 1780 intelligence about the quartering of American officers in houses in and around Paramus Church. This resulted on March 23, 1780 in a raid on Rebel positions in the area followed by another in April. Could it be the Loyalists informants resided at the Hermitage? Not only was a Dr. Joseph Browne, soon to be brother-in-law of Theodosia Prevost Burr, but also another American Doctor Samuel Bradhurst placed under house arrest at the Hermitage by the British.

A late nineteenth century tea parlor myth stated the body of Albert Zabriskie was found at the Hermitage after the war by the Rosencrantz family which had purchased the home after three other owners following Aaron Burr who had purchased the Hermitage from the estate of General Prevost. The new owners counting windows on the top floor from outside the home noticed an extra set not accounted for from within the house. Upon further exploration a secret room was found containing the possible remains of Zabriskie clothed in a Hessian Captain's uniform and draped in an American battle flag!

What were the circumstances of this strange finding, a Hessian officer draped in an American flag in a secret room in the home of a British officer? Albert Zabriskie of Prussian descent was a British army doctor who had somehow remained behind his fellow soldiers to attend to the wounded of Washington's army at Paramus. He had passed on information on the location of American officers in private homes thus acting as a spy which resulted in a raid by the British on Paramus and Hopperstown. The Americans must have realized the possibility that the British had inside information and confronted Zabriskie sometime after the April, 1780 raid. Perhaps finding or obtaining information from him about the secret room at the Hermitage the Americans also realized the possible complicity of Theodosia and her entourage, Drs. Joseph Browne and Samuel Bradhurst. Zabriskie was executed as a spy and placed in the secret room for those who would know of its existence and thus eventually find him. The American flag was a symbol of discovery and justice, and thus a warning to his accomplices.

During the early 1800s an elderly man would on many occasions stop near the home looking up at the north end of the Hermitage where the secret room was located holding his hat over his heart. Although a fabricated story of Lady Rosencrantz a hundred years later, no one except perhaps Burr knew the whole story. The Zabriskie family had bought land from James Prevost. They were early settlers of New Jersey and original patent holders of extensive land in and around Paramus, New Jersey. Many were rebels during the Revolution. Obviously, one strayed to the loyalist cause and paid the price during or after the war for corroboration with and spying for the British, Albert Zabriskie forever denied being a spy.

Both Aaron Burr and Doctor Joseph Browne were married at the Hermitage in a double wedding with Theodosia Prevost and her half sister, Catherine De Visme in 1782. Shortly after the time of the raids in 1780 Burr removed Theodosia, her children and her mother to Connecticut for safety in the care of his sister. It appears the two American doctors remained at the Hermitage with other relatives of Theodosia.

Thus the invitation to Washington to station his headquarters at the Hermitage after the Battle of Monmouth in July, 1778 was a direct act of espionage by Theodosia. Burr also must have been aware of this fact at the time, even though he was detached from the army at Paramus by Washington to independent service as observer to the retreat of General Clinton's British army to New York City.

That Burr would refer to this incident in 1809 to his daughter from exile in Europe suggests another example of Burr's use of his war time experiences and actions to parallel current events by reference. His daughter not then born in 1780 had to have been taught the war time stories as she was growing up as personally significant to the Burr family. Burr felt that as a yet undetected spy for England in exile in Europe for near conviction for murder and treason in his home country he was in jeopardy of the same fate as Dr. Albert Zabriskie, especially since his country was refusing him a passport and his enemies were still active at home. That *"Z."* was *"good"* meant he was a loyalist; *"meek"* meant Burr was remaining submissive or in hiding; *"timid"* meant Burr was fearful; *"rest assured"* meant dead.

Besides General Clinton, General William Tryon had his own intelligence network of which Albert Zabriskie was accused of being a member. Aaron Burr's reference to Z. implies that Burr himself may have been a part of the same spy network.

In a letter to Mrs. Burr in 1794 Aaron chides her for an unpleasant visit with the Z. family, her former neighbors; a visit perhaps chilled by her loyalist involvement with the incident alluded to above in 1809.

Dr. Samuel Bradhurst III's great grandparents were Thomas and Anna Pell related by marriage to Theodosia's grandmother, Mercy Sands. Her brother, Samuel Sands married Mary Pell. His family owned property next to the Watkins and Maunsells, both Theodosia's aunts, and Roger Morris property in Harlem. The latter two Tories left the country at the outbreak of the Revolutionary War. The last property became the Jumel estate mentioned by Theodosia and Burr in correspondence in 1804 prior to the duel with Hamilton and later to become Burr's second wife's home. Bradhurst would then marry Mary Smith, cousin of Theodosia, and niece of her mother Ann Stillwell, at the Hermitage in 1778. If true, was it coincidence that one or both (some say only Bradhurst) doctors were supposedly placed under house arrest at the Hermitage by the British as prisoners of war and would marry into the Hermitage family? Did the British acquiesce in placing possible British sympathizers in a position of trust at the home of a British officer? Were they active spies? Certainly the reference to *"Z"* in the history lessons for grandson, A.B.A. suggests just that.

Again Theodosia wrote a curious statement on May 31, 1809, *"Mrs. B. Moore, kind."* And again from New York on March 8, 1809, *"61 looks like 16* (The code is changed. 61 once was Burr, now B. Moore.) *There is a cipherical quibble for you. I forgot to tell you that Mrs. B. Moore has showed me more attentions, and given me more frequent marks of affection, by much, than any other person. Scarcely a day passes unmarked by some new proof of kindness."* B. Moore is Reverend Benjamin Moore. To which Aaron replied on February 15, 1809, *"Yourself and your concerns engross my thoughts; and, together with an extraordinary expression in a letter from 61, must occupy the residue of this."* Here the cipher code for Reverend Benjamin Moore, bishop of Trinity Church, Manhattan, New York is established as 61.

Not only does this establish a contact between Aaron Burr and Trinity Church during his exile in Europe, it also reinforces the idea that Burr has not fallen out of favor with the Loyalists in Manhattan. Remember that Mary Stillwell, sister of Theodosia's mother, Ann, was mother of Charity Clarke, wife of the Reverend B. Moore. Reverend Moore also reluctantly gave the last rights to a dying Alexander Hamilton.

Burr on November 10, 1810 wrote from Paris, *"I have many questions to ask you about Luther Martin. You can devise and answer them without their being put down. His devoted friendship has sunk deep into my heart."* On January 8, 1811 Theodosia wrote, *"I will obtain the opinion of Luther Martin, and send it to you."* On May 10, 1811 Theodosia wrote, *"I have written to Luther Martin, but have received no answer...I have immutable faith in the strength and sincerity of his attachment to you."* Luther Martin is Martin Luther the founder of the Protestant schism from Catholicism of which the Anglican now Episcopalian Church can be considered an equivalent. It might be surmised that this referred to Reverend Benjamin Moore likewise. Contact with Trinity Church continued up to the return of Burr from Europe.

Chapter Seventeen: Burr's Counterespionage

What did Burr glean from his short stay with Washington? Perhaps Burr gleaned a lot more than anyone has realized until now. During the period Burr was attached to Washington the American army was engaging the British on Long Island and Manhattan in 1776. At the same time we now know from the *Spy Master* the American Long Island Spy Chain was formed and operating behind British lines. By 1778 Major Benjamin Tallmadge was head of the chain of Setauket, Long Island inhabitants and reported to General Washington. Robert Townsend, code name *Culper, Jr.* operated a coffee shop on Wall Street. Information was forwarded by Austin Roe to Setauket and left for Abraham Woodhull, *Culper, Sr.* Then Caleb Brewster would cross the Long Island Sound in whale boats and deliver the information to Major Tallmadge, *John Bolton*, in Connecticut. Robert Townsend posed as a Tory in partnership with James Rivington. *Bolton* through a *Nancy* would send Roe to obtain 1/2 reams of blank paper from Rivington's press in which a secret message in invisible ink would be hidden on a predetermined buried blank paper in the 1/2 ream which was carried back to Major Tallmadge. At Setauket Roe would tend his cattle at the farm of Abraham Woodhull at Conscience Bay. Ann Smith Strong, code name *Nancy,* wife of Judge Selah Strong, would signal the location of Brewster's whale boats for rendezvous with Woodhull by the color of her petticoat, red or black, and number of handkerchiefs on her clothesline. It was this chain which discovered the Arnold plot to turn over West Point to Major Andre, *James Anderson*. This revelation led to Andre's capture following the bombardment of the British ship, *Vulture* eliminating his escape route. Tallmadge had been given warning of *James Anderson's* arrival by Arnold to facilitate his movement or free passage. Tallmadge put together the capture of Andre as spy and the letter from Arnold to him to watch out for a James Anderson and pass him on to his headquarters.

What is significant is the identity of this chain of spies was thought to be a secret even to Washington. However, Aaron Burr and Theodosia in their 1803-4 correspondence mentioned *La R.* (Roe), many times in cipher. Evidence has surfaced that the British had discovered the Culper ring and had a plan to shut it down, but decided to let it stand. It is easier to know a spy ring exists and feed it misinformation. Another would surely spring up in its place if it were removed. Did Aaron Burr discover the identities of this Long Island Spy Chain and reveal it to the British during the Revolutionary War? It would seem likely that he did since Burr and Theodosia used another incident in the war in 1775 at Quebec City for their cipher also. At the time of this cipher letter the identity of the Culper Spy Ring was still not public knowledge.

Then how far back does Burr's spying really go, to Manhattan, to Quebec? Did the British let Aaron lead a nearly trapped brigade of General Henry Knox with Alexander Hamilton in the attached artillery to safety by the Bloomingdale road and Sunfish Creek left uncut by the enveloping British forces? The story goes on September 15, 1776 the British landed at the foot of present day 34th Street in Manhattan on the East River at Kip's Bay Farm. Mrs. Robert Murray saved the army by entertaining the British officers with food and wine while General Putnam and 3500 men were able to slip past the Murray Farm (the location of the Waldorf-Astoria Hotel). Did the British tarry on purpose? Would a determined British force just landed on enemy held soil for the purpose of cutting off the retreating American army delay an attack to block the escape of a large force of the enemy because of the home cooking of a Rebel farmer's wife? Hardly! The officers would have been court-martialed. However a similar occurrence in World War II where the British halted offensive operations for the allotted tea time left the American army hanging speaks to its plausibility. This author thinks the delay story was a ruse to cover the complicity of Burr with the British in allowing him an escape route to improve his advantage with Washington. Among the officers were Generals Howe, Clinton and Tryon. General Tryon would prove himself an aggressive pursuer of the Whigs in North Carolina. He was implicated in the just failed attempt on Washington's life at Manhattan and would meet Aaron Burr at the head of the Yale student militia in New Haven in 1779 to Aaron's personal gain again. It would seem that Aaron Burr would outsmart Governor General William Tryon at the evacuation of

Manhattan and the defense of New Haven, Connecticut. Or were these two instances set ups to make Burr look loyal and glorious in the eyes of Washington and the Rebel cause? It is hard to fathom the good fortune of Burr without some collusion of the other side.

The reason for the ruse can be found in the prior event of June 22nd. An Irishman, Thomas Hickey had been confined to the Provost jail for counterfeiting. Hickey a member of Washington's personal Life Guard told his fellow cellmate, Isaac Ketchum confined for the same charge that Hickey was part of a plot to spike the cannon, burn the only bridge to the mainland and blow the magazine as soon as the British attacked. Members of the guard would execute Washington and all his generals and thus end the war before it had started. Ketchum seeing his opportunity for freedom got the story to Washington who arrested two life guard, six drum and fife corps members, a gunsmith on Broadway and the Mayor of New York, David Mathews. Among dozens of others was then colonial governor William Tryon and prominent Long Island Loyalist, Richard Hewlett. Hickey was the first execution by the American army on June 28th. Washington at the time of the British landing on September 15th was safely at Harlem Heights beyond their reach. If Burr, one of Washington's aides at the time was a part of the plot there was nothing he could do but make himself look good in the eyes of the General. What better way than stage a valiant retrieval of part of the army in the face of the enemy. Burr probably would not have had direct contact with the ordinary soldiers in the plot for fear of implication if a failure and maintaining his distance would assure his position of intimacy with Washington.

Joseph Hewes to Samuel Johnston of North Carolina from Philadelphia, July 8th, 1776, "...*one of Genl. Washington's guards has been put to death for being concerned in it, the Mayor of the City and some others are confined, I believe many of them are guilty, [stricken] it has been said the matter has been traced up to Govr. Tryon.*"

It seems not hard to believe that Burr might have known about the plot and help direct it through someone like the mayor of New York, or Royal Governor, William Tryon, perhaps by indicating the opportune time to attack Washington. Burr's mother's brother, Reverend Jonathan Edwards' son Jonathan Walter Edwards married Elizabeth "Betsy" Tryon, daughter of Navy Captain Moses Tryon. (William Tryon II was also married to Sarah Goodrich, the granddaughter of Timothy Edwards, Burr's uncle and surrogate father.) Jonathan Edwards, son of Timothy who raised Aaron Burr, married his cousin Lucy Woodbridge whose son William Edwards (born 1770) married Rebecca Tappan. Their son Ogden Edwards married Catherine Shepherd, daughter of Thomas Shepherd and Catherine Tryon of Northampton, Massachusetts, the ancestral home of Aaron Burr's grandfather, Jonathan Edwards.

William Tryon was born in England and his relationship to Moses whose family was from Springfield, Massachusetts is not known, however it may be that the ancestor William Tryon of Bibury, England who fathered children both in England and America by different wives is the great-grandfather of the Governor William Tryon and Moses (others place James Tryon of Bulwick, Northants the great-grandfather of the governor). It is not too hard to imagine a connection here of an uncommon surname that led to the near assassination of George Washington. How close Aaron Burr came many times to derailing the War for Independence! His close calls with General William Tryon during the War which made Burr the victor each time where General George Washington could hardly be so fortunate against the British suggest his possible involvement in the attempt on Washington's life in Manhattan also.

The difficulty connecting the American and British Tryon families is not unusual in genealogical investigation. Where a branch leaves one country as from England to America or from the United States to Canada the branch left behind often erases the memory of the departed who often leave under a cloud such as trouble with or disloyalty to the Crown in England or fidelity to the Tory cause in the United States. Thus the wayward brother or uncle is left out of the family history. Likewise the immigrant branch beginning anew states the progenitor of the family as the immigrant ancestor. One clue here in the Tryon family, as is often the case, is the similar given name of Moses who is the great, great, grandfather of Governor William Tryon and Burr's cousin. The story of William Tryon, Jr. the immigrant to Springfield, Massachusetts tells of William's impressments in the British navy despite his well to do status in the British hierarchy. His family gave him up for dead and his younger brother, the benefactor of his older brother's disappearance under the British system of primogenitor inheritance, denounced him as an imposter upon his return. His mother, however, acknowledged him the rightful heir. His siblings must have bought him off, as he *"purchased the finest estate on the Connecticut River in 1663."* This little story in itself would suggest a motive for British heirs erasing the memory of the Emigrant, William Tryon, Jr. (RootsWeb's World Connect Project: Raven Genealogy and Family History.)

Did Burr purposely lead General Montgomery into a trap at the walls of Quebec? At both battles at Manhattan and Quebec Burr an unseasoned junior officer tried to get his superiors to accept his battle plan and was miffed at their rejection. Neither seems plausible but how could one not wonder where did Burr's disloyalty to the cause of the Rebels really begin. Funny, now that we think of it he was the only one who survived that charge through the barricades at the foot of the walls of Quebec City (Prologue). In the block house at the foot of the walls of Quebec, where Montgomery and John McPherson (a name referred to by Theodosia *"J. M'Pherson is dead on the road"* in an 1804 letter from South Carolina, perhaps a code term for assassination by set up. The road is leading one to his death.) were cut down in front of Burr, was a militia volunteer John Coffin (later Major General in the War of 1812), a ship merchant and brewer, just recently from Boston, who had in August, 1775 defected to the British.

Did Aaron Burr know John Coffin from his stay in Boston prior to his joining Arnold's march through the Maine woods to Quebec City? Burr's closest friend at Princeton College was Reverend Samuel Spring born in Northbridge and from 1774 pastor in Newburyport, Massachusetts, the home town of John Coffin (born Boston) and future brother-in-law Joseph Browne, M.D. (some say of Philadelphia and the Pennsylvania Continental Line, born Bridgewater, Dorset, England). Newburyport was the rendezvous point for the Quebec invasion. Burr would surely have stayed with Spring and been introduced to his close friends in Newburyport. Samuel Spring accompanied Benedict Arnold to Quebec as chaplain and carried the wounded (?) Burr off the field. He later wrote about the duel between Burr and Hamilton.

More likely a plot to trap Montgomery at Quebec was hatched during the period when Aaron Burr disguised as a friar with the help of local clergy in monasteries went ahead of Benedict Arnold's army approaching Quebec to apprise General Montgomery at Montreal of Arnold's arrival. Alone and passing through enemy held territory Burr had every opportunity to meet with his British counterparts and make plans for the first assassination by Burr. In fact Canadian historians now claim that although the local populace was indecisive as to whether or not to help the rebels from the lower thirteen colonies or the British occupiers of French Canada the clergy was staunchly loyalist and pro-British. So how did Burr fare so well among them as a rebel and spy out of uniform if this was the case? Or was Burr setting up an espionage plot to throw the siege of Quebec for the British with the help and liaison of the clergy? The reference to J. M'Pherson in Theodosia's 1804 letter suggests this was so. For why else would she mention an event that occurred before her birth if only it had been told to her by her father as a significant event in his life?

The M'Pherson family was mentioned earlier in letters to and from Theodosia and Burr. The significance of these references is not clear except that Captain John M'Pherson and Alexander Hamilton were both aid-de-camps to General Montgomery and General Washington respectively. The parallel references could represent Alexander Hamilton in the current time frame of the letters which were just after Burr's loss of the Presidential election to Thomas Jefferson. Here Burr may be realizing that Hamilton had a lot to do with the outcome. It may be supposed that M'Pherson had interceded in Burr's position with Montgomery at the time of the Quebec campaign. Did a M'Pherson family live in South Carolina during the time of the letters? The references to them may be coincidence. Too many coincidences make a doubter. Remember Burr and Theodosia were masters in cipher and detail.

True to form in *The Charleston Times* of South Carolina on March 21, 1807 the notice of the marriage of Reid Pringle to Miss Eliza M. M'Pherson, daughter of the late Gen. John M'Pherson mirrors an earlier notice on April 1, 1801 *"at Prince William's parish __Alston esq. second son of William Alston (*brother of Joseph Alston, husband of Theodosia) *to Miss Sarah M'Pherson, daughter of __M'Pherson, esq. deceased."* There was a James M'Pherson of South Carolina who was a French and Indian War General and died before the Revolutionary War which places a M'Pherson family in South Carolina. However the John M'Pherson who died with General Montgomery at Quebec is called a Captain from Delaware by the Daughters of the Revolution, Patriot Index. A John M'Pherson, perhaps son of either man lived in Charleston in 1790 but not in the 1800 directory. A William Allston was present in both directories. Both men were planters or plantation owners who maintained residences in Charleston.

In either case the reference by Theodosia in her letter of 1804 to Aaron Burr was to a past event of the demise of either John M'Pherson of Delaware at Quebec in 1775 or Charleston, South Carolina between 1790 and 1800. The transposition of time to the present suggests an analogy which Aaron Burr would surely understand as referencing Alexander Hamilton's current betrayal.

But what about the story that Aaron Burr had attempted to carry the body of Montgomery (a relative of Peggy Shippen Arnold by marriage to a daughter of Robert R. Livingston, Janet, whose brother Henry married Hannah Shippen) through waist deep snow back toward the American lines in a hail of bullets? What better cover than a body carried across his back as protection from the bullets raining down on him? That is, if anyone was really shooting at him. Remember, some reported he was the only single soldier to return from that mission at the walls of Quebec. Was he really that lucky? Or was he wearing a coat of a different color to prevent him from being mistaken for the others in his unlucky party? We may never know the whole story. But taken in the context of the other events in his military career and later civilian escapades it makes sense that something like this might be closer to the truth than purely luck alone.

Curiously a family history of a Louis Alexandre Picard (University of Toronto Canadian Biography On-line), who was present in the block house with Francois Chabot and John Coffin that sprung the surprise ambush of General Montgomery, states they were forewarned of the attack by a deserter. Could this warning have come from Aaron Burr, who was instrumental in formulating the plan of attack as aide-de-camp to Montgomery? Lieutenant-colonel Allan McClean of the Quebec militia attributed the success of the blunting of the American attack to John Coffin whose home had been turned into the defensive blockhouse, *"in keeping the guard at the Pres-de-Ville under arms, waiting for the attack which you expected; the great coolness with which you allowed the rebels to approach; the very critical instant in which you directed Capt. (Adam) Barnfare's fire against Montgomery and his troops..."* (underlined for emphasis by author).

Are these words written in 1776 chosen carefully so as not to expose the source of the intelligence alluded to here? Could John Coffin have known of the plans for the attack and who among the enemy to shoot in its front, *"directed fire"*? Why is this unusual? It is unlikely that a deserter of the ranks would have detailed information on the plan of attack unless he was given it by an officer, such as Aaron Burr. A noncommissioned soldier giving orders for fire is extremely unusual in any army let alone the British army! Because, John Coffin was not the commanding officer at the time as he was given no title in this commendation yet he was attributed to the success of the defense and directed the fire on the enemy, perhaps picking out the officers and sparing the one informant, Aaron Burr! Why would fire need direction otherwise? Fire on the enemy was fire needless of direction unless there were ones to kill and others to spare. The reference to waiting on the approach of the rebels suggests a need to let them get close enough to identify the individuals marked for death and sparing. This contradicts the common American version of artillery fire cutting down Montgomery and M'Pherson simultaneously. It is possible in the blinding snowstorm the simultaneous volley of musketry from the blockhouse would sound like canister. There is no mention of artillery fire from the blockhouse in the Canadian versions.

Burr a man of 5 feet 6 inches could hardly have been able to carry Montgomery's body of 200 pounds through waist deep snow! In fact

Burr did not succeed in retrieving the body. His body was returned to New York in 1818 and buried at the Broadway entrance to Trinity Church Corporation's St. Paul's Church. He was found on the battlefield and buried by Governor Guy Carleton. Thus the story originated with Burr as sole witness; Burr became his own mythmaker.

Again another unexplained happening occurred at the end of that Canadian expedition. Burr had an urgent need to desert the army of Benedict Arnold with whom he supposedly quarreled to return to Boston. It seems his relative, Matthias Ogden, had obtained a position for him on Washington's staff. Washington himself had snubbed Aaron Burr when he first sought a position in the army before the trek through the Maine woods to Quebec with Arnold. How did Aaron Burr know of this appointment before the letter from Matthias reached him? Could there have been another route via the British in Canada for correspondence to reach Burr? This little analyzed event fits this new interpretation of Burr's complicity in Canada.

What made Burr turn traitor after that arduous march to Quebec? Maybe it was rebelliousness. Burr had as a child run away from the home of his strict uncle, and sought a position on a ship. When Uncle Timothy found him, he sought refuge on the mast top until he made his uncle promise not to beat him when he came down. Burr had been infuriated by Washington's refusal to post him at Boston. His actions at Quebec might suggest that he found more acceptance in the hands of his Loyalist relatives in Canada than with the strict Presbyterian authoritarian uncle, a Whig or Rebel as was General Washington himself that embodiment of authority.

Matthias Ogden was the brother of Rhoda Ogden, wife of Aaron Burr's uncle Timothy Edwards, and brother of Moses Ogden, father of Frances Ogden, wife of Burr's uncle Pierpont Edwards.

Apparently the Coffin family was related some 16 times to the Alstons. Joseph Alston future husband of Burr's daughter, Theodosia, in 1801 had graduated from Princeton College in 1795. His brother was Lemuel J. Alston and father William. William Alston was a wealthy South Carolina land owner and close friend of Thomas Jefferson. William Tryon had been a Royal governor of North Carolina and may have introduced Burr to the Alstons when he was governor of Loyalist New York in 1775. Burr's cousin, Jonathan Walter Edwards was married to Elizabeth (Betsy) Tyron (alternate spelling, Tryon), whose parents, naval captain Moses Tyron and Narcis Turner were from Northampton, Massachusetts where Burr's mother's ancestors, Rev. Jonathan Edwards had lived. Abiel Tyron was the progenitor of this family in Northampton.

There is a possible connection of Joseph Browne to the Coffin family of Boston and Newburyport, Massachusetts, revealed in the records of the Mormon Church. Joseph Browne was reportedly christened April 9, 1758 in Bridgeport, Dorset, England, son of Joseph and died in 1835 (or 1810). A Joseph Browne, son of Revolutionary Captain Jonathan Browne and Mary Garland of Rye, New Hampshire, born April 27, 1757(or3), married a Martha Coffin, born January 11, 1758 of Newbury, Massachusetts, on December 4, 1777 in Salisbury, Mass. and he died on March 4, 1841. They had one child Sarah Hook Brown, born November 10, 1778. Joseph Browne and Catherine De Visme had Catherine De Visme Browne who married Robert Wescott of Philadelphia in 1806 in St Louis. While the birth dates are close for both Joseph Brownes, the father or grandfather is also named Joseph. Likewise someone has misattributed the birth of a Martha Coffin in Dorset, England in 1741 without other evidence of parentage. This suggests a confusion of Martha's birthplace with her husband Joseph's. This could only be made if Martha of Newbury was married to Joseph of Dorset, England, the same man who later married Catherine De Visme on July 5, 1782 in the double wedding with Aaron Burr and her sister-in-law, Theodosia Bartow Prevost at the Hermitage in Paramus, New Jersey.

Herein lies the demonstration to the uninitiated of the frustration of the genealogical historian. Misinformation promulgates in archives of genealogical fact. Someone says one's father is Joseph and in actuality it is one's grandfather. Dates are misquoted in records because the family has just moved from one place to another. Baptismal dates become birthdates and visa-versa. Ancestral homes become birthplaces. Especially true in the period of the American Revolution not only are records lost or destroyed, but memories of expatriate Tory relatives are painfully erased from the history of Patriot families. Although it appears unlikely Joseph Browne of Dorset, England is the same Joseph of Rye, New Hampshire, the evidence does not clearly disprove it either. Joseph had a father or grandfather also named Joseph. Both Josephs had birthdates in April a year apart. The dissimilarity of years is not uncommon. Someone found records of Joseph Browne's christening in Bridgeport, Dorset, England. Thus may be the origin of the confusion of a Martha Coffin born in Dorset, England in the Mormon records. The Browne family may have immigrated to Rye, New Hampshire. If he had married a Martha Coffin in 1777 she could have died in childbirth shortly after delivering child Sarah Hook in 1778. Joseph, a physician, most likely would have studied medicine in a large city such as Philadelphia where he joined the Pennsylvania Continental Line at the beginning of the Revolution, just as his father Jonathan had in Newbury, Massachusetts. Joseph Browne appears on the scene at Paramus, New

Jersey, as a prisoner later in the war where he meets and eventually marries Catherine De Visme, the half sister of Theodosia Bartow Prevost (Burr) in 1782. The exact death date of March 4, 1841 is confused by someone as the marriage date to Martha Coffin. Other death dates for Joseph are 1810 perhaps the time Joseph is relieved of his duties in the Louisiana Territories by a new Presidential Administration and thus disappears from the St. Louis political scene, and 1835 the year before Aaron Burr died.

One can see how difficult the task is to sort the wheat from the chaff in genealogical investigation. The thread of truth is often hidden in the nuances of variable fact and fiction. It remains to be proven, but the possibility of the connection of Joseph Browne, brother-in-law to Aaron Burr, and John Coffin, one of the principals in the death of General Montgomery at Quebec, is tantalizingly close. Remember too, that too often the mere coincidences of Aaron Burr's life have led to startling revelations of truth. This author refers the reader back to the Preface of this book and the unraveling of the death of Charles Bulkley in the French and Indian War as an example of genealogical historical investigation.

Cavalry officer Major John Coffin (born Boston) of the New York Volunteers, nephew of John of Newburyport who fired upon General Montgomery from the block house at the walls of Quebec, had performed marvelously in Georgia and South Carolina from 1779 until 1782 when he was commissioned in the King's American Regiment. Cornwallis gave him a beautiful sword in acknowledgement of his services at Eutaw Springs, South Carolina. Uncle John served in the War of 1812 as Major General and corresponded with Benedict Arnold when both retired to New Brunswick, Canada. His brother, Isaac Bartholomew was a British naval officer who took part in Rodney's victory of 1782 and captain of the *Shrewsbury*, having served on the *Gaspe* as midshipman. All three Coffins fondly remembered their roots in New England, but their loyalty to the Crown outweighed their allegiance to Boston, their birthplace.

The *"circumstance"* of Burr's resignation at Westchester alluded to in Washington's acceptance letter was purposely vague and cool and not sympathetic to any illness. Washington must have suspected Burr of deeper duplicity as we have and so did Monroe. In light of the letter by Monroe to Prevost referred to above Monroe early in the war may have been more on the fence between sides than anyone has realized before. Because he hung out with Burr's gang at the Hermitage, he must have known the players in the underworld of espionage revealed here and may have passed that information on to Washington. He himself must have placed himself more firmly in the Rebel camp not too long after his parting with the Prevosts at the Hermitage, in Paramus, New Jersey.

Most importantly Monroe in 1803, just as we have seen Burr was hatching his plans for territorial secession and monarchy building in Spanish Mexico, upstaged him by blundering into the Louisiana Purchase from France. Jefferson sent Monroe to France to purchase New Orleans and was offered all of Louisiana for a pittance more by Napoleon. Monroe was almost as obstructionist to Burr's plans as was Hamilton, thus the reason for the insertion of the letter by Monroe to Theodosia Prevost in the *Memoirs of Aaron Burr*. Remember, with Burr no point is insignificant and without purpose. The proof is in the detail.

Chapter Eighteen: A Second Plan of Secession

During Aaron's drift down the Ohio and Mississippi Rivers to establish his domain he accepted the hospitality of his old friend from Congress of 1797 in Nashville, Tennessee, Andrew Jackson. Determining Andrew's lack of love for the Spanish allowed Burr to mislead Jackson into thinking there was a territorial incursion of the Spanish on United States soil. Given assurances Burr was Jefferson's emissary, Jackson offered his help with troops and river vessels. When in November of 1805 a Captain Foot from New York sent by Colonel Samuel Swartwout on the way to join Burr stopped at the Hermitage and thinking Jackson was privy to the details, that is the truth, spilled the beans on Burr's solo performance sans authority from the United States government. Jackson confronting Burr on another visit in December forced Burr to produce a blank commission signed by Jefferson. Jackson however had already alerted the Governor William C.C. Claiborne of New Orleans of the treachery of Burr and his accomplice General James Wilkinson head of the army of the Louisiana Territory. Though Jackson proceeded to release two vessels promised to Burr on the authority of the blank commission he withheld further support. Wilkinson, also in the service of Spain as agent number 13, had served with Burr and Arnold at Quebec.

Already Wilkinson in 1795 with Daniel Clark future US consul to Spanish New Orleans had attempted secession of Kentucky and parts of the Spanish territories to form their own country with the help of the Spanish. In order to save his own skin Wilkinson had himself already alerted President Jefferson to the plot and so Jackson was relieved of that position. In December, 1815 Burr might not have known the extent of Jackson's plot breaking and thus had encouraged son-in-law, Joseph Alston's consideration of Jackson preferable to Monroe for President. Alston declined to help in the matter because of poor health and subsequently died in 1816.

Another interesting aside has to do with a blank commission. Aaron Burr had already confronted President Jefferson in 1804 prior to the second term election about wishing a government post if not reelected as Jefferson's Vice President. Jefferson had indicated otherwise and in his diary had written about his distrust, disgust and distaste for Burr. It would be strange indeed for Jefferson in 1805 or 1806 to have personally given Burr a blank commission without even attaching Burr's name to it. General Wilkinson as head of the American Army would have such blank commissions already signed by the President in order to fill positions in the field without waiting for the President to return one from Washington, D.C. Thus Burr obtained this blank commission from Wilkinson, a co-conspirator, with or without his knowledge or consent.

A hint to this was in the deciphered letter, at the Treason Trial of Burr, to Wilkinson of May 13, 1806 delivered by Samuel Swartwout, outlining the plans of the conspiracy requested *"4 or 5 commissions of your officers which you can borrow under any pretence... shall be returned faithfully."* This suggests that Burr did not have the approval of Jefferson since he obviously needed Wilkinson's officers' commissions as false identities for his men during the passage down the Ohio and Mississippi Rivers; and perhaps to convince persons like Jackson that he did have a legitimate force with the tacit approval of President Jefferson in order to get their help and conjunction.

In contradiction Jefferson's knowledge of Burr's conspiracy came from Kentucky district attorney Joseph Hamilton Daveiss, who tried to indict Burr twice unsuccessfully in 1806. George Morgan of Washington County, Pennsylvania, whom Burr had tried to recruit, likewise wrote the President a warning on August 29 that Burr was talking treason. Then Jackson realized Burr's conspiracy and finally Wilkinson to save his position as spy number 13 for the Spanish and his job as General of the American army, both wrote Jefferson the facts of the matter. But even before all these revelations in December, 1805 an anonymous letter *"He* (Burr) *is meditating the overthrow of your Administration... A foreign Agent* (Spanish ambassador, Marques de Casa Yrujo), *now at Washington knows since February last his plans and has seconded them beyond what you are aware of... Watch his connexions with Mr. M----y* (British minister, Anthony Merry) *and you will find him a British pensioner and agent."* Just as Burr had feared in his letters to Theodosia, *"La R."* had been spying on his summits with Merry at *"Montalto"*.

Now it might be time to hazard an educated guess as to whom Burr was referring to as La R. Suppose La R. was short for La Roe as we suspected earlier in reference to the Culper Spy Ring of Long Island during the Revolutionary War. Knowing that feminine La usually stood for the masculine counterpart, who would most likely be in a position to know about Burr's tendencies toward the British in the distant past, say during the Revolutionary War, yet not wish to expose his own knowledge and inaction during that period, thus the anonymous letter? Also Burr or his wife Theodosia was responsible for introducing Monroe to his wife. For the sake of matrimonial harmony Monroe thought better of openly betraying their intermediary. Who indeed would sound the part of Roe by analogy? Who would be in a position to know then Burr's ongoing plans for Spanish, then French, then American Louisiana? Who beat out Burr for ambassador to France in 1794? In other words who replaced Alexander Hamilton as Burr's number one opponent? Burr gave us two hints in his *Memoirs*. One was the letter by Monroe to Theodosia Prevost in 1776 about his on the fence leanings among the Hermitage clique, and two, the letter to Joseph Alston in 1816 urging him to obstruct the nomination of James Monroe for President in preference for Andrew Jackson. Monroe sounds by alliteration like Roe. Monroe was in a position to know about Burr's dealings with the British from the Hermitage days with Theodosia Prevost. He also must have surmised the purpose of Vanderlyn's appearance in Paris to paint his portrait while he was negotiating with Napoleon for the Louisiana Territory. In fact Burr's dependent might have well let it slip during prolonged sessions Vanderlyn required for a portrait why Burr might be interested in the events occurring in Paris at that time. Monroe also had a vested interest in seeing that Burr did not succeed in upsetting what he had accomplished regarding the annexation of the Louisiana Territory with the United States. No one else fits these requirements in toto. Thus James Monroe had replaced Alexander Hamilton as Aaron Burr's watch dog. And Burr knew it.

Two other feminine names, La Planche, and La Binney appear in the same part of the letter denoting La R. as an impediment. Another guess would suggest that La Binney referred to Horace Binney, a prominent lawyer of Philadelphia who was appointed director of the First Bank of the United States in 1808 after this letter. Moreover Monroe was a lawyer also, but the claim to prominent lawyer certainly rested with Burr. The French word planche means board or plank. In nautical context to board means to come along side or go on board as to attack; plank means to put down forcibly; thus translated Monroe was attacking prominent lawyer Burr from afar in his post as minister to Great Britain at the time. In London one can suppose Monroe may have become privy to rumors about Burr within the British Government. Later Burr would write *poor Binney* in reference to his own predicament, not some casual amour.

But what of this word *"pensioner"*? Is this the smoking gun that proves our thesis herein that Burr was all along an agent of Great Britain? The reference to pensioner would mean for prior service not just the current conspiracy. Would prior service antedate the formation of the current government of the United States? By definition pension is "given when certain conditions, as age, length of service, have been fulfilled." And how did Burr receive his pension? Ah, one only has to look to the land transactions of Manhattan Island (Appendix B, D).

Then why did not Jefferson act on these warnings? Was he letting Burr self destruct or hoping maybe Burr would start something with Spain that he could capitalize on to solve the Spanish Florida problem then brewing? Was he waiting for others to show their stripes like Washington had at the Hermitage after the battle of Monmouth? Or, was he initially an accomplice himself as Blennerhassett later implied? In support of this theory are the appointments of Burrites to the Louisiana Territory when previously Jefferson had spurned Burr's suggestions for political appointments while Vice-President. As many have said, Burr's version of the conspiracy fits the listener's ears and Jefferson was probably led to believe a version he could buy into while Burr made other plans. When the secession plans of Burr became evident Jefferson had to act. Before that he was willing to let Burr run amuck with the Spanish outside the bounds of the American Neutrality Act, where after he could pick up the pieces without himself breaking that law.

Much has already been written about the Treason Trial of Aaron Burr in 1807 that nothing new can be added except that this was not the first or the last treason of Aaron Burr against the United States. Wilkinson asked the Spanish Government in Mexico for two hundred thousand dollars in compensation and reward for thwarting Burr's attack on them. The other co-conspirator Harmon Blennerhassett whose brother, John, had been among the first British casualties at New York in 1776, had sought from Joseph Alston thirty five thousand five hundred dollars hush money not to implicate him in the Treason of Burr. Blennerhassett threatened the publication of a book entitled *"A review of the projects and intrigues of Aaron Burr during the years 1805, 1806, and 1807, involving therein, as parties or privies, Thomas Jefferson, A. Gallatin, Dr. Eustis, Governor Alston, Daniel Clark, Generals Wilkinson, Dearborn, Harrison, Jackson, and Smith, and the late Spanish ambassador Yrujo..."* On May 10, 1811 Theodosia wrote Burr, *"...he* (Blennerhassett) *will publish a pamphlet containing documents which must ruin him* (Mr. Alston, her husband*) for ever... not indeed of Mexico, but of Alston, Jefferson, and Burr."* Burr implied to Blennerhassett that *"neither Mrs. Alston nor he would feel displeased at any steps I might take against Alston..."* Blennerhassett concluded Burr deranged, inconsistent in facts, noncommittal, but capable of confidence from all. He suggested for Burr a new source of wealth for Blennerhassett by inheritance whereupon Burr perhaps as a boast to counter the obvious bluff of Blennerhassett said *"I will again bury his credulity and rear upon it my aggrandizement."* Such were Burr and his ilk with no scruples.

Again in 1802 as vice-president Aaron Burr unsuccessfully entreated President Jefferson and others to appoint his future biographer, observer to the duel with Hamilton and closet friend and supporter for his last 40 years of life, Matthew L. Davis to the naval post of New York, collector of import fees, in place of the lame duck Federalist, Richard Rogers. Later during the Jackson administration in this post a friend and accomplice of Burr's in the Treason Trial about the secession of the Western United States and annexation of Mexico, Samuel Swartwout, had absconded with over one million dollars of federal funds and had to leave the country. Burr's most trusted friend within the administration and close friend of President Jefferson, Secretary of the Treasury Albert Gallatin's help was sought to no avail. Burr kept strange bedfellows indeed.

On December 4, 1803 Aaron had written to Theodosia *"At Mrs. General G.'s* (General Alexander Hamilton) *I met by accident Mrs. Rogers* (Richard Rogers*). She is a pleasant, cheerful, comely woman, to appearance not past thirty–eight or forty. You know we had heard otherwise* (the Federalist who held the post of naval officer of New York to the exclusion of his friend Matthew L. Davis) *... I am rejoiced at what you tell me of La Grec".* (Alexander Hamilton). Another reason to avenge his friend with Hamilton's blood, Burr must have felt Hamilton having thrown the election in 1801 to Jefferson over Burr encouraged President Jefferson to snub Burr's friend Davis' appointment to Roger's post. Thus Rogers was to Davis in the same league as Hamilton was to Burr in obstructing their political careers. Also perhaps more than political the post of naval officer at the port of New York meant a source of income that was corruptible.

Burr was successful in convincing President Jefferson to appoint the brother-in-law of his wife, Theodosia, Dr. Joseph Browne as secretary of the government of the upper district of Louisiana at St. Louis in March,

1805. Why on the eve of his second administration Jefferson did the favor for Burr whom he was replacing as his Vice-President is obscure. Either it was a pay off or a pay back to Burr for his help in garnering New York's electoral votes in the Presidential election of 1801, or, an initial acquiescence in a plan of Burr's to expand the Louisiana territory into the Mexican west. Burr bought land in the Bastrop Spanish land grant area of Louisiana from Colonel Charles Lynch. The appointment of Browne may have been the only success of the meeting between Burr and Jefferson in December, 1804. At that meeting Burr sought confirmation that he was not on the guest or patronage list of a second Jeffersonian administration. Perhaps Jefferson was unaware of the close connection of Browne and Burr (As are most historians today including those evinced by the History Channel program on the Duel between Hamilton and Burr, since they say Burr got nothing from the meeting with Jefferson). But for Jefferson to give any appointee suggested by Burr, related or not, any recognition must mean Jefferson was aware to some degree of Burr's intensions in the West. Harmon Blennerhassett obviously felt Jefferson was culpable in the plots of Burr as he was willing to expose his name in a book on the whole sordid affair. Even more telling John Bartow Prevost, Burr's stepson, became the federally appointed Louisiana Territory Supreme Court Justice from 1804 to 1808. Obviously, this was another plum appointment for Burr by President Jefferson even prior to the appointment of Joseph Browne.

As well the appointment of General James Wilkinson to be military Governor of the whole Louisiana Territory cemented a Burr conspirator in a place useful to Burr. Wilkinson had visited Burr in Philadelphia a few days before Burr announced his plans to British minister Anthony Merry.

Chapter Nineteen: Burr, Agent of the Crown

Even as early as his first session in Congress as the Senator from New York in 1791-2 Burr was engaged in suspicious activities. Davis says he spent much of his leisure time at the state department examining the secret correspondence of foreign ministers ostensibly to faithfully perform his duties as a Senator. These documents were kept secret even from the Congress. With Secretary of State Jefferson's permission he would outside of normal working hours examine and copy from these documents at will until President Washington ordered a stop to Burr's access. Burr then sought information pertaining to the surrender of western posts by the British which Jefferson denied. Surely with our suspicions of Burr now confirmed these activities suggest Burr was plotting at this early date a scheme of secession.

It maybe even more likely that Burr was already working with John Jacob Astor whose interest in the fur trade in the western expanse of the American and British territories required information about British and American control there. Because Burr sold many properties to Astor in Manhattan in the early 1800's when Astor had changed his emphasis from fur trading to real estate, one might infer that Burr was seeking this information on western British posts in order to pass on to help Astor determine where he could safely send his traders for furs without British harassment. Astor's fur trading was in direct competition with the Northwest and Hudson Bay Trading Companies. Although he later was allowed access to their controlled territories (perhaps as reward for some favor?), Astor initially was excluded from trading in British controlled areas.

Burr would speculate in Canadian land in 1797 with French money. His knowledge of these lands may have been obtained at these times at the state department or more likely from John Jacob Astor himself.

Burr's attachment to the federalist (loyalist) interests was not then evident as political parties were still loosely defined. In April, 1792 Burr with Rufus King was asked to determine the outcome of the election for the Governor of New York. The ballots from several counties were tainted by the handling of unofficial representatives of the election commission, namely an out of office sheriff. The ex-sheriff already holding another office and having knowledge of his replacement's appointment was no longer a representative of the election commission and as such was not allowed to touch the ballots. By the strict interpretation of the law as written in New York State which held a firm time limited term of office as opposed to English law which allowed for continuity of office until replacement installed, Burr threw the election to the anti-federalist candidate, George Clinton. Hamilton had supported Chief Justice John Jay for governor and his brother-in-law Stephen Van Rensselaer for lieutenant governor. Burr had already served as attorney general of New York under Governor Clinton in 1790. Clinton tried to reward Burr with a Federal Judgeship which Burr declined.

Not too much importance as evidence of Burr's agency can be placed on this event except that Matthew L. Davis himself devoted a great deal of time explaining Burr's role in this election. It might be more important that Burr was opposing Hamilton's choices rather than supporting the winning candidate. Rufus King had dissented on Burr's interpretation. King was the Hamilton candidate for senator from New York in 1789.

However, with subsequent events revealing the tacit support for Burr from the High Federalists of the Essex Junto a case could be made that Burr was continuing his undercover status as federalist (Tory) in republican (Whig or Patriot) clothing, much like present day Southern Democrats supporting current day Republican Party policy in Congress; a well crafted disguise from his earliest days in the revolutionary war.

As Vice President in republican Jefferson's administration he was most evidently out of favor and suspected of disloyalty. Even today Burr has been described as the *"hero of the imperialist Anglo-Americans"*.

Burr repeatedly asked Theodosia in his letters from exile in Europe to seek money from E. W. L. and Mr. C. Could these be a Lowell, Cabot or Cushing, members of the Essex Junto? E.W.L. could be in cipher spelled backwards, L-we-- and represent Judge John Lowell of the Essex Junto. Lowell is also spelled Lowe.

Even more telling is the lease of many lots as designated by a "Map" in June 16 of 1804 prior to the challenge to duel with Hamilton. From this transaction one might suspect influence of the Crown in the duel if one believes that Trinity Church is a land agent of the English Crown.

On January 21st, 1814 several transactions made to Burr previously were recorded. Burr bought 30 lots from Joseph Winter originally obtained from Nicholas Bayard in August, 1793 (104/297), lot 317 from a Kip for 456 pounds originally from Trinity via a Ferris (104/299). On the same day was recorded the transactions of Aaron Burr from Daniel Ludlow and Brockholst Livingston (104/302) made on July 1st, 1794 for a parcel of land between the lands of Mary Berkley and Leonard Lispanard leased by Nicholas Bayard on January 5th, 1786, 100 acres (lots 421-458 Houston St. between 5th and 6th Streets and Spring Street) next to Burr's home (Richmond Hill) once that leased by Trinity Church to Anthony Mortier in 1786. Likewise on May 5th, 1796 John W. Watkins released (104/305) for 832 pounds land (lot 21 Spring St. between 5th and 6th Streets) originally from Nicholas Bayard on November 21st, 1789 to Daniel Ludlow and Brockholst Livingston. These recordings all made at the request of Ezra Weeks were most likely for lands subleased to John Jacob Astor by Burr in 1803 and 1804. The twenty nine year term of the leases from 1786 was drawing near and Trinity Church Corporation needed to establish the line of succession of the subleases in order to renew the leases to Astor who had received the latest transfer from Aaron Burr in November, 1803.

Matthew L. Davis admitted that Burr in his diary remarked on *"The benevolent heart of J. B* (Jeremy Bentham, the father of British intelligence)*"* when anticipating an arrest for debt. Further Bentham continued correspondence with Burr long after his return to the United States. The British government acted coolly to Burr and even expelled him from the British Isles. Yet Jeremy Bentham continued to finance Burr's stay in England. If Bentham was grooming Burr for the next round of espionage in a new war between the United States and England he could not let it be known by openly supporting him and interceding with the overt actions of the British government. He could not say to lay off; he is one of us, lest Burr's cover become public. Burr left England for Europe and was unsuccessful in obtaining support for any scheme from Bonaparte. He could not obtain a passport from the American embassy to leave France. Eventually he left Paris under the assumed name of M. Arnot. His ship was seized by the British and he became the guest of Bentham once again. Adolphus Arnot eventually entered the port of Boston in mid 1812. It is interesting that Peter Arnot also obtained several leases from Trinity Church in 1819. Arnot is an alternate spelling of the family name of Benedict Arnold.

At Boston Burr, a thirty third degree Mason, the highest level of secrecy in the Freemasons (His membership is currently denied by the Masonic Lodge by authority of William R. Denslow, *10,000 Famous Masons*), was aided by the Essex Junto, a pro-British organization placed at Harvard, headed by John T. Kirkland in 1812 with Harvard University funds. George Cabot, Caleb Cushing and George Bancroft were names connected to the Essex Junto, located primarily in Essex County, Massachusetts (George W. Bush attended The Phillips Andover Academy in Essex County). Cabot and Cushing and others in the Junto would later figure in the China trade based in Newburyport, Massachusetts and London, England. The China Trade is well known as a euphemism for the importation of opium from Turkey to China. This trade first created out of the outlawed slave trade by Thomas Handasyd Perkins of Newburyport, Massachusetts was adopted in 1832 by the Russell and Company owned by Samuel Russell; second cousin to William H. Russell of Middletown, Connecticut. Together with Alphonso Taft, father of President William Howard Taft, William Russell founded in 1832 the secret society at Yale, Skull and Bones, legally the Russell Trust Association in 1856 exempted from corporate filings by Connecticut state legislature in 1943, to which Presidents George H. W. and George W. Bush and 2004 Presidential candidate Massachusetts Senator John Forbes Kerry belong. John Kerry's mother was a Forbes of Essex County. What choice in presidential candidate is there in 2004? The British connection to both is clear through Skull and Bones.

The Central Intelligence Agency was founded and staffed by Yale graduates of whom many were Bonesmen. George H.W. Bush was its director. Five Skull and Bones members were on the Atomic Bomb Commission which developed the Atomic Bomb. Bonesman Henry L. Stimson was secretary of war for Presidents William Howard Taft and Franklin D. Roosevelt, who appointed fellow Bonesman George L. Harrison in charge of the Atomic Bomb deployment with Robert A. Lovett, Averell Harriman, and Harvey H. Bundy, also all Bonesmen. This group stayed nearly intact in the President Harry Truman administration. Harriman continued on in the President John F. Kennedy administration as assistant secretary for Far Eastern affairs with Bonesman McGeorge Bundy as national security advisor.

The British have finally won the third war with the United States. If the Revolutionary War and the War of 1812 are the first two, then surely the latter is the war for control of the financial health of both countries by these elite intermarried British families as proxies for the Crown of

England. The argument of which country has control is a moot point. The dominant economy is obviously that of the United States.

The Junto supported the nomination of James Polk for President of the United States and ultimately the Mexican War in 1846 with George Bancroft as Secretary of War. Senator George Cabot of Massachusetts had failed to make Burr President instead of Jefferson in 1800. The families of Cabot, Lowell, Higginson, Forbes, Cushing, Perkins, Sturgis, Weld and Paine mostly of Essex County, Massachusetts reportedly comprised the Essex Junto. President John Adams from Massachusetts identified Senator George Cabot, Judge John Lowell and son John, *"The Rebel"*, Secretary of State Timothy Pickering under President Adams, merchant Stephen Higginson, Massachusetts Supreme Court Justice, Theophilus Parsons, and Judge Tapping Reeve of Connecticut married to Aaron Burr's sister, Sally, all part of the Essex Junto. This group represented by Timothy Pickering, Senator from Massachusetts, professed secession of the North in 1804 in the governor's race for New York of Aaron Burr mentioned previously, then later the South during the American Civil War. The British connection of the Essex Junto is well established as the British East India Company and wealthy families of Britain and Europe which generated their wealth in the fur trade and subsequently the opium trade with China. The Burr family was married to the Cushing family of Essex County. John Cushing born 1763 married Silence Burr, daughter of Jonathan Burr and Mary Lincoln. Aaron Burr's great great-grandmother was Elizabeth Cable. The Cable family endowed the Cable Memorial Hospital in Ipswich, Essex County, Massachusetts. This author was on the physician staff of this hospital in 1976. The Burr family is named as immigrants in the Winthrop fleet to Boston and northern coastal Massachusetts. These intermarriages further support the contention that Burr was again involved in espionage for Britain with his relatives against his own country during the War of 1812.

The Essex Junto was intermarried with the Perkins family. The Connecticut Russell family group consisted of Russell, Pierpont, Edwards, Burr, Griswold, Day, Alsop, and Hubbard families. The Samuel Russell father's family was related to Aaron Burr's grandfather, Jonathan Edwards. Their wives were sisters-in-law, the Pierponts. The Russell Connecticut group merged with the Essex, Massachusetts group through the Coolidge, Sturgis, Forbes, Delano, Low and Alsop families. The second wife of Judge John Lowell was Rebecca Russell whose grandson was the poet, James Russell Lowell. His first wife was Susan Cabot. The Griswold-Green family gave fortunes to Princeton and the Low family likewise to Columbia University. The Delanos were grandparents of

President Franklin Delano Roosevelt. The Forbes family financed son-in-law author Ralph Waldo Emerson (this author's ancestor) and the Bell Telephone Company. Aaron Burr's cousin and law partner after 1817, Theodore Dwight, was secretary to the secessionist Hartford Convention of Connecticut in 1814 uniting the Connecticut pro-British party with the Essex Junto of Massachusetts. Brother, Timothy Dwight, was President of Yale University from 1795 to 1817.

The connection of John Jacob Astor to these two groups was through the Cushing, Delano, Schermerhorn and Roosevelt families. Granddaughter, Laura Astor married Franklin Hughes Delano. Grandson William Backhouse Astor married Caroline Webster Schermerhorn whose daughter Helen Schermerhorn Astor married James Roosevelt Roosevelt. Great grandson William Vincent Astor's second wife was Mary Benedict Cushing and third wife was Mary Brooke Russell.

Ancestors Reverend Nodiah Russell of Middletown and Rev. Russell James Pierpont were among the ten founders of Yale College in 1701. Descendant William Huntington Russell founded Yale Skull and Bones, or Russell Trust Association. Pierpont Edwards, uncle of Aaron Burr, a thirty third degree Mason himself, the highest level of secrecy, had been installed the Master of the Masons in Connecticut by the occupying British forces in 1783, and administered the estate of traitor Benedict Arnold. Rev. John Pierpont, whose family relatives were denounced by President Jefferson as *"under the influence of the whore of England"* was connected to Burr's family during the secessionist attempt of Aaron Burr. The Reverend's daughter, Juliet married Connecticut born British banker Junius Morgan. Their son and namesake of the Reverend was John Pierpont Morgan, US financial wizard of the American House of Morgan.

The family connections do not belie the steadfast British influence over our present and past history.

On the eve of another war with England Burr suggested to Joseph Alston via Theodosia to seek a position in the army. Because of his governorship of South Carolina he could expect a high position of leadership. Alston obtained a brigade-general commission without a brigade. On July 26, 1812 Joseph Alston wrote Burr about the death of his son, Burr's grandson. Later in the letter he says *"I have great anxiety to be employed against Quebec and have a letter prepared asking of the president a brigade in that army... Then, be the event what it may, I shall gain something."* What would he gain from being in the army? Should he be employed against Quebec Alston would be facing the British General George Prevost, nephew of Theodosia's mother's first husband. The Prevosts had entertained Burr in London. Certainly he did not want to spill the blood of Theodosia's half brothers' cousin. Was there another scheme afoot? Alston's eagerness suggests so. Could Burr be seeking an insider to the American Army for more espionage? Burr had been supported upon landing in Boston under an assumed name of Adolphus Arnot by the Essex Junto, a secret group of Loyalist in Essex County, Massachusetts.

On August 12, 1812 Theodosia hinted *"a war with England would necessarily affect the plans of all Americans at home or abroad. In that case, suppose you should offer your services to government"*. By this she meant for Burr to offer his services to Great Britain certainly not the United States which had just attempted to prevent Burr from returning to the States by denying him a passport.

Chapter Twenty: Burr vs. Hamilton Once Again

Upon returning to the United States from Europe in 1812 one cannot believe that Burr had retired from the theatre of personal intrigue and masterful plotting. In 1803-4 Trinity leases were turned over to John Jacob Astor, a British agent in order to fund his Secessionist Plot and reward Burr's assassination of Alexander Hamilton. We know that Burr had continued to pursue funds for a take over of Spanish South America and Mexico while in exile in Britain and Paris, France. In 1816 he was offered *"management of our political and military affairs...."* of Mexico by Jose Alvarez De Toledo and again in 1819 another offer of generalship *"in favor of the emancipation and liberty of Venezuela and New Grenada, and all other countries of South America and Mexico...."* by J.Baptiste Arismendi, Vice President of Venezuela. Aaron Burr was not a reformed scheme addict. We know however that this letter from Venezuela did not come out of the blue. On June 5, 1809 Theodosia wrote Aaron, *"T. Sumter will set off immediately to the Northward, thence to go to Rio Janeiro. He contemplates a very long absence, for all his property is advertised. I hope to see Natalie before their departure...I beseech of you be more careful in writing with ciphers. Again I have been tantalized with something about X. Pray, pray do not let this happen again. Where did you meet with any of my grandmother's connexions?* (De Visme family in England)" Of course Natalie Sumter was the adopted daughter of Aaron Burr. Surely Sumter had something to do with it. Theodosia worries about the repeat of the failed attempt for secession of Mexico that led to the treason trial in 1807.

The inclusion of these letters in his *Memoirs* suggests a desire to make it known <u>now</u> that he was still actively seeking the success of his unhappy childhood. To rule a vast empire to spite his vituperative uncle was his childhood dream that he could not forego even in his twilight.

Thus history Will admire the VIRTUES and TALENTS of the incorruptible Alexander Hamilton and not Aaron Burr. The Loyalists of New York City had come to realize the true selflessness of a man whose intensions were given the character of the accuser by transference, just as Hamilton had accused Burr of his own indiscretions in love and politics. They had second thoughts about the man they misinterpreted as an outsider who only wanted to be accepted by them. Was this glowing tribute a remorseful epitaph or obfuscation of the true duplicity of the corporate body of Tories, Trinity Church, in his death? He sought fame, not of masses as one would today, but of recognition of the elite of the time. They ultimately turned on their gadfly Aaron Burr and he died in poverty and in debt a lonely man without an admiring country or a grateful relationship with Loyalists or the Crown. Although Burr felt vindicated when in 1836 Texas became independent just before he died, one must realize that Texas would not have been more than a member of the Empire of England ruled by himself and his precious Theodosia at his side.

In 1894 Robert Frost wrote *Kitty Hawk* while visiting the Outer Banks of North Carolina. He had just learned the story of Theodosia.

> *"Did I recollect*
> *how the wreckers wrecked*
> *Theodosia Burr off this very shore?*
> *"Twas to punish her*
> *but her father more."*

Theodosia means God's Divine Gift, and so were both the wife and daughter to Aaron Burr. Tragically, Aaron Burr may have played a hand in the death of his daughter who carried his papers. These papers could be seen as too delicate to reveal to the world or at least the newly liberated colonies. Aaron Burr was never aware of it during his life. While Alexander Hamilton could not attain that Supremacy of Royal Heredity, Aaron Burr could not reveal his connections there.

As Warren Goldstein, chair of the history department at the University of Hartford, in the Yale Alumni Magazine (Spring, 2004) so aptly describes the *"extraordinary power of privilege: the intense web of connections knitting together America's upper classes through family ties, business relationships, philanthropic and civic activities, social and recreational life, and of course, education,"* is applicable today as it was at the beginning of our colonial and national life. One could so correctly add one more, religion.

Part Three: The Mechanics of Manhattan

Chapter Twenty One: The British Bankers

A most intriguing fact is Aaron Burr obtained deeded leases from Trinity on June 16, 1804, just prior to the challenge to duel with Hamilton and subsequently resold the leases to John Jacob Astor on June 28, 1804, obviously for a profit. Aaron Burr also sold property to Astor in November 11 and 18, 1803 recorded on June 4th, and 11th, 1804 and in 1827 by attorney. Astor paid over $100,000 for this sublease of some 400 lots owned by Trinity Church. His net worth at that time was estimated at a quarter of a million dollars from the fur trade. It is inconceivable that he would risk nearly half his hard earned wealth on one transaction that did not even include full title to the property. John Jacob Astor was related to the loyalist De Lancey family. Was this a pay off for Burr's participation in the duel by the Essex Junto or the Crown in order to remove the pesky Hamilton from obstructing the plans, for succession of western territories of the United States and subjugation of adjacent Spanish lands in the Louisiana Territory?

There is evidence of a connection between Astor and the Junto through favors from the British East India Company in the China trade and trapping territory rights from the Hudson Bay and Northwest Trading Companies in Canada controlled by the British. Astor wrote Burr from Canada about his landlord (the Crown of England) in 1803 (cited previously). There is no direct evidence as yet of an earlier connection between Burr and Astor except our speculation on Burr's interest at the State Department in the British occupation of its forts in the Ohio Valley in 1795 counter to the Treaty of Paris of 1783. But clearly Astor's letter to Burr in 1803 implies a prior relationship of unknown duration.

John Jacob Astor was buried in 1848 in Trinity Church Cemetery and left a library which formed the foundation of the New York City Library.

Many historians would agree that Astor arrived in America on March 25, 1784 well after the conflict had ended. But some would have us believe he had some involvement in the War. However this could only be done from Canada and the favors of trade in British controlled China did not begin until well after that period. Likewise Astor was still in his early twenties then and began as apprentice to his older brother and thus not on his own yet. The Astor family claimed the China trade included tea, rice, matting, and sandalwood from the Sandwich (Hawaiian) Islands without mentioning opium, which some claim was the basis of his wealth, not furs. In addition the British East India Company gave Astor permission to trade in ports otherwise monopolized by it. This fact demonstrates one way the British can do business. In this case rarely does money exchange hands. Instead favors in kind are exchanged in disparate parts of the world beyond the borders of colloquial conception of the average American public. This methodology is repeated with compensation for Loyalist losses incurred during the revolutionary conflict with land grants in Canada to Loyal refugees of the War. Even now the privilege of doing business in the center for North American trade, Manhattan, might be meted out not for money but as a favor for like exchanges in other parts of the globe.

Because of Astor's conspicuous accumulation of property in Manhattan George Taylor acted as agent for Astor in many purchases to conceal the involvement of Astor. Descendants of Taylor became actively involved in the real estate of New York and particularly in 1855 son Moses Taylor became president of City Bank, which became National City Bank, formed in 1812 with the principals of the dissolved First Bank of the United States founded by Alexander Hamilton. Subsequently, Moses' son in law, Percy Pyne succeeded him as president of National City Bank. When Percy became incapacitated, William Rockefeller, brother of John D. Rockefeller, and big stockholder of the bank persuaded him to relinquish the helm to James Stillman in 1891, whereupon, John D. Rockefeller deposited his big oil income in the bank. The son of William Rockefeller married the daughter of James Stillman. The British connection and the nepotism kept expanding. James Stillman's father, Don Carlos, was a British blockade runner for the South in the American Civil War in Brownsville, Texas. In 1914 National City Bank purchased ten percent of the stock of the Federal Reserve Bank of New York. Together with the National Bank of Commerce and the First National Bank all three banks of New York City owned the majority shares of the privately held Federal Reserve Bank of New York. This implies there could be considerable control of banking operations in the United States from British interests in New York and London.

However each bank only had one vote no matter how many shares one bank owned. All nationally chartered banks and savings and loans in the jurisdiction of a branch of the Federal Reserve of which there are twelve had to buy shares in that branch of the Federal Reserve proportionate with its size. The Federal Reserve System is controlled by a Board of Governors (Board) and the Federal Open Market Committee (FOMC). The seven member Board is appointed by the President of the United States and confirmed by the Senate. The Board sets interest rates for loans to commercial banks and thrifts, the issuance of new currency by the Fed, and the reserve ratio of loans to deposits on hand which controls the ability of a bank to create new credit. The FOMC members consist of four presidents of a rotation of eleven branches and a permanent seat for the New York Branch of the Federal Reserve. The FOMC determines how much the Fed banks may buy and sell of government bonds, a monetary policy tool. These committees supply the check and balance against untoward influence of any one bank or foreign interests.

Although the New York Federal Reserve Branch has more permanency on the FOMC, the publicly appointed Board determines policy and overrides the FOMC. Only by size not number of votes do the large often multinational banks of New York have influence over this policy. It can not be denied that the sheer size of these largest banks is intimidating to smaller banks trying to share a piece of the monetary business of the United States. But there are checks in place in the form of the Board and FOMC to limit this intimidation. The largest member banks in 1997 were Chase Manhattan Bank, Citibank, Morgan Guaranty Trust Company, Fleet Bank, Bankers Trust, Bank of New York, Marine Midland Bank, and Summit Bank. Of these in 1997 only Citibank has foreign ownership of 5% or more disclosed by requirements of Securities and Exchange Commission for publicly traded stock. This consists of one foreign national. But as we can see below many American citizens hold allegiances to multinational firms as agents or partners. It cannot be said for certain how this effects our national monetary system for the good or bad. But Hamilton felt that only by participation of wealthy international investors would the American monetary system find stable footing. A stake in the well being of our nation served the interests of the rest of the financial globe and assured its longevity.

New York City mayor John F. Hylan stated in 1922, *"The real menace of our Republic is the invisible government which like a giant octopus sprawls its slimy length over our city, state, and nation... Rockefeller-*

Standard Oil interests and a small group of powerful banking houses generally referred to as the international bankers virtually run the U.S. government for their own selfish purposes."

First National Bank was controlled by the Baker family. A daughter married British George F. St. George of London, and granddaughter married grandson of Jacob Schiff, John M. Schiff, Honorary Chairman of Lehman Brothers Kuhn Loeb Company. The National Bank of Commerce was a J. P. Morgan controlled subsidiary of Junius S. Morgan Company of London and the N. M. Rothschild Company of London for which Kuhn Loeb Company acted as agent and co-owner. J. P. Morgan owned shares directly and through controlling ownership of shareholders, Mutual Life and Equitable Life. Through his control of National Bank of Commerce and part ownership of the First National Bank headed by George F. Baker, through stock ownership and directorships, Morgan interlocked them with other strong New York banks, Liberty, Chase and Hanover, while personally dominating New York Life, Equitable Life, and Mutual Life Insurance Companies.

J.P. Morgan was the American front man for the Rothschild banking interest in the United States. Journalist William T. Sillman said from the United States, *"Working through the Wall Street firms of Kuhn, Loeb & Co., and J. P. Morgan Co., the Rothschilds financed John D. Rockefeller so that he could create the Standard Oil Empire. They also financed the activities of Edward Harriman* [railroads] *and Andrew Carnegie* [steel]." Curiously the P. in J.P. Morgan's name is Pierpont, his grandfather's name on his mother's side. The Reverend John Pierpont openly pro-British was the son of a Yale University founder, James Pierpont. Pierpont Edwards was an uncle of Aaron Burr and a descendant of the same Rev. John Pierpont. Aaron Burr's maternal grandmother was Sarah Pierpont wife of Reverend Jonathan Edwards of the Enlightenment.

The widow heiress of the E. H. Harriman railroad empire financed by Jacob Schiff of Kuhn Loeb Company owned stock of National Bank of Commerce in 1914. The London branch of Brown Brothers Harriman, Brown Shipley Company, is among the seventeen merchant banks allowed to do business in London's financial district upon approval of the Bank of England. Prescott Bush, father of President George H. W. Bush was a partner in Brown Harriman & Company. The London branch of House of Morgan, Morgan Grenfell, as well as Schroder Bank, Lazard Brothers, and Rothschild are among the seventeen which actually control the New York banks which together had a controlling interest in the Federal Reserve Bank of New York at that time. The London Connection persisted in 1914. Fortunately, since 1947 profits of the Federal Reserve are rebated to the Treasury of the United States as much as 96.9%. Thus what is good for the wealthy and well connected is beneficial to the masses, at least in this case.

No wonder the King of England suggested to John Adams that he had only resisted the revolt of the American colonies for the sake of the British Empire, but that his heart was now with their Independence! *"... that I have done nothing in the late contest but what I thought myself indispensably bound to do by the duty which I owed to my people. I will be very frank with you, I was the last to consent to separation; but the separation having been made, and having become inevitable, I have always said, as I say now, that I would be the first to meet the friendship of the United States as an independent power."* For his money was still safely flowing from his obscured holdings in the new United States entrusted to loyal relatives. He had likewise been relieved of the burden of protecting the colonies with an army and collecting taxes from these reluctant subjects.

Hamilton died in the presence of his wife and family, in debt of about $55,000.00, or ten times that amount in today's money. He had not profited from his dealings with the wealthy aristocracy of New York and Europe. Though he had tried to be accepted as one of them, he never attained that status which he called fame. He included them in his institutions of the Bank of New York and the Bank of the United States; he defended their causes in the Congress and the courts of the land. He married one of them. He named his New York City home, the Grange, after the home of his guardian and mother's savior, Thomas Stevens who introduced Alexander to Nicholas Cruger. Also he may have aspired to the presumed Scottish ancestral home of the Hamilton's likewise named the Grange. Many had difficulty telling Alexander from his stepbrother, Edward Stevens, such that one would assume Thomas Stevens his true father. Edward Stevens would inherit his father's wealth, while Alexander Hamilton could not.

Chapter Twenty Two: The Land

The Edwards family has already come up twice, as Aaron Burr's mother's family who raised him after the death of both parents and a Robert Edwards leasing land to Aaron Burr and two Crugers in Manhattan. There has been much written about the Robert Edwards land in Manhattan which wound up in the hands of Trinity Church. There have been many law suits by heirs and supposed heirs to Robert Edwards against the holdings of Trinity Church. Rufus King, friend of Alexander Hamilton was involved in the suit against Trinity Church in 1784 involving the King's Farm and Annetje Jans land.

A Thomas Edwards (1631-1711) married Elizabeth Hall or Hael, daughter of Thomas Hael (one of first Englishmen to settle Dutch New Amsterdam), tobacco planter, who in 1654 had been deeded land in Manhattan located on the East River known as Beekman's Pasture by Isaac De Forrest and confirmed by Governor Richard Nicholls in 1667. This land was originally conveyed by Willem Kieft, Director to Philip De Truy in 1640. In 1647 a portion of this land was deeded to Isaac Allerton of the Mayflower, land now owned by the Mayflower Society. The remainder Susannah de Scheeve (De Chiney) widow of Philip De Truy deeded to Isaac De Forrest in 1654. Added to this lot was that of Grover Lockermans adjoining farm. William Beekman resided here until his death in 1707. Also adjacent was Beekman's Swamp or Bestevaer's Cripplebush which by a clause in the Dongan Charter of 1686 vested all waste, vacant, unpatented and unappropriated lands to the corporation of New York. This swamp land was granted to Jacobus Roosevelt in 1734 whose heirs partitioned the land. It is now known as Beekman Place.

This was deeded to the Church of England by Henry Beekman and wife on March 17/18, 1748 (v3?/p268, 270).

Likewise a 27 acre farm of 1638 owned in common by Edward Fiscock, Hans Hansen, and Maryn Adriensen, in common situated on the North or Hudson River on the opposite side of Manhattan Island formerly owned by Claes Cornelissen Swits and originally plantation land of Tonis Nyssen, was deeded to Thomas Hall by Maryn Adriaensen in 1642 for 1,000 Carolus guilders paid in 1644. This land similarly bordered a swamp known as Cornelis Maersen's cripplebush. This deed was not recorded or found. However, Willem Kieft, Director (Governor) confirmed this deed in 1642. To this was added in 1646 land of Garrent Jansen. This title in the name of Thomas Edwards was later confirmed by the English Governor Lovelace in 1673 as "Old Deed from Thomas Hall to him (Thomas Edwards)" along the North River between Old John's (Jan Celes) land on the south and Van Rotterdam's Road (now Christopher Street) on the north end. Again in 1674 English Governor Edmund Andros reaffirmed all titles and estates legally possessed prior to the abdication of the Dutch in 1674. This is the same land of 77 acres leased to George and John Cruger in 1778 by Robert Edwards. The lease in turn was turned over to Trinity Church Corporation of which the Crugers were vestrymen in 1779. In this lease the starting point is at the high water mark near Beathaven Kittlegil (Bestaver's Killetjie), a creek ending at the southwest corner of the Edwards property and the southwesterly end of Charlton Street and extending north to Christopher Street along the Hudson River. Witnesses to this lease were Anthony Barclay, a British officer, and the son of second rector of Trinity Church, and Nicholas Bayard. To the south lay another swamp granted to Anthony Rutgers in 1733 whose boundary with its southern neighbor was confirmed by exchange deeds to straighten the boundary line between Trinity Church property and that of Anthony Rutgers in 1772. The southern property was previously owned by Henry Bogardus first rector of Trinity Church, becoming the King's then subsequently the Queen's Farm, granted to Trinity Church Corporation in 1705 by Queen Anne of England. This clearly separates the Edwards-Hall land from that of Trinity Church by grant of Queen Anne in 1705. Subsequent claims by Trinity Church of inclusion of this Edwards-Hall land in the grant of Queen Anne of 1705 are not substantiated. In 1784 heirs of the widow of Henry Bogardus, Annetje Jans, asked the state of New York to repossess the Queen's, then the King's Farm in their name. But the legislature sought possession for itself against which Alexander Hamilton successfully defended for Trinity Church by finding the lease of the land from Queen Anne to Trinity Church. In the lease from the

Crown of England in 1670 to Annetje Jans is mentioned the northern boundary at the Palisades, now Charlton Street. This further supports the contention that the Queen's Farm did not include the land northward of Charlton Street to Christopher Street herein described as that of the 77 acre Robert Edwards land. This is important because many times Trinity Church would claim these 77 acres were always included in the northern part of the Church Farm quit rented to Trinity Church in 1705 by Queen Anne, the northern boundary being ill defined as above.

Their possession rather arises from the surrender of the 99 year lease of these 77 acres by Robert Edwards to George and John Cruger in 1779 to Trinity Church. The conveyance was written in Dutch and found in England, not the United States. Recent revelations place a recording now in the archives of the State of New York, not as originally in the county clerk's office of Manhattan, King's County, N.Y. City, NY book 43, page 139. The Crugers were of Dutch descent. The conveyance from Robert Edwards to the Crugers was found in Dutch in Wales perhaps because its transport across the ocean in time of war was perilous and if captured damaging to those involved and the continuation of title risked confiscation. Another copy was also found in English in Atlanta, Georgia presumably written before the 1970s translation of the Dutch deed, thus supporting the theory that the original was in English and the Dutch translation used to obfuscate its identity if captured in transit.

It is interesting to note that in the confirmation of Governor Lovelace in 1673 *"a yearly Quit Rent to his Royall Highness his use one Bushel winter wheate upon demand and the Obedience of his Royall Highness..."* If the deed to Thomas Edwards had come by inheritance from Thomas Hall by way of his only legal heir at that time through male ownership, daughter Elizabeth wife of Thomas Edwards, then why would there be a payment to the Crown of England of Quit Rent? The quit rent implies that title did not flow directly to Thomas Edwards from Thomas Hall but rather by way of the Crown. Also the title was not clearly Thomas Edward's but rested with the Crown. A quit rent instituted by the proprietors of New Jersey, Sir George Carteret and John, Lord Berkeley in 1664 and James, Duke of York in New York, was a feudal acknowledgement of tenure and payment symbolized servility. It represented imperial control of the land as it was instituted in the North American Colonies at a time when quit rents were declining in England itself. But more importantly, by levying quit rents, the government left open the ability to revest land in the Crown. Thus when heir Robert Edwards leased the same land to the Crugers for 99 years in 1778 to be used in the support of the British Army and then subsequently ending up in the control of Trinity Church

Corporation, was not the land reverting back into the control of the Crown, the rightful owner? At least prior to the War of Independence the Trinity Church charter was in communion with the Anglican Church of England whose ecclesiastical structure was divided in two parts at the archbishops of Canterbury and York headed by the monarch of England. Was this a subterfuge in order to hide the true ownership from the enemies of the Crown during time of uncertainty about the outcome of War? Two boards of proprietors, East and West, still exists today in New Jersey. The Eastern Board at Perth Amboy had power to give deeds of certain lands. Only in 1998 was this board dissolved for lack of interest in board members!

In a case brought by Bogardus et al vs. The Rector, Church Wardens and Vestrymen of Trinity Church, in the City of New York et al. (case 369 and 633, October, 1846) in the Chancery Court of New York before Honorable Lewis H. Sandford of First Circuit no mention of the conveyances above to Trinity are divulged by the voluminous defense of the Trinity Church enumerating the origin of the Queen's Farm and the leases and sales of its holdings subsequently. By implication the Church attempts to insinuate that these 77 acres are part of the original Queen Ann's grant of 1705 but by testimony within the defense admission by witnesses to the ambiguity of the northern border, either Charlton or Christopher Street, was evident. The plaintiffs did not prevail because of latches, or that of adverse possession (physical occupation or control without challenge) of the Queen's Farm by Trinity Church for over one hundred forty years. Judge Sandford was a descendant of the grandparents of Theodosia Bartow, Aaron Burr's wife and the Crown of England. The case originally filed on December, 1830 was not heard until January of 1847 partially waiting upon the advancement of Judge Sandford from Assistant to Vice-Chancellor of the Court.

What is revealed therein are the extensive real estate holdings and transactions by Trinity Church both leases and sales and the 1797 lease of Aaron Burr of Richmond Hill. In addition Aaron Burr was counsel for Trinity in the advice of eviction of Cornelius Bogardus from the property in 1784.

Testifying vestrymen made no mention of involvement of the Crown of England in the affairs of Trinity after a supposed separation of the Crown from the Episcopal Church of the United States in 1784 when all quit rents ceased. Lease payments were made by Trinity to the treasurer of the State of New York in 1738, 1750, 1768, and 1786. They did however state that all taxes were paid by the tenants of leased property. The plaintiffs made estimate of the worth of Trinity Church holdings of five million dollars and annual rent of three hundred thousand dollars in 1830, the original filing date, far more than the Church admitted to in 1856 report to the State Senate. Also thirty leases were given by the Church during the period of unincorporation by the Continental Congress of 1775 until reinstatement by the State of New York in 1784. A lot numbered "one" of seventy seven acres was leased for 21 years to Leonard Lispenard in 1758 surrendered in 1764 in exchange for other leases. Lot number one eventually was subdivided into two hundred lots of 25 by 100 feet each contained land adjoining the Broadway and the banks of the Hudson River. Again no northern boundaries are assured except that this lot number one which abutted Sir Peter Warren and Elbert Herring lands to the north and east matches the description of the seventy seven acres of Robert Edwards' lease of 1778.

Could it be that Trinity Church leased the land mistakenly and realizing its mistake recalled the lease in 1764? The mistake being that it did not own the property in question. Or, did the Church then lease the land to Robert Edwards in 1768 who then leased it to the vestrymen, the two Cruger brothers and Aaron Burr in 1778, intending to return it to the Church? The former seems likely because Trinity did not reveal in its extensive report to the court a lease to Edwards. In any event the Church regained possession in 1779 whereupon it began leasing it again to Lispenard on March 25. Thus the conveyance to Trinity by the Cruger brothers of the seventy seven acres of the Robert Edwards lease was made on or before March 25, 1779 or as stated before on March 12, 1779 in the extension of the leases in 1865 by heirs of Robert Edwards cited elsewhere.

From 1768 to 1831 Trinity made 620 leases and sold mostly by auction 491 lots of 25 feet by 100 feet in size from 1784 to 1825.

Thomas Hall also held title to 500 acres on the Hudson north of the Great Kill or Creek in Manhattan, in 1667, together with Jan Vigne, Egbert Woutens, and Jacob Leendert, which does not seem to have been disposed of before his death in 1669. Neither was the house and lot obtained in 1667 at the east end of Smith's valley. It would seem that Thomas Edwards might have inherited these parcels as well. Son Thomas Edwards held 50,000 acres of the Bayard or Freemason Patent now in New Hartford, Paris, and Bridgewater, Oneida County, and Winfield, Litchfield and Frankfort, Herkimer County, New York in 1771 which must have passed to Robert Edwards and his siblings.

These Edwards were from Edwards Hall in Glamorganshire, Wales. Thomas Edward's grandson, Sir Thomas Nathaniel Edwards, son of Robert, married Elizabeth Downing whose father was Sir George Thomas Downing, born 1623, M.P. (Member of Parliament), who was the keeper of the Palace at Whitehall and first occupant of Ten Downing Street, London, now the residence of present day Prime Ministers of England. Thomas helped the British until his death in 1781 with supplies in New York. His son Robert Edwards II was a Captain in the British Navy and later carried a letter of marques from the King of England to act as privateer along the Eastern American coast. In this capacity he became very wealthy from all the prizes his ships captured and brought into New York. He was given or bought several large parcels of land in Manhattan, New York and New Jersey from the Crown of England. These parcels are among those acquired by Trinity Church through the transfer of 99 year leases from Robert to Aaron Burr and several Crugers. Robert without children drowned in 1778 on his way to Wales to claim his right to Edwards Hall, the family estate just after these leases had been made.

Robert Edwards most likely acquired from Elbert Herring (Haring) descendant of Jans Pieterson Haring of three generations a 100 acre farm located from Bouwery Lane to Bedford Street both sides of Broadway. Elbert Herring had inherited the property, and turned it over to Trinity or Edwards in 1755. Adjacent northward was Sir Peter Warren's lands acquired by Trinity in 1758, 1773 and 1775 from his heirs perhaps the De Lancey family (ref. 3/13/1758 lease by City of New York to Oliver Delancey for children of Sir Peter Warren waterfront for $83 recorded 10/1/1813 103/434). These lands may have been part of the 80 acre parcel leased by Robert Edwards to Aaron Burr and the Cruger brothers in 1778 and turned over to Trinity Church in 1779. The 99 year lease to Burr and Cruger brothers stated the land was granted by King George II *"lying southeast and at waters edge, running north-east"* but gave no metes and bounds. *"Lying Southeast"* could alternately mean the land was on the East River side of Manhattan Island. This description may then include land owned by the grandparents of Robert Edwards. Robert Edwards Sr. owned 27 ships of the Dutch West India Company of which his wife Margriet Cuelen's father, Mathijs Jahson Van Kuelen, was an owner. Their property and that of the Dutch West India Company lay on the East River called Kuelen Hook.

The lease required 1000 pounds sterling nominal rent which if unpaid the land and improvements revert to brothers Joshua, Thomas, William, and sister Frankie (nick-name for Martha) all living in Virginia with families. Curiously brothers Jacob and Leonard were omitted from this lease as heirs whereas they all were included in the 77 acre Robert Edwards lease written two days later. These inconsistencies make this lease suspect. However at the same time without the knowledge of Burr's loyalist leanings during the Revolution revealed for the first time in print herein the addition of Aaron Burr's name as a Colonel in the American Army to a Loyalist transfer of land makes this document seem more authentic. That is because only Loyalists would know the truth at the time of the Revolution and in no other time period up to the present has anyone indicated suspicion of this fact.

The fictitious 77 acres of Elizabeth Hall, wife of Thomas Edwards, great grandmother of Robert Edwards II was actually given by the will of husband, Thomas Hall in 1669 with the whole estate to her mother, Anna Medford Quick as a life estate, who somehow was induced by Nicholas Bayard (ancestor of the above Nicholas, witness to the lease of Robert Edwards to the Crugers), council of New York City, to deed the land in 1670 over to William Beekman, now Beekman Place. Mr. Beekman of Esopus, now Kingston, gave a mortgage to widow, Anna Hall for fifteen thousand guilders and a lifetime only right to live on part of the property. Thus the land which rightfully should have passed down to Elizabeth, or rather her husband Thomas Edwards as was the tradition of the time, upon the death of her mother in fact was transferred out of the family before it came into the hands of Thomas Edwards and Elizabeth Hall. This land is then not that which came into the holdings of Trinity through Robert Edwards.

Thus we see that Robert Edwards through his ancestors Thomas Hall and Thomas Edwards and his own efforts as a privateer for the Crown of England had amassed great tracts of land in Manhattan and surrounding New York and New Jersey by the time of the Revolutionary War. What happened to this land during the War is illustrative of other lands owned by those loyal to and owing allegiance to the Crown of England.

Illustrative of the return of land to loyal descendants of Robert Edwards is the quit-claim deed of July 29, 1876, recorded August 7, 1876 at Bellefountaine, Logan County, Ohio, recorded August 16, 1876 in New York City, New York, in consideration of $1000 made before W.H. Moore and Samuel B. Taylor, Probate Judge, Logan County, Ohio by Justice G. Edwards, Amanda Edwards, Catherine Tennis (by X mark), Margaret Edwards (by X mark), Catherine Perry and James Taylor guardian of Catherine Perry to Henry W. Ingersoll and Harry Edwards of thirty or thirty-five acres on East Broadway from the Battery northward, perhaps including the New York Stock exchange *"formerly owned by one "Robert Edwards", who inter-married with Margaret Curlin* (Cruelin), *and leased said premises to the "Crown of England" for 99 years "The Robert Edwards Estate" so called. "which lease expired; in 1872, as supposed."* (volume 1336, page 174, and 175, 176, City of New York, New York).

Obviously, the Robert Edwards heirs in this case regained control of the land from the Crown at the expiration of this 99 year lease made in 1773.

Another parcel of land of 24 acres was deeded to Symon Congo in 1644. This was conveyed to Cornelius or Lucas Vanderburge in 1755 to Dirck Dey, of Bergen Co., New Jersey and to Trinity Church in 1758 (3/25/1758, v54/p528). This is the property Trinity leased for the term of 99 years to Abraham Mortier, Deputy Paymaster to his Majesty's Troops on May 1, 1767 and who died before June 7, 1775. His widow died before April 30, 1787 and daughter Elizabeth Banyar inherited *"my house and farm in the Out Ward of New York, which I hold by lease from the Corporation of Trinity Church"* which Aaron Burr subleased in 1797 for his home, Richmond Hill, now the middle of Charlton Street, and a little east of Varick. 37 Charlton street built by John Jacob Astor in 1826 is now the rectory for Trinity Church which Trinity Church museum claims was part of the original Church Farm. Richmond Hill was used by General George Washington as headquarters during the battle of Manhattan and later as home for the first Vice-President of the United States, John Adams. The parcel was east of King Street. Van der Burgh's granddaughter, Maria, daughter of Susannah Van der Burgh and Richard Lewis married James Reynolds in 1783 at age 15. Her sister, Susannah married Gilbert Livingston, ancestors of the Presidents Bush, and her brother, Henry married Eleanor Ter Bush, and sister Sarah married John Ter Bush. Maria would later be involved with Alexander Hamilton in the Reynolds scandal of 1791 which became public in 1796. The 24 acres of land would also be sold by Aaron Burr to John Jacob Astor on November 23, 1803, concluded in August 20, 1804 after Burr's flight from justice for the Duel with Alexander Hamilton, for a presumed considerable profit to fund his secession scheme.

The Church Farm land originally was leased in 1641 by Dirck Jansen Dey for 600 guilders from the Dutch West India Company at the corner of Broadway and Dey Street including the Trinity Church location. He died in 1687. His son Theunis Dey married Anneken Schouton who remarried Joris Ryerson in 1691 after Dey died in 1689. Their son Dirck Dey returned in 1752 from New Jersey to the property or that further north in 1755 where city hall is today. In 1745 a lot on Dey St. sold for 75 pounds whereas in 1747 a mere 25x28 foot lot sold for 50 pounds. However since 1705 this was the Queen's or King's Farm the 75 and 50 pounds must represent leases not sales.

Chapter Twenty Three: The Church

Reading the numerous histories of New York, Manhattan, the Revolutionary War, and the biographies of Aaron Burr and Alexander Hamilton strangely very little is mentioned of Trinity Church. Yet already we have seen how pervasive and pivotal a role the Corporation of Trinity Church has played in the political and economic well being of these historical topics from the very beginning.

Indeed, author Jim Marrs has said *"religion and politics, particularly in the past, have been inextricably intertwined. To exclude religious matters would be a failure to tell half the story."*

Trinity Church although functioning much earlier, got its legal beginning in 1694 by act of the colonial legislature for a ministry and the raising of taxes upon the inhabitants of the city of New York to maintain it. In 1697 the legislature provided the title of corporation with a grant of the Queen's Garden of about 310 by 395 feet between Broadway and the Hudson River just south of the acre of church and cemetery original grant. In 1704 rights were given to the corporation by Queen Anne to purchase, receive, acquire, use and enjoy lands, tenements and hereditaments... to demise, lease and improve to the benefit of said church not exceeding five hundred pounds yearly rent or income to be run by two church wardens and twenty vestrymen. The authority of the rector is by instructions from his Britannic Majesty, through the Archbishop of Canterbury of the Anglican Church of England. In 1705 these rights were expounded upon with permanent use of lands called variously the Duke's Farm, Queen's or King's Farm or Bogardus property formerly Dominie's Bouwery of 62 acres located adjacent to and northeast of the Trinity Church and deeded to Governor Lovelace in 1670. This land is bounded by Broadway and the Commons on the East and partly by the swamp (northerly Rutger's Swamp?) and on the West by the Hudson River and the Queen's Garden, lying South of the Church and Cemetery... for yearly rent of three shillings. The northern border was not specified. This omission has led to extending the boundary by claims of the Church to include the Robert Edwards land north of the Rutger's Swamp. The inclusion of Rutgers Swamp with the Queen's Farm after 1772 must make up the difference in acreage. These repeated leases from Governor Fletcher in 1697 and Lord Cornbury in 1702 *("including the whole tract of land owned by the English Crown",* which could be construed to mean more than the original 62 acres of Dominie's Bouwery or farm). Heirs to the Annetje Jans Bogardus property claim that not all the six principals named in the transfer signed as it excluded a Cornelius Bogardus. This has led to attempts to reclaim by squatting and physical occupation of a sixth portion of the land, with physical confrontations and removal by the Church representatives in 1784.

As was the Dutch custom to allow the widow property rights, upon the death of Domine Everhardus Bogardus in 1654 *"Peter Stuyvesant on behalf of their High Mightinesses, etc... has given and granted unto Annetje Jans, widow of Sir Everardus Bogardus deceased, a piece of land lying on the island of Manhattan along the North River; beginning at the Palisades* (now Charlton Street)... *running north by east to the division line of the Old Jan's land... then east by south to the marsh* (Anthony Rutger's Swamp)... *containing 31 morgans* (more than 60 acres)." This describes the northern boundary of the Queen's Farm given Trinity Church by Queen Anne in 1705 which in later years Trinity Church tried to claim included the Edward's Land north of Charlton Street to Christopher Streets. This land was added to the Rutger's Swamp and the land assumed by the English Crown from the Dutch West India Company to the south in 1664 thus constituting the Queen's Farm in 1705. Failed lawsuits in the 1800s were based on latches or statute of limitations of twenty years and adverse possession of 150 years and did not attempt to define these boundaries.

In 1775 Continental Congress dissolved all churches deriving their authority from the Anglican Church of England: the state of New York repealed and annulled that part of the charter of incorporation that derived rights and authority from the Crown or the Anglican Church and the use of taxation to support it. In October 23, 1779 the legislature vacated the offices of warden and vestrymen because the activity of the Church in occupied New York City *"could endanger the peace of said city"* while occupied by the British. Little is said of the fact that Aaron Burr represented Trinity Church in Albany as state legislator and was instrumental in passing the law in 1784 to reinstate the state corporate charter. The 1784 law repealed the 1775 suspension of activities of Trinity Church while annulling its taxing authority and references to the Anglican Church of England. Also it repealed its preferential status as the tax supported authorized church of the State of New York above all other religions. The 1784 act was specific in restoring all title to holdings prior to the act of 1775, which effectively meant all lands it held before and incidentally subsequent to the act of 1775.

A deed granted on 5/10/1848 (500/498) by Trinity Church to the Mayor and Aldermen of the City of New York for $1 consideration a lot of land on the Queen's Farm within Washington, West, Duane and Reade Streets for the express purpose for the City of New York to build a chapel and hospital. It does not appear the hospital was built on property mentioned in this deed. However a most likely result is the New York Infirmary, a hospital for women and children founded in 1853 on William Street by British born Elizabeth Blackwell, M.D. first woman physician in the United States and on the British registry of physicians. She later removed to England and died there. The Infirmary merged in 1979 with the Beekman Downtown Hospital on Beekman Street, perhaps where the St. George Church once stood, founded in 1920 ostensibly because of a terrorist attack on J.P. Morgan, and together are now called the NYC Downtown Hospital. Despite the divorce of the American Protestant Episcopal Church from the Anglican Church of England and the Crown of England, this deed states for the benefit of "*British Emigrants*" with reversion to Trinity Church for failure to execute within three years. In the same deed the City of New York deeded lot 73 in the 12th Ward between 53rd and 54th Streets on Fifth Avenue perhaps once the property of Hilton Hotels just north of the Rockefeller Center to the Anglo American Free Church of St. George with the proviso that it build the hospital and chapel for British Emigrants. Is this a means of hiding the fact that Trinity Church Corporation initiated the idea; Trinity to New York City to Church of St. George?

St George's Chapel was founded by Trinity Church in 1749, opened 1752 on Beekman and Cliff Streets, burned in 1844, and sold in 1868 to serve its growing congregation, now at Rutherford Place and East 16th Street at Stuyvesant Square near Second Avenue since 1846. J. P. Morgan was a lay officer of the church and built the New York Babies Hospital and the St. George Memorial House nearby. The parish of St. George established St. Luke's Hospital.

Trinity Church owned a hospital on Varick St. until 1906.

Now this deed demonstrates several issues. As of 1848 the American Episcopal Church in New York City still maintained a British point of view. That is one *Emigrates* or leaves a country to immigrate into another. A truly American institution should first not have limited the benefits to British ancestry solely and regard all immigrants equal status of care. And is it not the British who pride themselves in the precise use of the English language? If to those in England the persons who leave are *emigrants* to America, then should not the America viewpoint classify the British who enter the continent as immigrants? In fact most Americans do not know there is such a word as emigrant since their only exposure is to immigrants to North America from elsewhere. Create yourself an experiment and ask several friends, what is an emigrant?

Then one can only surmise that the usage of *Emigrant,* the capital *E* for the grantor's emphasis, was specific and demonstrative of a British point of view, even perhaps Royalistic in origin, certainly British, not European or continental.

In addition the use of reversionary rights was not unusual in the nineteen century law of title transfer of property, yet its placement here seems a little excessive use of power and control. The acceptance of the wording and the terms of the transfer by the City might suggest impotence or collusion at best. That the City of New York which prided itself, even then before the Statue of Liberty was erected, of accepting many diverse peoples to it's shores, so the Dutch in 1666 accepted the British, should limit public money to benefit one group alone, even if not intended in execution, is morally unacceptable and astonishing. The precedence, of course, existed in the Anglican Church's primacy as a tax supported institution of Faith in the late 17th and early 18th century; until the Revolutionary War supposedly put a stop to tax supported churches of any denomination. It seems as though still in 1848 it was business as usual.

In 1784 Trinity Church was enabled to take the name The Rector and Inhabitants of the city of New York in communion of the Protestant Episcopal Church in the state of New York. In 1814 it became The Rector, Church Wardens, and Vestrymen of Trinity Church in the city of New York in order to allow other churches the rights of incorporation as Protestant Episcopal Church in New York.

In 1801 the legislature passed an act to provide for the incorporation of religious societies specifically mentioning Protestant Episcopal Churches. The limit of three thousand dollars was placed on the annual value or income of these corporate churches; further they must report the annual revenue arising from and the inventory of all the estate of the church triennially to a judge of the court of common pleas or justice of the supreme court of New York or cease to be a body corporate. In 1814 the account and inventory duly exhibited need not be repeated unless the church has purchased or acquired any lands, tenements or hereditaments within this state letting Trinity Church off the hook. This bill was supported by a pamphlet published by Robert Troup, Esq., vestryman of Trinity Church, former associate of Aaron Burr and Alexander Hamilton. It should be noted that earlier, Robert Troup had been involved in land deals on the Genesee River upstate New York with known Loyalist Charles Williamson, the go-between for Aaron Burr and British minister Anthony Merry in 1804.

In 1855 the New York State Senate resolution required a long overdue report of Trinity Church holdings. In 1856 a detailed report as reported in the New York Times February 21, 1856, was submitted under protest by the trustees of Trinity Church against the power of the Senate to exact such information. They stated they had made similar reports twice to the Houses of the Legislature within the few years. Total value of property was $2,668,710 in 1855 assessed value for taxation purposes. Annual rents were $71,301.97. Total value of ground rents was $1,984,332. Total lots sold in last five years are 113. Total value of landed estate of the Church excluding value of rents was $1,446,371.71. The original 2,068 lots owned have been reduced to 691by gift and sale for charity. Total income is $96,423.32 of which a total of $123,746.51 in expenses for church related activities leaves a deficit of $27,818.19. Gifts of aid to churches in the City of New York from 1807-1855 have totaled $172,590.92 plus $58,418.00, and grants of $48,852.50 outside the City. A new Trinity Chapel cost $227,164.82 in land and building. From 1790 to 1855 Trinity gave to Churches in New York City 192 lots and $493,125.70, 146 lots and $721,419.50 total and another 172 lots in 1848 to 1855 and $286,111.83. Finally this all totals $1,287,292.75 in aid to other institutions of learning and faith, diminishing its holdings to one-third of the original extent, as stated above was worth $2,668,710 in 1855 assessed value. This leaves an approximate value of $5,400,000 dispersed of which they account only for $1,287,292.75, even when calculating for fluctuating market values and accounts only for assessed properties. Many of the leases provided that the tenants pay the tax on the improvements and this added tangible value may not have been calculated in the above assessed values of Trinity holdings. Assessed valuations have historically always been significantly below appraised or actual value, sometimes lower than 50%.

Three lots in 1832-3 were sold for a total of $48,800 (305/556 Wardell lot# 143, 297/116 Minton lot# 57, 296/200 Lenox lot# 105), average $16,367. By extrapolation 113 lots were sold between 1851 and 1856 representing at least $1,200,000 income in five years in 1833 prices. Trinity diminished its holdings by 1400 lots of which 510 are reported gifted. The other 900 at the average price of $10,000 would yield a $9,000,000 income. The remaining 691 lots might be valued in 1833 prices at $7,000,000, not the

$2,668,710 assessed value in 1855. *Manhattan History, Trinity, Child of Empire* written in 1931 (found on line) estimated the worth of the 986 retained lots at $5,000,000 in 1857 and $75 to $100,000,000 in 1931. They also reported 318 lots gifted away and 1059 sold. This article concluded "Trinity Parish remains in its age the most important vestige of British Imperialism in America". Its net worth at that time $63,647,638 and income of $1,798,528. It paid $511,529 in real estate taxes, had expenses of $515,227 and gave the remainder to charity or less fortunate churches.

The GSGA Survey Atlas of 1885 by Joseph Biens located at Clinton College, New York, page 3 lists Manhattan section #18 of 80 acres, #19 of 77 acres, #20 at Beekman Place, and #21 of 40 acres on the northeast corner of Trinity Church King's Farm and Broadway St. including City Hall and County Court House owned by Trinity Church Corporation obtained from Anthony Rutger's Swamp after 1772. Note the 80 acres corresponds with that which Aaron Burr and John and Robert Cruger accepted from Robert Edwards and the 77 acres that of grantees John and George Cruger from Robert Edwards in 1778. Presumably both of which were turned over to Trinity Church on March 12, 1779. Twenty four acres of the former 80 acre parcel may include the land obtained by Trinity from Dirck Dey on March 25, 1758, (book34/page523) and subleased by Aaron Burr for his Richmond Hill home in May 1, 1797 (65/513). Other lands adjacent to his home may have come from Nicholas Bayard and Elbert Herring of 1755. The Beekman Place is that located on the East River deeded to Thomas Edwards and Elizabeth Hael after 1707 (or Henry Beekman and wife to Church of England, March 17-18, 1748, book 35/pages 268, 270). The last parcel of 40 acres is probably the land deeded to Trinity Church Corporation after 1772 by Anthony Rutgers and for which Trinity Church Corporation renews the deed presumably to each newly elected Mayor and Aldermen installed in office in the Church. (Leases as deeds are not indexed and thus may not be recorded.)

The act of renewing the lease and installing the new government of New York City each time in the Church of Trinity Church Corporation in effect controls the government itself by inference alone.

The lease of the 77 acres to Trinity Church was extended in 1865 by some heirs of the Edwards Loyalist line for 49 and possibly an additional 50 more years until 1974. But again in 1925 apparently another extension was made with other Edwards heirs. The first extension perhaps facilitates the planning and building of the first underground transportation system which included a pneumatic tube in 1870. The latter extension coincides with the plans for the Holland Tunnel finished in 1927. The Port Authority of New York and New Jersey in 1931 assumed control of the tunnel and collected tolls which sustained the Authority for floating bonds for its other projects including the George Washington Bridge. The entrance to the tunnel at the western end of Canal Street and Spring Street was at the northern edge of the Queen's Farm and feeding streets came from the location of the Edwards lease to the north and east over the land of once Richmond Hill. Thus it was probably to assure a 99 year uncontested access to the tunnel from the Edwards 77 acre lease that the lease was extended early, that is before 1974. The new termination of the 77 acre lease then would be 2026.

In 1921 the Port Authority of New York and New Jersey was formed. In 1964 the Port Authority acquired the property of the World Trade Center from the Hudson and Manhattan Railroad and others which includes some 16 acres near 34 Church between Church, Greenwich, Washington Streets, and West Street on the Hudson River including Liberty, Cortland, Dey, Fulton (Partition), Vessey, and Barclay Streets extending into the Hudson River several blocks on filled land. This land is located on the original Queen's Farm of Trinity Church some of which is most likely still owned by the Trinity Church Corporation. The original leases of the Hudson and Manhattan Railroad were obtained from individuals between 1847-50 such as John Jacob Astor, Pell family, Delano, Wood, Striker family (see Loyalist confiscations in 1779 Appendix A), Ward, Knapp, Kimberly, Thompson, Ogden, Lawrence, Low, Barclay, Fernando Wood (Mayor of New York City), New York and Harlem Railroad Company (leased to them by Mayor and Aldermen of Manhattan), De Peyster, Wolfe, James Monroe, Waldo, Cutting, Oliver, and Eliza B. Jumel (second wife of Aaron Burr), and others. Many of these same families have earlier transactions with Trinity Church and possibly were turning over unexpired land leases from Trinity to the Railroads in succession. 44 of 110 leases or deeds to Hudson and Manhattan Railroad from 1847 to 1850 have family connections to grantee lists of Trinity Church in the early half of the nineteen century. Six names are identical on both lists, of course, John Jacob Astor, Samuel Thompson (Thomson), William Williams, John Lawrence, James N. Wells, Joseph Carter, and Eliza B. Jumel who has direct connection to the Aaron Burr lands of perhaps the deeds of 1833/4 as his second wife at that time. However most of these six above recordings are fee simple purchases of subsurface water rights adjacent to property north of the Queen's Farm or eminent domain acquisitions of rights of way from John Jacob Astor and family by the City of Manhattan for the use of the Hudson and Manhattan Railroad north of the Queen's Farm.

Plans by the Port Authority for the acquisitions of property for the World Trade Center (Damage Map April 15, 1968, Map of Real Property being acquired for World Trade Center purposes) called for fee simple title transfer. Since most of the Hudson and Manhattan Railroad tunnels and accesses are on both the Queen's Farm and the Robert Edwards Lease it stands to reason that perhaps these transfers of lease ownership revert ultimately to Trinity Church. No direct title transfer to the Hudson and Manhattan Railroad was made by Trinity Church during this initial acquisition phase of the construction of that railroad, in 1847-50. Since PATH acquired the property and thus presumably the leases of the Hudson and Manhattan Railroad directly in 1964 then ultimately should not Trinity Church still own the land under the World Trade Center where the Manhattan Hudson station was located, unless there are direct transfers to the Port Authority by Trinity Church Corporation subsequent to the take over of the Hudson and Manhattan Railroad property not yet evident to the author? However the acquisition plot of the World Trade Center does not indicate ownership by Trinity Church Corporation of any of the property to be purchased, but rather property owned in many individual names, mostly real estate corporations. Alternately, the property thus enumerated could be only the improvements on the land already owned by the Port Authority or even Trinity Church.

Curiously all the above named streets enumerated on the acquisition plans called Damage Map (money to compensate for an injury or wrong, thus by eminent domain) have unknown owner of the bed of streets. Since this is on the Church Farm proper and since the City of New York does not claim ownership of these streets, then must Trinity Church still own the land of the street beds? So must Trinity Church derive rights to a direct lease payment along with the Port Authority of New York and New Jersey? In other words Trinity Church and the Port Authority may be co-owners of the land of the World Trade Center or silent partners. Otherwise there is no assessed valuation of the streets proper and thus no visible intent to purchase the street beds, unless there may exist a later, separate, and unrevealed acquisition document for these streets. The surface area of the streets proper represents a considerable area of the total Trade Center site, at least a quarter to a third since there are four north-south and six east-west streets within the World Trade Center site. In early Trinity deeds and leases the grantee was directed to pave the street to the midline adjacent to the property according to the directives of the City of New York which indicates control of the street by Trinity Church (i.e. Samuel B. Ruggles 3/11/1830,Varick St. leases 268/203,207). Otherwise would not the city pave the street with tax money?

However, many of these leases by Trinity are not indexed and/or also not recorded, making the trail of ownership difficult. It is also noted that these indexes were rewritten several times since 1858. As proof the later indexes photocopied in 1972 include records up to 1866 whereas the 1858/1863 versions could not. Earlier versions such as that copied for the Mormon Library in 1958 from the New York files by Recordak Corporation included Grantor Index (C) for 1858/1865 omitted book numbers that correspond with the year of recording, giving page numbers only. Many earlier versions include early leases or recordings of transactions in the 1700s whereas many Aaron Burr leases from Trinity Church in early 1800 to 1804, 1813, 1827 are omitted perhaps because the original dates are undecipherable in the older handwritten indexes. In the most recent 1972 copied index no transactions of Trinity Church or Protestant Episcopal Church before 1818 are listed whereas many earlier leases are still recorded in the individual lessee name prior to 1800. Look at Appendix B wherein Aaron Burr as lessee occurs in only three instances in newer version of index indicated by book/page numbers. This makes researching the titles nearly impossible without all versions of indexes. The difficulty imposed is stifling to accurate research as the original documents are often now nearly faded and illegible. How much of this is intentional is subject to conjecture. The most recent grantor list of Trinity Church is only a little more than a page long whereas the Appendix B list is twenty-eight pages long derived from several different earlier indexes.

The Hudson and Manhattan Railroad connected New Jersey with the Island of Manhattan and in 1961 was in poor financial and physical condition. The plans of the Rockefellers for the World Trade Center on the East River were moved to the Hudson River to include the terminus of the Hudson and Manhattan Railroad (H&M) beneath the to be built World Trade Center. The Port Authority assumed operations of the H&M Railroad and changed the name to PATH (Port Authority Trans-Hudson line). Thus the land of the H&M now PATH terminus on Manhattan probably remained a lease from the Queen's Farm of Trinity Church Corporation and the World Trade Center obtained sky rights over this location.

Another branch of the H&M line crossed beneath the Hudson River at Christopher Street, the northern boundary of the 77 acre Edwards lease. In the early 20th century the H&M Railroad had twin office towers, then in 1909 the largest office complex in the world, over the Hudson Terminal replaced in 1971 by the twin towers of the World Trade Center, then the highest towers in the world.

In 2003 Trinity Holding Company possesses 255 properties in Manhattan in the environs of Wall Street, representing some of the most valuable real estate in the world, making it one of the wealthiest corporations in the world. In the early 1900s its income was estimated at $900,000 a year. Trinity Corporation admits it has benefited by the land leases on which its tenants build and make improvements. When a recession or depression like 1929 occurs it takes possession of these improvements from defaulting and bankrupt tenants.

It would appear that the method of land lease, described as Quit Rent by Governor Lovelace in 1673, rather than outright warranty deed, beginning with the Queen's Farm lease of three shillings a year in 1705 to Trinity Church has mushroomed into a multimillion dollar bonanza surely unforeseen in 1705 or 1778.

Was there another reason besides money that land leases rather than warranty deeds were used by the Crown in colonial New York City? Quit rent is a feudal holdover where tenants pay a portion of their harvest to the proprietor. This system was applied by the British Crown to the assumed Dutch holdings in New Jersey and New York after 1673 continuing that which had already been similarly put in effect by the Dutch. The quit rent also represents tenancy or temporary occupancy with a finite term where the grantor retains ultimate control and ownership into the future. Thus the Crown of England considered itself the ultimate titleholder of the land assumed from the Dutch removal in 1673, and as late as 1705, Queen Anne granted the Queen's Farm to Trinity for a quit rent of three shillings a year. Does the Crown still consider itself the proprietor of these lands? Had Trinity Corporation become the agent of the Crown?

It appears that Trinity Church Corporation has accounted for all of its income and outflow in the 1856 report to the Senate of New York. Assuming that there are no other assets held by other entities outside of New York within its control, does a total of 1.2 million dollars outlay disperse a yearly income of 100 thousand dollars over fifty or more years? Suppose an inflationary figure over a 50 year span could account for the difference. If there was any slack left over where could it have gone?

A more recent transaction in 1977 may be illustrative. Australian newspaper magnate, Rupert Murdock supposedly bought two parcels, 217 Broadway, the Astor Building, and 225 Broadway, the Transportation Building, from Trinity Church Corporation with 42 million dollars borrowed from the National Bank of Tennessee. This transaction probably was not completely financed until 1984 when another 30 million dollars borrowed from the Union Bank of New Jersey was used to finance the land. He subsequently in 1987 may have formed a privately held Bank or Trust Company in Nova Scotia reportedly the Second Bank of Nova Scotia no longer extant with only three shareholders including his wife. He may have put the two properties on Broadway into a trust in British Columbia,

Canada, named Trinity Holdings, N.A. in 1993 listing newspaper assets of 11.5 billion dollars. These Broadway properties were then leased by Merrill Lynch Corporation, not currently. A recent report of a purchase of 225 Broadway in 2004 for approximately 72 million dollars from Trinity Holdings has surfaced. Since Trinity often retains control of property in Manhattan by securing long term leases with reversions to Trinity upon termination, it makes sense that these properties might be held in a Trinity Holdings trust. The proceeds of the transaction may possibly represent a mortgage or refinancing whose proceeds were then transferred to Nova Scotia, Canada and reinvested through Trinity Holdings of British Columbia formerly deposited in the bank or holding corporation in Nova Scotia with Rupert Murdock as principal representative. In this way assets in Manhattan are seemingly reinvested and dispersed outside the United States without relinquishing control of these assets.

An internet search of the name Trinity Holdings reveals another newspaper publishing conglomerate in Pennsylvania seemingly unrelated to the British Columbia corporation above; a portfolio and asset manager of South Africa, Trinity Holdings (Pty) Ltd.; a gold reserve company in South Africa including the Africander Lease; a Russian oil company, described as an *"obscure business believed to be a front for organized crime"* (Wow!? Perhaps not!); a truck manufacturer, Dennis Brothers, part of Trinity Holdings, 1904-1989 in Great Britain; Trinity International Holdings plc publishes newspapers in England, Wales, Scotland and North America; and another Canadian firm for mineral exploration in New Foundland located on Mountbatton Drive. Lord Mountbatten, born at Windsor Castle, was of German descent and uncle to Prince Phillip, consort of Queen Elizabeth. He was killed while fishing in Northern Ireland in 1979 by the Irish Republican Army (IRA).

The Queen of England has publicly reported on public television that a large portion of her income originates in a Bank of Nova Scotia.

Epilogue: The Crown's Jewel; The Twin Towers

Suppose:

To say that the Royalty of Europe that still exists intact today is disinterested in the economics of the world is to ignore the facts. The Queen of England is one of the largest holders of property in the world and one of the wealthiest people in the universe. She has been thought to have representation in the secret meetings of the Bilderbergers along with the royalty of Sweden, Spain, and Holland. The Bilderbergers have a vested interest in a global economy and a world government which in the past would have run counter to the goals of a royal family of any one country. But royalty now without political power has only its own economic self interest to care for. This secret society is credited by some for the origination of the European single currency and the concept of the European Union. Their counterpart in the United States has been often stated as the secretive Council on Foreign Relations and the more open Trilateral Commission. The latter is a prodigy of the powerful David Rockefeller and derivative of the former older stepchild of J. P. Morgan among others. Both wealthy men have strong ties to London banking interests which have influence on the central bank of the United States through holdings in the Federal Reserve Bank of New York which has a principle seat in the Federal Reserve System of the United States, a privately held banking system formed in 1913. The Federal Reserve is a direct descendant of the First Bank of the United States, formed by Alexander Hamilton in 1791 and the Second Bank of the United States in 1816.

Queen Elizabeth hosted President George W. Bush in the spring of 2003 for two weeks just following his successful invasion of Iraq. This is longer than any other Presidential visit abroad to any country's government and supposedly the Queen has no political power in England. However Prime Minister Tony Blair admits to daily visits with the Queen at which her opinion on matters of state are openly expressed and sought. On that visit it could be surmised that Bush was boning up on his world history at the royal college. The press seemed strangely silent and disinterested in the host and the subject of their conversations. Would that be because the Queens has a considerable interest in world media companies? The timing of the visit might indicate the subject matter, the nature of the colonial occupation of the Middle East and the residual ownership rights. What prompted the history lesson was the disastrous attack on the World Trade Center in New York City. The connection of interest of the Queen with this event is more than sympathetic as we can now surmise from the history of ownership and banking interests of the British in Manhattan.

The Crown of England had given the land by lease to Trinity Church Corporation in 1705 which in turn leased or supposedly sold fee simple some of the Queen's Farm to the Port Authority of New York and New Jersey (via the lease to the Hudson and Manhattan Railroad for one changed to PATH) on which the World Trade Center was built in 1972. The bed of streets owner unknown might imply continuation of ownership of the original grantor, the Crown of England or at least Trinity Church, the grantee. It would appear the Queen's interest in the World Trade Center bombing might include self interest if indeed she were to still consider herself a rightful liege or owner of the property by Feudal ground lease. It is hard to imagine Trinity Church Corporation has changed its long pattern over three hundred years of maintaining control of property indefinitely by use of lengthy ground leases known as deeds for as long as 99 years. Some sales known as warranty deeds have been found for Trinity land transactions in Manhattan. This might reflect the fact that Trinity obtained these lands by long term leases also and thus has no clear title by which to convey to others, even if it wanted to release control completely.

At St. Paul's Church founded by Trinity Church in 1766 on Broadway there is currently a display of six flags on the rear balcony surrounding the Crest of the Crown of England Facing the display the observer sees the flag of Great Britain to the left of the Crest and the Irish flag and French flag in succession to the left. To the right is placed the first flag of the United States consisting of thirteen stars in a circle and thirteen bars, followed by the headquarters flag of General Washington, thirteen stars on a blue field. Finally to the far right or stage left is the current flag of the United States. Flag etiquette dictates the flag should be to the viewers' far left or stage right, not left. If not a mistake, this is a subtle reminder of the influence of the Crown of England today on Manhattan Island and its former Church of England, Trinity Church

In 1785 the State Legislature of New York concluded "*From this state of facts, the said Committee reported, that it appears to them, that the right and title to said lands, called, the King's Farm and Garden, were of right, before the late Revolution, vested in the King of Great Britain, and now belong to, and are of right vested in the people of this State.*" (Journal of Assembly: 1785, pp 22-27). A report of the Tax Reclamation and Reduction, Inc. of Oneonta, New York, W. Bernarr Clancy, Legislative Agent on February 28, 1951 concluded that Trinity Church Corporation acquired the Queen's or King's Farm property as an extension of the Crown of England. Both concluded, wrongly, that the property should now belong to "THE PEOPLE OF THIS STATE" by virtue of the conclusion of the Revolutionary War. To the victors go the spoils of war, so to speak. But this is to deny the terms of the Treaty of Paris which reinstated the ownership of property in the United States by the Loyalists of which the Crown is primary, as Alexander Hamilton so prevailed in *Rutgers vs. Waddington* in 1784 against his eventual nemesis, Aaron Burr.

Likewise the origin of the 77 and 80 acres of land deeded to the Cruger brothers and Aaron Burr by Robert Edwards is not clear. One can surmise the Crown of England granted the land to its privateer, Edwards for loyal service. In fact the 80 acre lease states "*by grant of King George II*". Thus Robert Edwards is a vassal granted land holdings by the lord or liege for military service or other duties favorable to the Crown. Like all Feudal grants of land the loyal subject is free to sell the title to the land to other loyalists keeping in mind that if the chain of loyalty is broken the land reverts back to the Crown. This is exactly what happened to these tracks of land. The attempts of nonloyalists to recover the land in court have been frustrated by strict adherence to latches all the while Trinity Church Corporation may be releasing the land with direct descendants of loyalists Edwards branches. Under Feudal title the Crown of England truly owns the land even today. No warranty deed as we know it today may ever have been given by the Crown. The Treaty of Paris that ended the War of Independence stated all loyalist lands were to be returned or compensated for confiscation given. The ultimate loyalist can not be excluded from this treaty.

Forty nine of the fifty states, New York being the exception, have adopted the laws of England where they don't conflict with the Bill of

Rights or the Constitution of the United States or the individual states. Maine 1985 c. 782 (new), *"The Legislature further finds and declares that his public trust is part of the common law of Maine and generally derived from the practices, conditions and needs in Maine, from English Common Law and from the Massachusetts Colonial Ordinance of 1641-47"*. Virginia 1-10, *"The common law of England, insofar as it is not repugnant to the principles of the Bill of Rights and Constitution of this Commonwealth, shall continue in full force within the same, and be the rule of decision, except as altered by the General Assembly."* This in effect by definition promulgates the use of fee simple ownership of property wherein the right of clear title does not exist beyond the duty of payment of taxes. In other words property is subject to reversion to the higher level of authority in the case of failure to pay taxes. The only owner of property without this duty is the Crown of England, in allodial title meaning free of all encumbrances. The incorporation of the States and the District of Columbia gives these entities the same rights as corporations entrusted with the right of ownership, fee simple, derived from the Crown of England by continuation of English law by the states. In theory at least the Crown of England still holds allodial rights to the United States. The Treaty of Paris of 1783 did not remove this reversionary feudal system of land ownership. Also the ownership of mineral rights in the United States still reverts to the Crown. Notably in Georgia the wetlands are still owned by the Crown of England, except where proof of prior ownership exists. This rather foreign and convoluted thinking evidently has some validity in the courts of the United States today.

In any event if the Crown of England still controls Trinity Church Corporation and considers its holdings the property of the Crown as in original feudal control, then the interest in the World Trade Center is economic. It is part of the income of the Crown of England which flows through the Bank of Nova Scotia, or perhaps that of Rupert Murdock. The first Bank of Nova Scotia was decidedly a Tory institution founded by the same interests and men that started Hamilton's Bank of New York.

An analogy to a wagon wheel can help explain the interconnections of all the elements of this book. One can place the British Crown on the axel around which the hub, the Corporation of Trinity Church revolves. From the hub emanates the spokes or the different components of Manhattan, different churches of all denominations, Loyalists, fire departments, the city hall and courts of Manhattan, King's now Columbia College, currently the World Trade Center and Port Authority of New York and New Jersey, banks, insurance and brokerage companies and most importantly Wall

Street, all of which have had real estate transactions mostly through long term leases with Trinity Church Corporation.

Thus we come full circle. Burr was using the interests of the British in North America to further his own ambitions of power and monarchy; a megalomaniacal rebellious fantasy of a strict childhood upbringing by a tyrannical uncle. Hamilton the idealist would sacrifice his own political health, matrimonial harmony and ultimately his life for the good of a strong central economy and government not unlike the British system which he fostered, encouraged, and from which he sought help for his fledgling country; equally a product of his early lack of a strong father figure. These diametrically opposed strong willed individuals alone in their own ideals of the one, selfishness, and the other, selflessness met on the banks of the Hudson River at Weehawken, New Jersey on July 11, 1804 to determine the fate of a nation unaware of the sacrifice of one and the perfidy of the other. Until this day not even the descendants who staged a reenactment of the duel on the 200th anniversary have a clue as to the reasons for the duel and the reasons for the strong British support for our War on Terror. At least the support comes from the heads of the British Government if not from the populace indifferent to the vested interest of its monarch.

It might be surmised that the global interest of all the monarchies left in the world lies in the fact that the majority of their income derives from abroad in their former colonies and not from their own governments or people. Thus the interest in the Bilderbergers secret planning for a new world order is one of uniform currency with no barriers to commerce, trade or exchange of ideas. Ideal as it may sound it would extinguish the pride of heritage of a national history and identity of a people subjugated to the power of untrammeled wealth all over the world.

It could be said the use of outsourcing, establishment of economic free trade zones and international corporations are the beginning of such a move in this country. Whether or not it is desirable or unavoidable is beyond the scope of this book.

Had Burr succeeded in just one of his schemes of secession, or during the Revolution thrown Washington to the British, or in the War of 1812 had his daughter and son-in-law lived to help him plot against the United States again, the United States would not be as we know it today. Thanks to the steadfast opposition of Hamilton who read Burr's political will but not the total extent of Burr's personal debauchery, we are here to honor a true American hero as free Americans. And perhaps James Monroe took up the mantle of protector of the country from the avarice of Aaron Burr after the death of Alexander Hamilton at the hands of Burr.

The truth is that in the end Great Britain gained a true ally and America gained a true friend. King George III stated some time in the 1780s, *"...it is to be hoped that we shall reap more advantages from their trade as friends than ever we could derive from them as Colonies; for there is reason to suppose we actually gained more by them while in actual rebellion, and the common open connection cut off, than when they were in obedience to the Crown..."* (www.nationalcenter.org/GeorgeIIILossof Americas.)

Hamilton was not a President of the United States, but his image on the ten dollar bill should now mean something to those of us who rely on the selective teaching of American History in our publicly supported education. Great as the achievement of President Ronald Reagan was in ending the Cold War, he did not stop our sunder from within. He should not replace Hamilton, but find an equal position of tender in the hands of everyday Americans.

Governor Jonathan Trumbull of Connecticut, namesake of one of Yale's residential Colleges, wrote General Tryon on April 23, 1778, *"The British nation may, perhaps, find us as affectionate and valuable friends in peace as we now are determined and fatal enemies, and will derive from that friendship more solid and real advantage than the most sanguine can expect from conquest."*

Aaron Burr died on September 14, 1836 age 80 on Staten Island, one hundred sixty five years before the World Trade Center destruction. Without legitimate descendants and a legacy of Aaron Burr perhaps this single event, the attack on the United States, is a reminder to us that history does repeat itself. Burr's law office on Church Street and Fulton (Partition) Street was owned by the City of New York prior to its acquisition by the Port Authority for the World Trade Center. Thus *Aaron Burr* is perhaps the truly eternal *American Enigma*.

THE END, BUT NOT THE END OF THE STORY

On July 24 of 2001 a **99 year lease** for the **World Trade Center** Property was signed for $3.2 Billion dollars on original property of the Dirck Jansen Dey Farm of 1641 first leased from the Dutch West India Company for 600 guilders and filled land of the Hudson River.

Appendix A: Loyalist Land Confiscations; Trinity Church Corporation, grantor, Return To Relatives.

<u>1783 Confiscation Act of New York</u>
<u>Loyalists Confiscations of New York City and Long Island (misspellings original)</u>

Loyalist	Position	Location	Trinity Church Deeded Back Relationship to
Thomas Betts		Queens, LI	wife Elizabeth Smith,11 Smith deeds by Trinity
Waldron Blauw (Blewitt)	Merchant	NY, NY	(Blue) in Cruger Family
Archibald Campbell	Lieut. Col.	NY, NY	Alexander (Allistar) Campbell 12/3/1805 son p530
James Campbell		NY, NY	Charles, John S., William Campbell, 1822
Jaques Dennice		Gravesend, LI	w. Ida Stillwell, related Moore, Bowne, Watkins deed
John Emmons	Farmer	Kings Co, LI	Taken prisoner by British, escaped, not a Loyalist
James Hubbard	Yeoman Gravesend	Kings, LI	Helen Watts, Samuel Hubbard 2/7/1816 re DeLance
James Marr (Erskine)	Lieut	Queens, LI	Fought in Jacobite Wars to restore King James
Johannis Polhemus	Innkeeper	Jamaica, Queens, LI	Cornelius Paulis Deed
Abraham Rapeljie	Innkeeper	Bushwycke, Queens, LI	George Rapeljie 4/4/1810,(Robert M. Rufielle)
Johannus Remsen	Cordwainer	Flat Sands, Kings, LI	Garrett Remsen 5/23/1799(Crueger Fm). son(s)
Volkert Sprung, Jr.	Yeoman	Flat Lands, Kings, L.I.	(Sprong) grandmother Sodelaers, William Southerland deed
Johannis Stothoff Jr.		Flat Lands, Kings, L.I.	Bogardus, Henry Robert, William B. Bayard (several 1825-26, 1833), and James Barclay (several 1816) relatives of rectors of Trinity Church, Harris Van Buren, related to Remsen, Rapeljie
Samuel Striker (Stryker)	Yeoman	Gravesend, Kings, L.I.	Robert A. Striker1814sRichard A.Striker1826gs Voorhess Family on LI Richard A. Striker 1833
Dowe Van Dyne (Duyne)	Captain	Newton, Queens, LI	wife Annetje Remsen, Garret Remsen 5/23/1799
Gerret Williamson	Yeoman	Gravesend, Kings, LI	related to Rapeljie

(Many of these family names appear in deeds in the early 1800s between themselves. The Rapeljie family was early Dutch settlers of Manhattan in 1624. Sarah Rapaelje was the first European birth in New Netherlands in June, 1625. Maria Vigne daughter of the earliest settlers married Jan Roos whose son, Gerrit Jansen Roos', the great-great granddaughter, Cornelia Hoffman, married Isaac Roosevelt in 1726, grandfather of Franklin Delano Roosevelt) www.fulkerson.org/The Vignes

List of Act of Attainder 1779 for Manhattan and Long Island

Indicted	Location	Trinity Church Deed Grantor
*William Axtell	Flatbush, King's Co.	(bought by Col. Aquila Giles)
Robert Bayard		9//1825 367
William Bayard		9//1825x2 360,367
*Christopher Billopp	Staten Island, Richmond Co.	(Manor of Bentley)
#David Colden	Queen's Co.	numerous, see Appendix B
#James DeLancey		
Richard Floyd	Suffolk Co	wife Arabella Jones; 5 Jones, one Hutchinson (mother)
George Folliot	merchant NYC	wife Jane Harison; Gen. George Harrison 1828, Mary H. 1812
Charles Inglis	clerk of New York City	
Margaret Inglis	wife of	
James Jauncey	merchant NYC	wife Maria Smith; 9 Smith leases
Daniel Kissam Sr.	Queen's Co.	wife Peggy Treadwell; Ephariam Tredwell lease, son Daniel's wife Phebe Oakley; Charles Oakley lease
#Isaac Low	merchant NYC	mother Johanna Gouverneur; 3 leases 11/30/1817-84 10/13, 23/1818 Nicholas, Michael Gouverour p 210, 217
#Jabriel Ludlow	Queen's Co.	Robert, Peter 11/1812 469
David Matthews	Mayor of New York City	Andrew 1804 446
William McAdam	merchant NYC	
Mary Morris (wife of)	King's Co.	John L. Morris
#Roger Morris	King's Co.	of Council of New York Colony left during war
George Muirson	Suffolk Co.	wife Anna Smith; 9 Smith leases
*Frederick Philipse	Westchester Co.	(92,000 acres) mother Catherine Van Cortlandt
#John Rapalje	King's Co.	(bought by Tory Comfort and Joshua Sands), George 4/4/1810
Beverly Robinson	King's Co.	received unknown date

Suannah Robinson (wife of)	King's Co.	James W., John x2
Miles Sherbrook	merchant NYC	born England 1734, Died Westchester, 1804
Alexander Wallace	merchant NYC	James 3/3/1819
*John Watts	merchant NYC	Helen 2/7/1816
John Whetherhead	merchant NYC	
Thomas White	merchant NYC	
Parker Wickham	Suffolk Co.	mother Abigail Parker; Sarah Parker 3/22/1819 p 329

(It is not known if any of these listed lost any property through court action)

    * late or separate confiscations by end of war.

    # known confiscations also.

Appendix B: Land Transactions of Trinity Church Corporation as grantor; grantee relationships to loyalist families, and Bank of New York, 1784-1855

(absent data means illegible entry on microfilm)

(Bank of New York represented by majority of Loyalists to the Crown of England)

Grantee	Date	Page or volume/page	Loyalist Relative (D) De Lancey (H) Heathcote (V) Van Cortland (British Officer not necessarily a relative of grantee)
George Abbe	3/6/1847	491/371	
Samuel Abrams	6/7/1830	411/279	
Samuel Abrams	11/1/1844	515/484	
Abraham Ackerman	1811, 1830	268/203, 360/333	lot 71 Varick St
Abraham Ackerman	1811, 1830	268/207, 405/133	lot 70 Varick St.
David Ackerman	8/18/1795, 7/9/1813	103/115	Hudson River and Greenwich St Lot 1173,1174 Lease 500 pounds
John Adams	7//1824	76	Lt. Gideon Adams Jessup Loyal Rangers
John J. Adams	4//1827	125	
John J. Adams	1833/4		
Don Alanson		183-4	
Samuel Albertson	1826		
William Alexander	1/2/1822	114	
Alexander Allaire	7/5/1821		Peter Allair 8 Shares Bank of New York

Grantee	Date	Page or volume/page	Loyalist Relative (D) De Lancey (H) Heathcote (V) Van Cortland (British Officer not necessarily a relative of grantee)
John Allen	6/7/1831	307/606,611	lot 177 15 yrs.
John Allen	3/6/1834		Isaac and William Allen Lt Col. Brit Offi
Mary Penn Allen			Wm. Allen Lt Col Penn Loyalists
Jacobus Allgett	1/18/1787	94	
Jacobus Allgett	9/17/1788	178	
Jacobus Allgett	7/13/1796	316	
Isaac Alston	8/18/1818		Lt. James Alston 42nd Brits Regiment
Elbert Anderson Jr	4/12/1812	203	Joseph Anderson, Ensign 22nd Brit Regi
James Anderson et al	5/9/1807	366	1 share Bank of New York
James Anderson	1/13/1816	486	Robert Anderson Lt. 80th Brit Regiment
Elbert Anderson Jr.	4/17/1812	162, 203, 524	
William Anderson	7/25/1815	377	
Peter Aritt(Arndt Arnott)	4/29/1819		
John C. Armings	10/26/1816	524	
John Ashfield	8/8/1806	13	
John J. Astor	6/28/1804	517	
John J. Astor	2/29/1807	586/221, 224, 227	
John J. Astor et al	5/12/1807	386	
John J. Astor	9/18/1810	517	
John J. Astor	3/15/1814 (7/27/1819)	138/272	
John J. Astor	7/24/1819	242	
John J. Astor	12/31/1828 (2/24/1829)	248/62	
John J. Astor	3/13/1832	283/86	
James Aymar (Eymar)	11/26/1799	188	Kennedy-Burr
John Auchincloss	1834/5	356	son of Hugh Auchincloss
John Auchincloss	9/27/1839	400/398	

Grantee	Date	Page or volume/page	Loyalist Relative (D) De Lancey (H) Heathcote (V) Van Cortland (British Officer not necessarily a relative of grantee)
John Auchincloss	2/25/1851	589/278	
Jacob Badgley	11/14 1804	220	
Daniel Baker	11/14/1804	217	John Baker, 4 shares Bank of New York
Daniel Baker	11/30/1804		
Benjamin Bailey	3/27/1816	114/82	lots 540,547 $5000 Chamber St.
James Bailey	1824		James W. Bailie Capt. 7th Brit. Regiment
Joseph Balastier	2/6/1824	216	
Thomas Ball	6/24/1832		Isaac Ball Est. Mate General Hospital Bent Ball; Capt 63rd Brit Regiment; John Ball Ensign 80th Brit Regiment; Matthew Ball Ensign 80th Brit Regiment; 1st LtJacob Ball, 1st LtPeter Ball Loyal Rangers
Tunis Banta mentioned	2/2/1831	269/199	lot 938 Greenwich St $140 21yr lease
Joshua Barker	12/6/1805	13, 13	
Joshua Barker	3/5/1831		
James Barclay	5/1/1804, 2/20/1816	114/106	lot 37 $1250
James Barclay	2/20/1816	116/114	
James Barclay	2/20/1816		Major Thomas Barclay Brit Officer
James Barrow	1824	309	
James Barrow	11/13/1832		
James Barrow	5/7/1833	49	John Barclay Ensign Nova Scotia Volunteers
James Barrow	8/24/1833		
James Barrow	11/24/1833		
John Barton	8/2/1831	61, 64	Henry Barton Ensign 1st NJ Volunteers
William Barton	6/27/1799		James Barton Ensign 1st NJ Volunteers

Grantee	Date	Page or volume/page	Loyalist Relative (D) De Lancey (H) Heathcote (V) Van Cortland (British Officer not necessarily a relative of grantee)
Henry Bayard	12//1826	219, 220, 221, 229, 304	Rector Trinity Church
Henry Bayard	5/21/1833	219, 224, 304	Lt. Col. John Bayard Brit Officer
Henry B(a)yard	recorded 1811,1830	268/203, 360/333	lot 71 Varick St. lease
Henry B(a)yard	recorded 1811,1830	268/207, 405/133	lot 70 Varick St. lease
Robert Bayard	9//1825	367	Director, Bank of NY, Maj. Samuel B.
William Bayard	9//1825 x2	360, 367	1 share Bank of NY, Director, Hamilton died in home
Henry Martin Beare	12/21/1809	114/82	42 yr lease lots 540, 547 Chamber St.
Deborah Beekman	8/18/1826	123	
Elizabeth Beekman	8/18/1826	123	
John L. Beekman	11/14/1804	295	Captain under Butler
John Bedwell (James Barrow)	7/19/1833	126	Crugar-Livingston Family
James Bell et al	3/24/1802	222	James Bell Supernum Mate General Hospital
James Bell	3/24/1807		
Robert Benson	8/24/1833		
Governour S. Biddy	3//1824		(D)
Henry Billings	802	319	
Leonard Bleecker	1811	360/333	Varick St. lease lot 70 $60
Leonard Bleecker	1811	405/133	Varick St. lease lot 71 $60
Henry Bloodgood	3/17/1807	51, 56	
Anthony Boardman	5/2/1820		(D)
Daniel Board (man)	5/1/1810	220	
Daniel Boardman	3/20/1819	284	
John Boddin	4/30/1832		
Adrian Bogart Jr.	7/20/1829	240	
James L. Bogert	6/6/1814	555, 556	
Tunis Bonte et al	5/4/1827		
Daniel Bowie	8/22/1790		James Bowie Ensign 22nd Brit Regiment
Daniel Bowie	6/4/1795	33	

Grantee	Date	Page or volume/page	Loyalist Relative (D) De Lancey (H) Heathcote (V) Van Cortland (British Officer not necessarily a relative of grantee)
Daniel Bowie	9/29/1806	383	
Daniel Bowie	12/16/1817	547	
Robert Bowne			4 shares Bank of NY, Director John Bowen Capt. Prince Wales Am. Vol.
Walter Bowne	1/8/1805	480	Bank of NY Director, NY Stock Exchange York
John Boyce and others	6/6/1844	449/448	
Samuel Boyd	5/20/1813, 1/12/1814	104/250	lot 350,1 $6000 Murray St. John Boyd Est. Mate General Hospital
Samuel Boyd	1823		James Boyd Ensign 44th Brit Regiment
Samuel Boyd	6//1825		Bank of NY, Director
William Bradford	11//1824	452	
Robert Braham	1833/4		
Christian Bramon	6//1826		
Phillip Brasher	4/13/1817, 10/29/1818	457	sold lot 549 for $1850
Phillip Brasher	5/1/1818		
Phillip Brasher et al	12//1825	491	
Paul A. Brez	5/1/1837	378/200	
Thomas Brooks	4/3/1817	331	
Abraham Brown	8/12/1800	400	
Cynthia Brown	1833/4		
Mathias Brown	3/27/1813	28	
Peter Brown	1//1822	216	
William Brown	8/12/1800	400	
William Brown	1/25/1827		
Henry Bruce	7/2/1807	464	Andrew Bruce Brig Gen. Brit. Officer
William Bruce	7/2/1807	467	
_ Bruck			
Mathias Bruen	3/27/1813	102/28	sold lot 529 Broadway $6600
Jacob Brush	9//1827		
Joshua Buchede	9/14/18?	317	

Grantee	Date	Page or volume/page	Loyalist Relative (D) De Lancey (H) Heathcote (V) Van Cortland (British Officer not necessarily a relative of grantee)
William L. Buchnor	1/26/1829	96	
James Buckley	2/20/1816		
Aaron Burr	12/2/1795 (3/17/1797)	55/425	(lots 33, 35, 35(sic) lease Church Farm)
Aaron Burr	5/1/1797 (11/16/1803)	65/512	(300+ lots leased on 5th St. and Houston)
Aaron Burr	5/17/1796	p 372 see Map	3 shares Bank of New York
Aaron Burr	5/1/1799 (sic7?) (1/21/1814)	104/307	(straighten lot southern lot lines with Church as on 5/1/1797)
Aaron Burr	1800	?	
Aaron Burr	6/16/1804	p 372 see Map	
Aaron Burr Ttee, Elijah Reeve	10/11/1823	167/351	
Aaron Burr	6/14/1826		
Aaron Burr	1827	?	
John Butler			Lt. Col. Loyal Rangers Major Jessup
Lodwick Cagstaff	3/14, 18/1807	200, 202	
James Cahill	1833/34		
Hugh Caine	10/11/1820		
Alexander (Allistar Stewart) Campbell	12/2/1805	530	Officer, Bank of US
Alexander L. Campbell	1822		John Campbell Lt. General Brit Officer
Alexander S. Campbell	1822		John Campbell Brig Gen. Brit. Officer
Charles Campbell	1822x2		George Campbell Lt. Col. Prov. Brit Off
John S. Campbell	1822		Officer, Bank of US

Grantee	Date	Page or volume/page	Loyalist Relative (D) De Lancey (H) Heathcote (V) Van Cortland (British Officer not necessarily a relative of grantee)
William Campbell	1822		Alexander Campbell Major Brit Officer; Thomas B Campbell Supernum MateGenHosp; Archibald Campbell Supernum MateGenHosp; T.B. Campbell Lt. 38th Brit Regiment; George Campbell Lt. 42nd Brit Regiment; Robert, Duncan Campbell Lts. 71st Brit Regim Colin Campbell Capt 71st Brit Regiment; Archibald, Duncan, Colin, Kenneth Lts., Alexander Ensign, Dougald, John Capts., Alexander Major, Colin Qtr. Master, John Lt. Col. 74th Brit Regiment
Lewis Carden	2/13/1816	113/465	lot 150, 149
Edward Carey	11//1821	238, 242	
John S. Carey	1824		Isaac Carey Lt. 17th Foot
Henry Carey	11//182	231, 238, 242	
Henry (Wm) Carey	1825		w Mary Boelyn sister to King Henry VIII wife Ann Boelyn, and aunt to Elizabeth I
William E. Carey	1825		
Robert W. Carnies	1/13/1834	307/338	lot 824 Hudson and Christopher St. release 21yrs.
Henry A. Carter	2/4/1817		Christopher Carter Supernum Mate Gen Hosp
Joseph Carter	3/22/1834		
David Catson	1/3/1818	229	
Thypolite Chardownay	1822		
Hon. W. Chardavoyner			
James Chesterman	7/2/1817	291	
William Chew	3/1/1832	1	
Alen Child	4//1827		
James Christermon	7/2/1817	291	

Grantee	Date	Page or volume/page	Loyalist Relative (D) De Lancey (H) Heathcote (V) Van Cortland (British Officer not necessarily a relative of grantee)
John Barker Church	5/25/1812	44	w. Maria Turnbull, Silliman-Anderson Family; Cpt. Turnbull, Butler's Rangers see *Duel* p 13.Catholic Arch Diocese, Bank of NY investors
Jim Church	2/16/1820		
Benjamin T. Clark	6/24/1828	502	Robert Clark Lt. 80th Brit Regiment
James C. Clark	12/6/1826	213	
James D. Clark	4//1824		
Scott L. Clark	5/5/1819	772	
John Clarke	5/12/1810	718	Thomas Clarke Surgeon Brit Gen Hospital
John Clarke	12/29/1815		Robert Clarke 1st Lt. Royal Artillery Brig; Allured Clarke Lt. Col. 7th Brit Regiment
David Clarkson	7//1825 x3		Director Bank of NY
Matthew Clarkson			Bank of NY, Director, President
Levinus Clarkson	4/29/1813	102/284	lot 775 sold $1420 Hudson River& Provost St
Levinus Clarkson	6/4/1814	49	
Levinus Clarkson	6/13/1819	49	
Louvinna C. Clarkson	4/1, 29/1813	102/286	lot 774 sold $2800 Hudson River & Provost
Thomas Clarkson	4/1, 29/1813	102/284	lot 775 sold $1420 Hudson River & Provost
Thomas C. Clarkson	6/4/1814	49	
Thomas S. Clarkson	4/29/1813	102/286	lot 774 sold $2800 Hudson River & Provost
Thomas Streatfield Clarkson	12/14/1807	114/469	sold $3250 lots 41, 42 between rec. 11/5/1816 Washington St. and Hudson River
Francis Cochran	4//1823		
Abraham Coddington	1804		
Abraham Coddington	1815		
David Coddington	5/23/1809	106	
Isaac Coddington	11/12/1811	38	

Grantee	Date	Page or volume/page	Loyalist Relative (D) De Lancey (H) Heathcote (V) Van Cortland (British Officer not necessarily a relative of grantee)
Moses Coddington	10/3/1809	258	
Moses Coddington	7/31/1818		
Levi Coit	5/10/1834		
Josiah Concklin	7/12/1810	183	
David Cornelius			
John Cornelius	7/12/1810	184	
John Cornelius	3/20/1814	213	
Henry A. Coster	2/4/1817		
Henry Cothout	11//1833		
Thomas A. Cooper	2/19/1818	133	Richard Cooper Ensign 3rd NJ Vol.
James Cowling	1833/4		
Frances Ann Jones Cruger et al	10/23/1833	306/148	John Cruger Lt. Col. Prov. Brit
John Cunnard	10//1822		Dutch West India Co.
Matthew Daniel	7//1829		
Thomas Danson, adm. of "	?1833		
John Darg	3/12/1807	170	
Anthony Day	10/14/1800	536	
Jacob Day	5//1824		
Abraham Delamator	7/13/1810	187	
John Delamator	9//1826	441	
Jacob DeLamortagime	6/24/1812	181, 192	
Samuel Demarest		164	
William Demming	5/22/1821		Director, Bank of NY
David Deneson	6/7/1831	307/598, 603,	4 lot178 Barron & Greenwich St David Deneson 3/6/1834 $52.50 lease 15 yrs.
Louis De Paul	4//1825	281	
Joseph Dephew	1823		
Samuel Derieck	2//1825		
Benjamin DeWitt	4/27/1812	305	
John Dickson	1833		
Joseph Didera	8//1826		

Grantee	Date	Page or volume/page	Loyalist Relative (D) De Lancey (H) Heathcote (V) Van Cortland (British Officer not necessarily a relative of grantee)
William Dikemon	2/20/1807	124	
Peter Dobbs	3/25/1807	327	
John H. Douglas	11/18/1818		George Jr., Director, Bank of NY; Robert Douglas Capt. Royal Artillery; Boleyn Capt 37th Brit Regiment; Benj. Douglas Ensign Kings Carolina Rangers
George Downing			Edwards Family
John W. H. Drukmille	7/5/1816	492	
Hugh Duncan	6/24/1795	544	Campbell Family Capt Richard Duncan, 55th Regiment
Henry G. Dunnol	12/71833		
Medcaf Edson	3/11/1809	257	
Medcaf Edson	3/16/1810		
Thomas Edwards	1/3/1833	346/489	
Thomas Edwards	4/15/1834	358/537	
Thomas Edwards	3/20/1835	379/296	
Thomas Edwards	1/31/1842, 2/11/1842	456/591	
Samuel Ellis	1804, 4/29/1813	102/286	lot 1014, 1015 2nd St. Greenwich St.; Daniel Ellis Lt Kings Carolina Reg.
Samuel Engle	6/8/1819	201	
Effingham Embree	5//6//1795	533,537 see Map	Emory Embury Emerson
Charles A. Evers	7/21/1812	53	
Widow of Fagon	8/22/1828		
John Fell	1//1830	16	3 shares Bank of New York
Peter Fenton	6/8/1812		James Fenton Ensign 43rd Brit Regiment
Robert Ferguson	9//1826		David Ferguson Lt. Col. Brit Gen Staff
Benjamin Ferris	4/24/1812	302	
Benjamin Ferris	4/5/1812, 4/27/1812	104/275	lot 317 $6000 lease 69 yrs.
Benjamin Ferris	5/1/1812	271	

Grantee	Date	Page or volume/page	Loyalist Relative (D) De Lancey (H) Heathcote (V) Van Cortland (British Officer not necessarily a relative of grantee)
Benjamin Ferris	5//1823		
Peter Fetner	7/29/1800		
Owen Flanagan	10//1800		
Thomas Fleming	4/10/1811		John Fleming Ensign Kings Orange Rangers; Garret Forbes, Alexander P. Forbes Lt., John Forbes Capt. 40th Brit Regiment
William Force	1800	129	
Nancy Forman	1833	321	
Derick D. Foster	10//1827		A. Foster Major 44th Brit Regiment; M. Frederick Foster Lt. 64th Brit Reg.
Vincent Foure	1800	275	
Benjamin Franklin			Abraham, John, Samuel (Director), Bank of New York (D); Robert Franklin Lt. 42nd Brit Regiment
David Franks		3/280-1	NY Banker (D)
Moses Franks		9/327	NY Banker (D)
Phineas Freeman	6/30/1813	103/91	release of Hudson Sq and Beach St.
Hugh Gaine	10/11/1820	193	3 shares of Bank of New York
Robert Gaston	6/14/1817	505	
Motby Gelston	12/20/1815		David Gelston, Bank of New York
William Geery	3//1824	4	
Thomas Gibbons	1//1824		
Thomas Gibson et al	5//1824		
William Giffing	1810/11	398	
Samuel Giffy	1833/4	363	
William W. Gilbert	1/20/1814	104/275	release lot 317 69 yrs. $6000
John Gillaton	5//1823		
Henry Gilson	2/19/1813	217	
Abraham Gip			
Christopher Givyer	10//1823		
William Glitzon	1802	125	

Grantee	Date	Page or volume/page	Loyalist Relative (D) De Lancey (H) Heathcote (V) Van Cortland (British Officer not necessarily a relative of grantee)
Jacobus Glogett	1/13/1798		
Eliza Glover	3/21/1818		John Glover 1 share, Bank of New York
Hugh Goble	12/20/1795	47	
George Goltman		349	
George Goltman	9/18/1817		
George Gosman	9/18/1817		3shares, Bank of New York, Robert 2shares
Michael Gouvenor (Gouseworth)	11/30/1818	84	
Nicholas Gouvenour Jr.	10/13/1817	210	5 shares, Bank of New York
Nicholas Gouvenour Jr.	10/23/1817	217	Director, President, Bank of NY
Nicholas Gouvenour	2/13/1816	113/465	lot 150
John Graham	12//1824	197	Charles Graham Lt. Col. 42nd Regiment
John Graham	12/15/18 26 x3		James Graham Lt. 64th Brit Regiment
John J. Graihon	8/6/1829		
John J. Graishen			
Abraham Green	8/2/1800	402	Temperance Green 25 shares, Bank of NY
Henry Green	1802	548	Joseph Green Major Brit Prov. Gen Staff
James Green et al	9/25/1825	534	Joseph Green Major 1st Batt. De Lancey
John Green	1802	548	
Thomas Green	1826		
William Green	8/2/1800	402	
William Green	3//1824	4	
William Green	3//1829		
Thomas Griffin	12/6/1813		lease lot 658A Rutger's Estate
Levi Guernsey	9//18 25 x2		
Benjamin Haight	5//1835	458	
Alexander Haire	5/25/1815	211	Cornelius Heyer, President, Bank of NY

Grantee	Date	Page or volume/page	Loyalist Relative (D) De Lancey (H) Heathcote (V) Van Cortland (British Officer not necessarily a relative of grantee)
Thomas Hall	1/3/1833		
Thomas Hall	4/15/1834		
Thomas Hall	3/20/1835		
Jacob Halsey			Anthony P. President, Bank of NY
Ledyard H. Halsey	1//1824		
Stephen Halsey	10/10/1800		
John D. Halstead et al	1//1824		
John D. Halstead	1827		
James Hamilton	3/3/1834	18	son of Alexander Hamilton 1½ share Bank of NY Alexander, Director, Bank of New York and founder
Joseph Hanna	4//1825		
Elizabeth Hanshaw	5//1826		
A. Haring	7/5/1815	113/152	sold lot 594 $3000 Chambers St.
Benjamin James Harris	2/13/1816	113/465	quit claim $1 lot 150, ½ 149
John Harris			John Harris Surgeon Brit Genl. Hospital
General George Harrison	11//1828	86	Richard Harrison 1 share, Bank of NY
Mary Harrison	8/22/1812	563	
Bernard Hart	1804	229	
David Hasselck	7/21/1815	463	
Peter Hattrick	2/28/1805, 4/2/1813	102/113	sold lot 61 $1025
Peter Hattrick	12/19/1807, 4/4/181	102/118	sold lot32 $775 Greenwich & WashingtonSt
Peter Hattrick	3/14/1811	449, 152	
Peter Hattrick	8/1/1814	341	
Rensselear Havoos	5/6/1814	199	
Mary Hays	6/24/1821	190	
Isaac Haws (Hawes) et al	6//1827		
Margaret Haws	4/23/1833	23	

Grantee	Date	Page or volume/page	Loyalist Relative (D) De Lancey (H) Heathcote (V) Van Cortland (British Officer not necessarily a relative of grantee)
John Hazlet	1//1825		
John Hazzard	1795/6	477	
Aaron Heath	1//1824		
John Heath	1823		Heathcote Family (H)
Andrew Heiser	6/21/1800 x3	314	
Henry Heiser	1/15/1812	94	
John C. Hemming	12/261/1806	524	
John A. Herring	1/23/1816	152	
Thomas Hewitt	1/8/1813		George Hewitt, Major Brit. Gen. Staff
Christian Mathias Heyl	4/7/1813	102/157	lot 325 450pounds Warren St.
James Hill	11/16/1830	45	William Hill 3 shares, Bank of NY; Hill 2nd Lt. 23rd Brit Reg.; Lloyd Hill Lt. 43rd Brit Regiment
Miles Hitchock et al	9/10/1831		
Richard Hogden	1833		
Andrew Hogg	11/11/1830		
Alexander Hoiazk	9/28/1815		
Ephraim Holbrook	2/2/1831	269/190	lot 938 lease $800
Joseph Horne	5/1827		
David Hosack	5/2/1814	151	
Michael Houseworth		72	
Alexander Howell	9/25/1815		
David Howell	7/21/1815	463	
Thomas Howell	3/3/1832		Loyalist, large land holders
Christian Hoyt	4/4/1813	157	
Christian Hoyt	12/30/1819		
Frederick Hovemeyer	1822/3	397, 400, 419	
William Hovemeyer	1822/3	397, 400, 419	
Samuel Hubbard	2/7/1816		LI Loyalist (H)
Samuel Hudson	6/13/1815		
Christian Hugh	4/4/1813	157	
John S. Hunn	11/19/1810		

Grantee	Date	Page or volume/page	Loyalist Relative (D) De Lancey (H) Heathcote (V) Van Cortland (British Officer not necessarily a relative of grantee)
H. Samuel Hunte(r)	1834		
Asorid V. Husted	5/13/1834		
John Hutchinson	4/1831		
Garit Hyon (Hagon, Hedgon)		423	
George Ireland		91	John Ireland 2 shares, Bank of NY
Henry Irving	1822		related Dr. Peter Irving, Thomas Illman
John T. Irving	7/29/1822 x2		Charles Irving Capt. 57th Brit Reg.
Henry Jackson	4/8/1828		Robert Jackson Lt. 57th Brit Reg.
Anthony Jacobs	1833	269/269	lot 146 lease $300/yr. builder
Phillip Jacobs	5/23/1823		
Anthony Jacobus	1833	269/704	lot 146 lease $300/ yr. builder
John D. Jacques	7/22/1813	244	
Thomas James, exec. of	7/18/1817	373	James and Alexander 1 share, Bank of NY
Pierre Jarvis et al	11/18/1831		
William Jenkins	7/12/1810	176	
William Jennings	1812	230	
Jerokimous Johnson	4/1/1821		Robert Chase Johnson 6 shares Bank of NY
Jeremiah Johnson	10/20/1821	52	Lt.Col. Sir John Johnson King's Loyal Reg. 1st; Ensign Johnson King's Loyal Reg.; Henry Johnson Lt. Col. Brit Gen Staff; John Johnson Apothecary Brit Gen Hosp.; Christopher Johnson Surgeon 17th Dragoons
John Johnson	6/2/1802	113/239	21 yr lease lot 477release $3500 Warren St.
William Johnson	2/2/1831	269/190	lot 938 Greenwich St $800 lease
Edward R, Jones	10/23/1833	306/148	trade lot 549 for 462, 463 Chambers St.
Isaac Jones	10/3/1833	306/151	lease Chambers St. lot 463

Grantee	Date	Page or volume/page	Loyalist Relative (D) De Lancey (H) Heathcote (V) Van Cortland (British Officer not necessarily a relative of grantee)
John Jones	7/8/1812	313	Capt John Jones Mjr. Jessup Loyal Rangers; Director, Bank of NY; Lt David Jones Mjr. Jessup Loyal Rangers; Capt Jonathan Jones Mjr. Jessup Loyal Rangers
Joshua Jones	11/15/1813	104/314	lot 549 sold $3000; Solomon Jones Mate; Jessup Loyal Rangers
Joshua Jones	10/23/1833	306/148	trade lot 549 for 462, 463 for $1 Chambers St
Robert Jones	7/8/1812	313	John Jones Lt. 17th Dragoons
Robert Jones	1//1824	373	John Jones Adjutant 17th Dragoons; George W. D. Jones Lt. 7th Brit Regiment;
Thomas Jones, exec. of	7/18/1812		Thomas Jones Lt. 57th Brit Reg.; 42 members of Jones in (D) (V)
Naphtali Judah	1804		started synod NY, Maiden Mill Lane
Naphtali Judah	1815	100	
Eliza (Burr) Jumel	6/30/1849	525/167	grantor
Samuel Keaton	8//1826		
John Kempe	1814/15		Congressman
Joseph Ketchum	1//1824		
Peter Keviston	4//1824		
Abraham Kidney	2/6/1824		
William Kimble et al	6/1824		
Rufus King	5/15/1833	14, 51, 54	Director, Bank of NY
Luke Kip	1/20/1814	104/277	lot 317 release 69 yrs. $9000 Murray St.
Lukel Kip	2/6/1824		
William Kip	1814/15		
Daniel Kipman Jr. et al	320		
Thomas Knox, trustee of?	11//1825	566	
Li L. Kuaag	4//1825		one of 13 Illuminati Families
Abraham Labagh	9/4/1810	468	

Grantee	Date	Page or volume/page	Loyalist Relative (D) De Lancey (H) Heathcote (V) Van Cortland (British Officer not necessarily a relative of grantee)
John Labagh	9/4/1810	468	
H. Lacy et al		183/4	
Cornelius LaForge			
Salome Lake			
Robert De (R or H.) Lamontagime			De Lancey Family (D)
William Landford	4/12/1796	45	
Aaron Lawrence (Laurounce)	5//1826	319	Austin2 and Jonathan 1 share of Bank of NY
John R. Lawrence	5/15, 22/1812		Capt. Campbell's Brigade Isaac, Dir. Bank of NY
John R. Lawrence	5//1826	319	Major John Laurence 3 shares, Bank of NY; Samuel A. Director, Bank of NY
John C. Leake (Lake, Loake, Locke)	11//1822	435, 167	2nd Lt. Philip Leek; Lt. Col. Butler Rangers; Maj. Robert Leake King's Loyal Reg.
William Lee			
Thomas Leggett	3/14/1812	85	
James Lenox	5/1/1833	296/200	lot 105 sold $12,500 Barclay and Church
Robert Lennox	3/15/1813, 4/2/1813	102/131	lot 988 sold $1859 Leight & Collister St; 1 share, Bank of NY
Hermon LeRoy	12/11 1804	393	1 share, Bank of NY, Director
Herman LeRoy	1819		Bank of NY, NY, Canada, Jacob, Director, President, Bank of NY
Alan Lewis	2/20/1819	376	Francis Lewis 6 shares Bank of NY
William Lewis	1834		
Mable Lions			
Leonard Lisponnard et al	6/24/1814	542, 549.555, 556	Second to Burr at duel
Leonard Lisponnard et al	5/1/1817	561	
Edward Livingston	4/19/1796	307	served Butler's Ranger (D)
Rev. John H. Livingston			

Grantee	Date	Page or volume/page	Loyalist Relative (D) De Lancey (H) Heathcote (V) Van Cortland (British Officer not necessarily a relative of grantee)
John R. Livingston	7/30/1814	278	(D)
Phillip 2nd Lord of Manor, Livingston	1811-4	67	(D)
Phillip Livingston	9/1824		Loyalist (D)
Robert Livingston		307	Loyalist, Ambassador to France (D)
Robert H. Livingston et al	9/1824		Loyalist (D)
Robert M. Livingston	4/10/1811	67	Loyalist (D)
Robert M. Livingston	1826		(D)
Robert S. Livingston	4/10/1811	67	Ambassador to France (D)
Robert M. Ludlow			Daniel 2, Thomas 2½ shares of Bank of NY
Peter Ludlow	11//1812	469	Julian Director, Bank of NY; Chris Ludlow Est. Mate Brit Gen Hosp.; Gabriel Ludlow Col. Prov. Brit Gen staff
John N. Luff	11/24/1818	46	
Mathias Luff	1//1819	376	
Peter Lugdan	1804	484	
Abraham Lyon	2/20/1819	376	
Moses Lyon	11/22/1819		
Deal Magee	/20/	419	
Charles March			
Benjamin Marshall	10/18/1817		
James Marshall	x6		
John Marshall			Chief Justice of Supreme Court
John Martin			William Martin Brig Gen. Brit; Also Lt. Col Royal Artillery
Andrew Mathers			
Andrew Mathews	1804	446	
Margaret Mayer			
Matthew McAllister	6/2/1807, 2/5/1814	104/425	lot 155 Robinson St. $3000
Auley McAuley	/26/	249	
Peter McCarter	9/24/1811	395	

Grantee	Date	Page or volume/page	Loyalist Relative (D) De Lancey (H) Heathcote (V) Van Cortland (British Officer not necessarily a relative of grantee)
Charles McEvers Jr.	7/12/1812	53	Director, Bank of NY
Robert McGill	2/20/1818		Butler's Rangers granted 100 acres two days before leaving US, denied 100 acres in Canada
Ferrell McGowan			
John McKee	12/26/1800, 5/20/1833	297/426, 428	pocket lease lot 804 500 pounds Moore St.
William M. McKenny	1804	136	
William M. McKenny	3/21/1807	84	
Sanady McLachlon		122	
Sandy Mc Lachton			
Archibald McVickers	3/11/1815		23 yr lease $150 Chambers St. lot 463
John R. McVinoy	4/2/1810	298	
William Miles	8/6/1821	4	
John Mills	7/13/1814		
Charles Minton	5/1/1833	297/116	of Morristown, N.J. sold for $21,700 lot 57 Greenwich and Fulton St.
John Moffett			
Joseph Mongin	7/23/1807	97	
Benjamin I (J.) Moore	8/2/1814		Blaze Moore 12 shares, Bank of NY; Dep. Chaplain General Hospital Brit
Frances Moore	1801	422	lease lot 111 to Benjamin Swan 1833; Chapel and Church St
Judith Moore	4/9/1811	200	
Lawrence Moore	8/28/1800		
William Moore	8/28/1817		
John R. Montgomery			
John L. Morris			Roger Morris Col. Prov. Brit Gen staff
Ann Morrisette			

Grantee	Date	Page or volume/page	Loyalist Relative (D) De Lancey (H) Heathcote (V) Van Cortland (British Officer not necessarily a relative of grantee)
Abraham Mortier	5/1/1767, 8/20/1804	222/43	99 yr lease Richmond Hill, Houston and rec. 5/25/1827 Varick St Subleased to Aaron Burr 5/1/1797
Jacob Morton	7/5/1810	142,144	
Lorenzo Moses	6/7/1831	307/603	4 lot178 $350 lease Barron and Greenwich St
Lorenzo Moses	1/8/1834	307/606, 611	lot 177 15 yrs. $350
Beaulah Murray Hoffman			Thomas Murray Major Brit Gen staff
Hannah Murray	x2		Major Murray, Brit. Officer
John R. Murray et al	1817/1833	366/533	lot 84 Chambers St. for 35 yrs at $100/yr; Loyalist, Butler's Rangers 1 share Bank of NY, Director
Mary Lindley Murry			Murry Hill, Murray and Sanson 6 shares
Henry Myers			Capt John W. Meyers Mjr. E. Jessup Loyal Rangers
Henry Myird		197	
Daniel Nager			
John Neafie			
Russell H. Nevins	5/1/1824	180/147	
William Newcomb	3/20/1835	329/	
William Newcomb	10/21/1836	369/	
Benjamin Newhouse	12/1/1844	450/617	
Benjamin Newhouse	5/13/1858	575/158-169	
Joseph Neiton (Newton)	5/8/1797x2		1 of 13 Illuminati Families, (Henry Newton 2 shares Bank of NY)
William Nexon (Nixson)	12/14/1793		Elias Nexsen 1 share Bank of NY
John Nolier	7/8/1773		63 yr lease to for lots 540,547 Chamber St.
Charles Oakly			
Andrew Ogden			
Thomas Ogden			

	Date	Page or volume/page	Loyalist Relative (D) De Lancey (H) Heathcote (V) Van Cortland (British Officer not necessarily a relative of grantee)
William Ogden	4/2/1810x2	391	
Alexander Ogilbury	4/12/1792		
Ralph Olmstead			
John O'Neil			
John Oothout	4/8/1826		Director, President, Bank of NY
John Oothout	10/3/1833	304/251	sold $1.00 lot 549 Chambers St once; Philip Brasher 4/13/1817 $1850
Samuel Osgood	1804	349	
Henry Overing	8/8/1811	144	
George Oxfold			
David Parid			Spanish
Sarah Parker	3/22/1819	329	
Daniel Paris	8//1822	268	
Silas Partelow	1812	341	
Aaron Picte (Pazte)			French
William Paulding Jr.	5/20/1812	475	Anglican Church of the Advent
William Paulding Jr.	3/30/1813	102/79	lot 155 $800 Greenwich St.
Cornelius Paulis			
Henry A. Peare			
Harry Peters			Capt John Peters Mjr E. Jessup Loyal Rangers; Ensign John Peters Loyal Rangers
John Phillips	10/9/1800	168	N. Phillips Capt Adj Genl's Dept; Phil Phillips 2nd Lt. Royal Artill
John Phyffe			
Lewis Pigmolet			
Gerardus Post	1/17/1814	104/217,219	$2750 lot 413 Murray St, lot 793, 4, 5
William Post	1/17/1814	104/217,219	$4600North Moore and Washington; Henry, Director, Bank of NY

Grantee	Date	Page or volume/page	Loyalist Relative (D) De Lancey (H) Heathcote (V) Van Cortland (British Officer not necessarily a relative of grantee)
Catherine Prevost, widow	11/25/1789	274/214	grantor Broad and Wall St. opposite City Hall
Michael Price	1800	113	Alexander Hamilton's sons duel 16 shares, Bank of NY
Richard Price			
Henry Rankin	1/15/1812	96	
George Rapeltje	4/4/1810		Long Island Loyalist Family 8 shares, Bank of NY
Cornelius Ray	9/8/	341	Director, Bank of NY
Eliokin Raymond	9/21/1811	338	
Henry Reare	6/22/1810	59	
Elijah Reeve et al Aaron Burr Trustee	10/11/1823	167/351	
Garrett Remsen	5/23/1799		William Remsen and Co. ½ share Bank of NY
Frederick Rhinelander			
Henry Rich	7/14/1800	506	
Jasper Ricketts	5/30/1810		
James Rikes	8/28/1817		
James Riller			
Mary Robert	6/24/1817	243	
Beverly Robinson			Sarah Robinson, 3 shares, Bank of NY; Beverly Robinson Colonel Prov. British
James W. Robinson			William T. Robinson 3 shares, Bank of NY
John Robinson	x2		Officer, Bank of US
Margaret Rodman			(D)
William Roe	3//1822	425	
Cornelius E. Roosevelt	12/5/1814	432	Isaac 5, John I. ½ share, Bank of NY; Isaac, Director, President, Bank of NY
Daniel Rosemond			
Samuel B. Rosemine	6/1/1816		
John E. Ruckles	1804		

Grantee	Date	Page or volume/page	Loyalist Relative (D) De Lancey (H) Heathcote (V) Van Cortland (British Officer not necessarily a relative of grantee)
Samuel B. Ruggles	12/11/1830	268/203	21 year release $60 lot 71 pave street
Samuel B. Ruggles	12/11/1830	268/207	21 year lease lot 70 Varick St. pave street
Abraham Russell	1/26/1818	783	
Robert M. Russell Rufiell			
Abraham Ruyter			
Richard Ryerson	7/28/1800		
James Samuel			
John Samuel			
Charles G. Sandford			Nathan, Director, Bank of NY
Charles W. Sandford		x3	Bank of NY
William Sandford		167	
Tyle Schermerhorn	1833		Bank of NY, Butler's Rangers (Peter Sr. 1 share, Bank of NY, Director)
Frederick Schwartz	5/1/1815, 4/3/1833	622, 273/617	lot 687 $80 lease renewed
Robert Scott		x2	Helena Scott, 1½ share, Bank of NY
Walter Scott			James Scott and Co. 1 share
William Scott et al			Lewis A. Scott 2 shares Bank of NY; William Scott Capt Adj. Genl's Dept
Aaron Sergiant	3/11/1819		1789 Trinity Vestryman
Malty Seton			William M. Seton and Co. 1 share Bank of NY, Director
William Sharp	2/14/1818	709	Lt. Guisbert Sharp Brit. Officer, NY
Robert Sheldon			
Isaac Sherwood			Capt Justus Sherwood, Corp of Loyal Rangers Mjr.Jessup; Ensign Thomas Sherwood Loyal Rangers
Lemuel Skidmore	1802	369	
Lemuel Skidmore	1/28/1814	104/348	lot 770 $3200 Provost & Washington St

Grantee	Date	Page or volume/page	Loyalist Relative (D) De Lancey (H) Heathcote (V) Van Cortland (British Officer not necessarily a relative of grantee)
William Slow	12/11/1817	342	
Charles G. Smedberg			
Arthur Smith			Alexander Smith 1 share Bank of NY
Floyd Smith			Charles Smith and Co. 4 shares
James W. Smith			Elias Smith 2 shares
John A. Smith	9/28/1814		James R. Smith 2 shares
Luff Smith	12/31/1797		Richard Smith Jr. 4 shares
Platt Smith			Charles, Director, Bank of NY
Tangier Smith Fm			Lt Thomas Smith Butler's Rangers (D) (V)
Walter M. Smith			Adj. William Smith Lt Col. Butler's Rangers
William Smith			Son in law of John Adams
Garrit Smythe			Surgeon George Smyth Loyal Rangers
Thomas Smythe Admin of	?		
William Southerland			2nd Lt. David Sutherland Butler's Rangers; Lt Walter Sutherland King's Loyal Reg.
Lewis St. John			
Anthony Steinbeck	2/17/1802	113/447	21 yr lease MarieDuffy to FideleBoisgerard; lot 552 $11500 release
Anthony Steinback	12/9/1812x2	414	
Anthony Steinfarde	4/21/1817		
David Stepson Jr.	5/25/1815		
Alexander Stewart	3//1825	326	Brit. Brig. Gen. (D)
Alexander C. Stewart	7//1826	194	(D)
Alexander L. Stewart	7/30/1813	104/215	Boone, and Varick, and Clark St; Col.Campbells Brigade Developer (D)
Alexander L. Stewart	7/28/1821x2		Robert Stewart 5 shares, Bank of NY (D)
Alexander L. Stewart	3//1824		Lt. Colonel Prov. Gen Staff (D)

Grantee	Date	Page or volume/page	Loyalist Relative (D) De Lancey (H) Heathcote (V) Van Cortland (British Officer not necessarily a relative of grantee)
Alexander L. Stewart	6//1825		(D)
Alexander S. Stewart	3//1824		(D)
Charles Stewart	3/3/1819 x2	444	(D)
Charles Stewart	3/24/1819		Surgeon's Mate James Stewart Butler's Rangers (D)
John Stewart	4/1/1819		Chapl'n John Stewart King's Loyal Rangers (D)
William Stewart	1800	167	(D)
Alexander Stevens			
John Stillwell			Col. Campbell's Brigade Provost
Garrit Storm	4/9/1812	205	
Richard A. Striker	1826/renewed 1833		Butler's Rangers 8th Ward North Farm lot 165 Hudson and Morton St.
Peter G. Stuyvesant	10/26/1818		Cruger De Lance Family (D) (H) (V)
John Sullivan	6/18/1794		
William Sully			
Daniel Sutton			
George Sutton	12/6/1821 x2	360	
Benjamin Swan		269/269	lot 111 Chapel and Church St. lease
Bernardish Swartworsh	2/28/1792		
John Swarthout			Collector Port Tax embezzled $
John H. Talmon	6/22/1819		
Abraham Tanner	3/191836, 1/16/1852	501/76,593/154	
George Taylor	2/2/1825, 11/4/1834	277/605	War of 1812, Signer of Declaration
Thomas Taylor	5/20/1813	102/ 419	lease lot 4 $15 Moore St, Beach St Hudson Square, Officer, Bank of US
Thomas Taylor	4/10/1833	376/349	John Taylor 1 share, Bank of NY
Thomas Taylor	4/30/1835	376/355	

Grantee	Date	Page or volume/page	Loyalist Relative (D) De Lancey (H) Heathcote (V) Van Cortland (British Officer not necessarily a relative of grantee)
Henry R. Teller	11/2/1814, 5/13/1828	235/265	
Anthony Ten Broeck	2/27/1847	525/146	
Catharyne Ten Broeck	6/6/1833		
Henry A. Ten Broeck et al	11/5/1824	182/447	
Henry A. Ten Broeck et al	1/14/1824	173/18	
Henry A. Ten Broeck et al	5/1/1833	300/74	
Phillippes M. Ten Broeck			Capt Peter Ten Broeck Lt Col Butler Rangers
John Thacker	4/15/1845	482/203	
Garrit Thew et al	11/1/1824	389/128	rec 7/18/1838
Garrit Thew et al	1/15/1825	389/132	rec 7/18/1838
Daniel Thomas	3/13/1816	310/375	rec 3/22/1834
Daniel Thomas	5//1837	397/540	
Henry E. Thomas	5/1/1825 x2	190/449	
Timpson Thomas			
Samuel M. Thompson	5/8/1818		John H. Thompson, 1 share Bank of NY, Director Adj. Matthew Thompson Loyal Rangers; Benjamin Thompson Lt. Col. Prov Brit; George Thompson Major Brit Gen staff; Ensign Timothy Thompson King's Loyal Regiment
Francis R. Tillon			
Robert Tillotson	3/5/1834		(D)
Robert Tillotson Esq.			Guardian Howard and Charles Gouvenour (D)
Thomas Tillotson			(D)
William S. Toole	3/29/1847	489/9	
Mary Tooler		658/361	
Frank A. Tracy			
Joseph Travis			

Grantee	Date	Page or volume/page	Loyalist Relative (D) De Lancey (H) Heathcote (V) Van Cortland (British Officer not necessarily a relative of grantee)
Ephariam Tredwell			
Robert Troup	x3		Friend of Burr and Hamilton
Richard I. Tucker	200		Daniel Toocker ½ share Bank of NY; Thomas Tucker Cornet 17th Drag
Daniel H. Turner			
James Tuttle et al			Richard and Timothy Edwards
Anthony Underhill	9/23/1823	254	
Anthony Underhill	12/15/1826x2	516	Long Island Loyalist Family
Lancaster Underhill	7/25/1800	433	
Daniel C. Urmyplans			
Simon Vanantroup	8/16/1814		LI Underhill Family (D)
Henry Valentine	8/18/1820	177	Adj. James Valentine Butler's Rangers
David Van Anderwort			LI Voorhess Family (H)
John Van Blarcourt Jr.	11/21/1815		
James Van Brackle	9/25/1815		Pieter Johan Van Berckel 9 shares, Bank of NY
Tunis Van Brackle			(D)
Abraham Van Buskirk			Abram Von Buskirk Lt. Col. Prov Brit Gen staff (D) (H)
Tunis Van Horn			Ann 1, Cornelia Van Horn 1 share Bank of NY
Garret Van Horne	9/16/1817	70	
Garrit Van Hosen			(D)
Jacob Van Ogden			Bank of NY 1788 (D)
James Van Pelt			(D)
Lavinia Van Pelt			(D)
Hubert Van Wagemon	5/11/1790		Herbert Van Wagener 1 share, Bank of NY (D)
James Van Winkle	12//1821	269	
Wyant Van Zandt			Director, Bank of NY (D)
David Vanderwort			LI Voorhess Family (H)
Jacobid Varme		168	
Richard Varrick	8/17/1800	117	7 shares, Bank of NY

Grantee	Date	Page or volume/page	Loyalist Relative (D) De Lancey (H) Heathcote (V) Van Cortland (British Officer not necessarily a relative of grantee)
Richard Varick	1812		Bank of NY, Elting and Varick 1 share
Daniell C. Verplanck	7/15/1820		12 shares, Bank of NY, Gulian 8, Director, President, Bank of NY
Henry Vervalon	1800	290	
James Vincent			D. Vincent Lt 22nd Brit Regiment (D) (H)
Jocobid Virwickson			
James Votey	6/15/1815		
James Walker	6/1/1795, 1827/33	297/244	lots 38, 39 Duane St and Greenwich
William Walker			Robert Walker Lt. 7t Brit Reg.; William H. Walker 1st Lt. Royal Artill.
John D. Waldron			Blauw Family (H)
James Wallace	3/3/1819		(H)
Van C. Wannamaker Fm			(D)
Samuel Ward	4/19/1817	230	2 shares, Bank of NY (H) (V)
J. Charles Wardell	3/5/1833	305/556	sold lot 143 for $14,400
James Warner	8/7/1792		(H)
James Warner	7/2/1822	719	Loyalist Richard Edwards Fm. (H)
James Warren			
John L. Watkins	12/2/1820	418	
Joseph Watkins		114,115	
Joseph S. Watkins	12/2/1820	418	
Charles Watts	3/25/1802		10th Ward Warren St. lot 50 (H)
Charles Watts	1809		lot 54 Bloomingdale Rd. Cedar St. 6 acres Lease $62.50 12 years left
Helen Watts	2/5/1816	113/239	lot 477 $3500 WarrenSt release 21yrs (D) (H)
Edward J. Webb			(H)
Ezra Weeks	1802 x2	157,395	(H)
Ezra Weeks	12/26/1816	412	
Johannes Weeks			(H)

Grantee	Date	Page or volume/page	Loyalist Relative (D) De Lancey (H) Heathcote (V) Van Cortland (British Officer not necessarily a relative of grantee)
Benjamin Wells	3/29/1813	102/70	lot 54 sold $700
Henry Wells	3/29/1813	102/70	lot 54 sold $700
James N. Wells	3/18/1819	136	builder
James N. Wells	10/1/1824	296/606	lot# 3 21 yr lease $10/yr. rent Hudson and Christopher St.
John E. West	3/25/1804, 6/30/1813	103/91	99 yr lease Hudson Square and Beach St.
John E. West	1/16/1816		
Daniel Westervelt	4/29/1813	102/286	lot 1002, 1003 Greenwich St.
John Westerville			
John A. Wheaton			m. Bethya Baldwin (H) (V)
Stephen Whiting			
Samuel Whitmore			St Lukes Church (H)
Charles Wilkes			Popham Morris Fm 1 share Bank of NY, (H); President, Bank of NY
Henry Williams	7/31/1792		Ed Williams Capt Adj Genl's Dept. (V)
Owen Williams			Jemiah Williams m. Harrison Samuel Ward Bank of NY (D) (H)
William Williams			
William J. Williams			Lt 17th Brit Foot
James Wilson			
Harold Wilson			
William Wilson	7/31/1792, 1827/33	297/244	lots 38, 39 Duane St and Greenwich (H) (V)
Jacob C. Winas			(H)
Gabriel Winter			(H)
John G. Wood			(H) (V)
Jonas Wood	7/9/1800	248	(V)
Evert Woomanormon et al			
Grove Wright			James Wright Major Prov. Brit staff (H)
Albert Wunnenberg			
John Young	2/27/1811		Lt. Henry Young King's Loyal Regiment

Appendix C: Trinity Church Corporation, grantor to other Churches, Schools, Banks, Fire Departments, and Politicians of Manhattan

Church	Date	Page or Book/Page	Grantee
King's College	1754		
African Methodist Episcopal Ch.	9//1827		Charles Tredwell
Anglo American Free Church of St. George the Martyr	10/15/1852	636/2	
Associated Reformed	3/20/1843	452/533	
Catholic Arch Diocese	1833/34		William Walker
Cedar Street Presbyterian	5/1/1834	?16/40,8, 11, 14	
Christ Church	9/1823, 6/26/1828	291	
Christ Protestant Episcopal	1/24/1828	238/291	
Christ Protestant Episcopal	4/1, 5/1/1835	350/256, 348/249	
Christ Protestant Episcopal	4/29/1853	639/246	
Church of the Ascension	1826		
Church of the Ascension	4/23/1836	346/512	
Church of the Avenues	1833/34		Now United Nations Church
Church of the Nativity	7/28/1840	407/527	
Church of the Nativity	5/20/1847	489/386	
Church of Utica	7/13/1833		Owen Bervian and Schermerhorn Loyalist
De Saint Esprit French	4/7/1832	383/22	

Church	Date	Page or Book/Page	Grantee
Episcopal Church of St Peters	1812	547	
First Episcopal Charity School	6/1822	458	
Free School Society	3/1/1815, 9/25/1820	39	
Grace Episcopal	3/29/1820	278	
Grace Episcopal	6/27/1837	376/523, 6	
K.G. Protestant			
Episcopal Public School	10/19/1829	436	Henry Cothval et al
Methodist Episcopal	1/10/1798	342	
Naphtali Judah	1804/5	100	Jewish Synod in NY
Protestant Episcopal Society	1/24/1811	277	
Protestant Episcopal Society	3/25 1811	302	
Protestant Episcopal	1833/4		
Scotch Presbyterian	10/2/1786	163/169	
Scottish Presbyterian Church	1822		
St. George's Church	4/1/1814	106/140	
St. George's Church	3/9/1820, 8/15/1820	138,140	
St. George's Church	11/29/1829	84	
St. George's Church	11/30, 12/10/1850	561/48, 561/104	
St. George's Church	2/11, 7/21/1851	561/530, 595/111	
St. George's Church	5/31/1854	695/214	
St, George's Church	2/20/1852	583/604	
St. George's Church	1/14/1856	697/490	
St. James Church	5//1823	427	
St. James Church New Town (Newton)	7/20/1814		
St. Luke's Church	5/2/1825	193/5	
St. Luke's Church	2/14/1831		
St. Luke's Church	7/2, 5/1828	98	
St. Luke's Church	1833/34	369	
St. Luke's Church	7/9/1838	230/98	
St. Marks Church		352	

Church	Date	Page or Book/ Page	Grantee
St. Michaels Protestant Episcopal	8/14/1810	348	
St. Peters Church	9/27/1820	214	
St. Stephens Church	12//1826		
Third Congregational Church	7/2/1828	423	
of the Associated Reformed	7/11/1828	418	
Third Methodist Society Associated			
Methodist Reformed Church	9/18/1831		original Trinity pastor
Trinity Church of Utica	6/10/1811, 9/13/1816	114/36	lot 610 $1 reverts to Trinity if not used for Divine Services Reade St to Rutger's deceased
Zion Church	2/16/1820		
Greenwich Bank	1833/4x3	356	used by NY tobacconists RJ and D.C. Reynolds
Leonard Lisponnard et al	6/25/1814; 5/1/1817	542, 549, 555, 556	
New York Bank	10/13, 23/1817		
Eagle Fire Co.	3//1824		
Robert Tillotson, Mayor, Aldermen et al	3/5/1834	269/4	
Robert Tillotson, att. Guardian et al		269/4	Trustees of Rourvard,Hannabe,Charles,Gouvenour,
Robert, Emily, Maria Louise		470	
Mayor, Aldermen et al		269/420	
Mayor, Aldermen et al	2/25/1814, 12/1/1814	104/629	move Greenwich St between North Moore and Christopher St.
Mayor, Aldermen et al	7/10/1815	269/316	Streets deeded to City, Harrison, Provost, North Moore, Beach, Hubert, Wright
Mayor, Aldermen et al	1825	44	
Mayor, Aldermen et al	6/25/1831	273/511	lease of lot 269 next to Rutger's land for 21 years, remainder of lease to Thomas Griffin 1813 Read St. East opposite Hudson Square, Hudson St. and Greenwich St.

Church	Date	Page or Book/ Page	Grantee
Mayor, Aldermen et al	6/9/1831	272/	
Mayor, Aldermen et al	7/10/1815, rec 2/17/1831	269/316	sale $1 land for streets,Harrison and Watts Sts.
Mayor, Aldermen et al	3/22/1848	500/474	lot 51 Clark St. 21 yrs. remainder from 1830 lease
Mayor, Aldermen et al	3/22/1848	500/476	lot 53 Clark St. 21 yrs. remainder of lease to Catherine Ducarre 5th Ave, 53rd and 54th St.
Mayor, Aldermen et al	5/10/1848	500/498	for $1 for benefit of British Emigrants, Hospital and Chapel at Washington St., West St, Duane St., Reade St. reverts to Trinity if not built, also City to Anglo American Free Church of St. George (the Martyr) 5th Ave 53rd and 54th St.

Appendix D: Grantor Deeds by Aaron Burr

Name of Grantee	Liber #	Page#	Date Executed	Date Recorded
John Agnew & others	167	351	12/1/1828 as trustee	10/2/1830
Jacob A. Arden	61	220	8/18/1797	11/21/1801
Jacob A. Arden	61	223	9/23/1797	11/21/1801
Jacob J. Arden	73	84	12/8/1800	8/21/1806
Jacob J. Arden	288	125	8/18/1797	9/29/1832
John Jacob Astor	67	2	10(11)/22/1803	6/1/1804
John Jacob Astor	67	11	11/18/1803	6/4/1804
John J. Astor	138	518	5/1/1804	8/24/1819
John J. Astor	138	521	11/17/1800	8/24/1819
John J. Astor	222	2	6/11/1804	5/25/1827
John J. Astor	222	11	6/4/1804	5/25/1827
John J. Astor	222	43	8/20/1804	5/25/1827
Theodosius Bartow	43	116	2/26/1784	
John Batchelor	64	232	9/8/1801	6/29/1803
John Batchelor & others	67	64	10/23/1802	6/14/1804
John Berry	59	284	5/4/1797	11/18/1800
James O. Bostwick	356	179	4/26/1800	5/11/1836
Anthony L. Bowronson	66	436	10/23/1802	4/17/1804
Anthony L. Bowronson	66	438	10/23/1802	4/18/1804
Samuel S. Breeze power of attorney	59	287	11/4/1800 as trustee	11/19/1800
Joseph Browne	68	502	10/23/1802	1/14/1805
William Buckland	63	218	9/16/1801	1/5/1803
James Constable	176	346	1/20/1800	5/4/1821
William Crotty	221	483	6/22/1797	6/2/1827
First Presbyterian Church	47	343	1/18/1790	7/13/1790
William Cutting	213	210	3/18/1804	1/17/1827
John De Lancey	114	500	7/23/1801	11/6/1816
James Davis	254	73	4/8/1801	8/4/1829
Matthew L. Davis & others, power at.	67	394	8/10/1804	8/21/1804
Thomas Eagles	233	279	12/24/1800	3/3/1812
Phillip E. Eckert	63	99	9/9/1801	11/10/1802

Name of Grantee	Liber #	Page#	Date Executed	Date Recorded
Rachel Eden, trustee	230	226	12/19/1827	12/28/1827
Rachel Eden, trustee	231	6	9/1/1827	1/21/1828
Rachel Eden, trustee	249	198	4/10/1829	4/19/1829
Medec F. Eden, executor of	257	254	12/11/1829	12/12/1829
Rachel Eden, executor	256	550	12/10/1829	12/23/1829
George De Grasso	64	351	11/16/1802	7/18/1803
David Gelston	56	79	3/9/1797	1/4/1799
David Gelson	100	117	11/1/1803	9/29/1812
Matthew Goul	292	185	6/20/1797	1/30/1833
Amos Green	287	305	9/21/1801 &others	6/25/1832
Stephen Halsey	63	55	9/9/1801	10/25/1802
John Hazard	57	79	3/9/1797	1/4/1799
William N. Hennel, B. Nash Ttee	270		8/18/1830	
William Hughes	317	533	8/29/1801	12/12/1834
John Kelly	277	495	1/15/1801	10/20/1831
John Kingsland	80	229	12/17/1800	5/19/1803
Henry H. Kip &others	295	405	1/6/1795 trustee&others	4/8/1833
Henry H. Kip	549	403	10/21/1850	trustee
Benjamin Knapp	206	20	9/21/1801	6/14/1826
James S. Lewis, Seaman Lawerre	588	109	9/20/1851 by public Administrator	
Israel Lewis	240	58	11/15/1801	7/25/1828
Edward Livingston	301	52	1/7/1803	6/14/1833
Charles Loss	67	437	10/23/1802	8/28/1804
Charles Loss	67	439	10/29/1802	8/28/1804
Seaman Lowerre	549	403	10/21/1850 by public Adm	10/22/1850
Manhattan Company	65	458	12/15/1802	11/4/180
Manhattan Company	65	462	10/23/1802	11/4/1803
Manhattan Company	65	466	10/23/1802	11/5/1803
Manhattan Company	65	471	10/23/1802	11/7/1803
Manhattan Company	65	475	10/23/1802	11/7/1803
Manhattan Company	65	479	10/28/1802	11/8/1803
Manhattan Company	65	483	10/23/1802	11/8/1803
Manhattan Company	65	487	10/23/1802	11/8/1803
Manhattan Company	65	401	12/15/1802	11/10/1803

Name of Grantee	Liber #	Page#	Date Executed	Date Recorded
Manhattan Company	65	495	10/23/1802	11/10/1803
Manhattan Company	65	498	12/15/1802	11/11/1803
Manhattan Company	65	503	10/24/1802	11/14/1803
Manhattan Company	65	507	10/22/1802	11/16/1803
Manhattan Company	65	508	12/15/1802	11/16/1803
Jacob Mark (Foundry, 5, 7 Worth St.)	69	23	7/11/1804	1/26/1805
Broadway and Trinity Church Cemetery, (? office of Aaron Burr) (Jacob Mark grantor Joseph Browne lot: Carmine and Bedford St.)	69	21	12/26/1804	1/26/1805
James Martin	221	489	8/30/1797	6/2/1827
James Martin	221	491	8/30/1797	6/2/1827
James Martin	292	187	8/30/1797	1/30/1833
John Martine	186	44	9/3/1801	1/22/1825
John Martine	282	269	9/3/1801	3/9/1832
William Martine	71	439	6/30/1797	1/28/1806
Phillip O'Keefe	221	487	6/27/1793	6/2/1827
John Oothout	58	183	9/18/1799	5/16/1800
Moses Pike	289	73	8/13/1802 (? 32) & others	6/25/1832
Richard Platt	46	161	4/3/1790 & Theodosia	6/7/1790
Richard Platt	46	163	4/3/1790 & Theodosia	6/8/1790
Jacob Post	245	103	4/8/1801	12/12/1828
Charles Sandinger	66	498	10/23/1802	5/21/1804
Peggy Slave (Burr's Slave?)	61	321	12/24/1801	1/14/1802
John Swartwout	7	535	10/23/1802	9/13/1804
John Targay	221	490	7/21/1797	6/2/1827
Francis S. Thompkins	622	496	12/3/1852 by public Adm	1/12/1853
Joseph Townsend	65	397	12/1/1825	10/2/1830
Simon Van Antwerp	301	50	4/15/1801	6/14/1833
William Van Ness	63	513	10/23/1802	4/25/1803
Joseph Watkins	66	80	10/11/1800	9/6/1830
Ezra Weeks	63	158	10/22/1802	12/2/1802

Name of Grantee	Liber #	Page#	Date Executed	Date Recorded
Ezra Weeks & others	63	201	10/22/1802	2/15/1803
Jesse West	266	573	9/25/1830	10/26/1830
Matthew West	107	212	9/11/1801	7/22/1814

Appendix E: Genealogical Descendancy Charts.

Genealogical Descendancy 1: Lowell, Russell, Cabot, Burr, Cushing, Prevost, Bartow, Stillwell, Pell, Vanderburgh, Lewis, Dubois, Shippen Families

(+ denotes marriage) (Oldest generation higher than younger generation) (Siblings on same line or beneath parents in column) (Underline denotes persons mentioned in book)

Lowell-Russell-Cabot Families

Rev. John Lowell+Sarah Champney Frances Cabot+Mary Fitch
2. Rebecca Russell+JD.John Lowell+3.Sarah Higginson+1.Susan Cabot, Lowell, Mass.

b. 1747   m. 1778 b. 1713 m.1767   Frances Cabot Lowell
Rebecca   John Lowell
Charles   b. 1769
Elizabeth   +Rebecca Armory

Sarah   b. 1771
Grandson poet   John Armory Lowell
James Russell Lowell
b.1819

Burr-Cushing Families

Henry Burr+Ann Fisher
Simon Burr+Hester   Henry Burr
John Burr+Mary Warren
b. 1659   Thomas Lincoln+Sarah Lewis
Jonathan Burr+Mary Lincoln
Silence Burr+Peter Cushing
        b. 1742
John Cushing b.1763

Burr-Ward-Pell-Ogden Families

lJehu Burr+ Elizabeth <u>Cable</u> (i.e.Cable Memorial Hospital, Ipswich, Mass.)
2m2Jehu Burr +Hester <u>Ward</u>+m1 Joseph Boosey, Nathaniel Burr+Sarah Ward, John Burr+Mary Ward//
b. 1625 England b. 1634 Phillip Pinkney+Jane b. 1640 Middletown,Conn. 2Samuel Ward+Hannah <u>Ogden</u>
3DanielBurr+Elizabeth <u>Pinkney</u>,EstherBurr+<u>JohnBulkley</u>/NathanielBurr+SusannahLockwood/2WilliamWard b 1670
+Hannah <u>Pell</u>
Cornelius Hull+Sarah <u>Sanford</u>
4Elizabeth B+Nathaniel <u>Hull</u>, Peter Burr+Abigail <u>Hall</u> b1664//4Anna Burr+John Silliman 2John Ward1679+
Rebecca Fowler
4Esther Burr+Daniel <u>Bradley</u>, Nathan Beers+Ann Burr   3John Ward+Mary <u>Pell</u>-Thomas P
4Rev. Aaron Burr+Esther Edwards   3 ThomasWard1718+Jemima <u>Pinkney</u>
5<u>Aaron Burr, Sally Burr</u>   3Elizabeth Ward+Gilbert <u>Thompkins</u>, Rebecca W+Nathaniel <u>Underhill</u>
4Hannah W.+<u>Peter Bulkley</u>1684

Prevost Family

Jean Louis Prevost+Clermonde Passavant
Augustin Prevost+Louise Martine

James Marcus Prevost	Augustin Prevost+Anne Grand	Jacques Prevost
b. 1735+Theodosia Bartow	b. 1723	b. 1725
m. 1763 Trinity Ch	<u>George Prevost</u> Born 1767 Hermitage with Wm. Johnson Indian Agent	
Augustine James Frederick P.	Governor General Canada 1811 <u>Geo. Croghan</u>-Indian agent	
b. 1767	<u>Augustine Prevost</u>+Susannah Croghan Catherine C.+<u>Joseph Brant</u>	
John Bartow Prevost	b. 1744	<u>Tory Indian Chief</u>
<u>b. 1766</u>		
Anne Louisa P. d.y.		
Sally P. d.y.		
Mary Louisa P. d.y.		

Bartow-Stillwell Family

Thomas Bartow+Grace//John Reid+Margaret Miller//Nicholas Stillwell
Richard Stillwell+Mary Cook
<u>Rev. John Bartow</u>+Helena Reid //Lydia <u>Bowne</u>+<u>Rev.Richard Stillwell</u>+Mercy <u>Sands</u>
Anglican Church+Westchester, NY   b. 1762 Presbyterian Ch of NYC

Theodosius <u>Bartow</u>+   Ann <u>Stillwell</u>   +Philip <u>DeVisme</u>
b. 1712 d. 1746 m. 1742   b.1714   m. 1752 at Trinity Church b.1719

Thomas,John,Basil,Anthony,Theophilus,Theodosia//Elizabeth +, <u>Peter,</u>   Samuel,
De Visme, Brit.seaman, Brit. Officer, +<u>Joseph Brown</u>
J. Duvall Brit Officer

Stillwell Family

Nicholas Stillwell+Anne   James Sands+Sarah Walker+William Hutchinson+Ann
Richard Stillwell+Mary Cook   Samuel Sands+Deborah Ray
Richard Stillwell+m1 Lydia Bowne+m2 Mercy Sands   Samuel Sands+Mary Pell

---

Mary Stillwell+, Richard+,   Ann+,   Deborah+,   Catherine+(b1716),Elizabeth,   Lydia+
ThomasClarke,Mary Bowne, TheodosiusBartow, RichardSmithd,   RevEbenezer + Peter Wraxell/   John Watkins   I
d. 1776   m2 Lydia Leonard   m2Philip DeVisme Mary Smith m 1778 Pemberton +   m2John Maunsell   I
Maria Theresa+Wm. Barrington s. of John BO +   Samuel Bradhurst   (Boston) both BritishOfficers   I
m.1778 JohnWatkinsJr+   b.1755
Mary-Richard Vassel//Samuel Hazard Brad, John Maunsell Brad//William Livingston-daughter-Judith Livingston
                                                            I
Clement-? Bayard   daughter--Sarah Livingston +John Jay
Charity+Rev. Benjamin Moore
        Clement Clarke Moore

Bartow-Pell Families

John Reid   Philip Pinckney

John Bartow+Helena Reid //Thomas Pell Sr+Lucy Brewster John Pell+Rachel Pinckney

---

Basil, John, Thomas, Theodosius, Theophilus B. + Bethseda Pell,
        Thomas   Joseph Pell Fairfield
                        Mary B.+Thomas Pell, Theophilus B, John B.+Ann Pell
                        Jeanne B.+James Achard   Sarah Pell+Wm Bagley
                                        Thomas Pell+Wausage Indian Anna

---

                        Mary Pell, Ann Pell,   Thomas Pell
                        +Samuel Sands +Samuel Bradhurst//Samuel Pell

                        Samuel Bradhurst NY Regiment

                            Samuel Bradhurst
                            +Mary Smith m. 1778
                    Samuel Hazard Bradhurst, John Maunsell Bradhurst

Vanderburgh-Lewis-Dubois Families

Lucas Vanderburgh
Dirck Vanderburgh Thomas Lewis+Anna Maria Vanderburgh
Louis Dubois+Jannetje Van Vliet   Henry Vanderburgh+Magdelena Knight
Elias Dubois--- + Susannah Vanderburgh-+--m. 1758 Richard Lewis
b. 1722 d. 1756   b. 1725

Lewis Dubois b. 1744   Thomas Lewis b.1759
Magdelena b. 1746   Susannah b.1761 m.1779
Henry d.y.   Gilbert Livingston
_____ancestor to Pres. GHW Bush, GW Bush
Garret b. 1751   Sarah b. 1763
Jan b. 1753   John Ter Bush-Catherine Van Wyck   +John Ter Bush
Henry b. 1755-Eleanor Ter Bush

James (Jacobus) b. 1766
Elizabeth b. 1772
Mary (Maria) b1768+m1783James Reynolds+ m2 Jacob Clingman
(Maria m. 1783)   (Mary m. 1792)

Barclay-Rutgers-De Lancey Family

John Barclay
Rev. Thomas Barclay//Col. Anthony Rutgers
Rev. Henry Barclay+Mary Rutgers
Rector of Trinity Ch. 1746, King's College
BeverlyRobinson+Anna DorotheaB,StephenB+Cornelia DeLancey,ThomasB+SusanDeLancey,AnthonyBTory

Todd-Dandridge-Astor-Madison-Washington-Lee Family

John Dandridge+m1 Anne +m2 Bridget Dugdale//Orlando Jones+Mary West Macon
Nathaniel West Dandridge Sr+m1Dorothea Spotswood+m2Jane Pollard, John Dandridge+Frances Jones
ColWilliam Dandridge+m1Unity West+m2 Euphan Wallace//Martha D+m 1 Col. Daniel Parke Custis+m 2 Gen George
Washington

John Todd PA//Archer Payne+Martha Dandridge// Adam Todd NYC//George Washington Parke Custis+Mary Lee Fitzhugh

m1John Todd+Dolly Dandridge Payne Todd+m2 James Madison //Jacob Astor// Mary Ann Randolph Custis+
Gen RobertELee

Sarah Todd+ John Jacob Astor, Henry Astor

Eliza,William Backhouse Astor+Margaret Armstrong,Magdalen+Dr. John Bristed,Dorothea+Walter Langden

John Jacob Astor III,	William Astor
b.1822	b. 1830 Florida Railroad
William Waldorf Astor	John Jacob Astor IV
Waldorf Hotel, NYC	b. 1862 died on Titanic

Shippen Family

Joseph Shippen+Abigail Grosse   Robert of Clermont Livingston

William Shippen MD, Edward Shippen+Sarah Plumley   Robert R. Livingston+Beekman
+Susannah Harrison Edward Shippen+Margaret Francis,Hannah Shippen+Henry L, Janet L+Gen Richard Montgomery
Peggy Shippen+Benedict Arnold
b. 1760

Genealogical Descendancy 2: Stoddard-Downing-Pickering-Pierpont-Pinckney-Pell-Hopkins-Edwards-Burr-Reeves-Alston-Browne-Coffin-Tryon Families

Geoffrey Downing+Elizabeth Wingfield   Thomas Hall

I   +Elizabeth Drury

George Downing+Dorcas Bois   Thomas Edw.+Elizabeth Hall

George Downing+Bellamy   Adam Winthrop+Anne Browne Mathijs JahsonVan Kuelen

William Stoddard Emmanuel Downing+Lucy Winthrop Robert Edw. +Margriet Cuelen

Anthony Stoddard+Mary Downing, *Sir George Downing*, Lucy Downing,   Isabella Downing

b. 1614   b. 1620   b. 1623 +Francis Howard,+Sir Richard Bulkeley,+Thomas Edwards b1690

Philadelphia Downing b. 1644+Sir Henry Pickering b.1634

Rev. Solomon Stoddard+Esther <u>Warren</u>   John Pickering   <u>Robert Edwards</u> b. 1716

b. 1640   Wm. Harris

William Edwards+Agnes Harris+Mary Eure//   <u>Rev. James Pierpont</u>+Mary Hooker

Richard Edwards+Elizabeth Tuttle

Jehu Burr+Elizabeth Prudden

Rev. Timothy Edwards--+--Esther <u>Stoddard</u>   b. 1669   b. 1672

Daniel Burr   Rachel Burr

+Elizabeth <u>Pinckney</u>   +<u>John Pell</u>

Esther Edw.   Rev. Jonathan Edwards+Sarah <u>Pierpont</u>   11 children

+<u>Samuel Hopkins</u>   b. 1709   Fairfield, Conn   <u>Timothy Pickering</u>

Esther Edwards-----------+-----------<u>Rev. Aaron Burr</u>

b. 1731   2nd Pres. Princeton College

Sally Burr+<u>Tapping Reeves</u> Aaron Burr+<u>Theodosia Bartow Prevost</u>

b. 1754   b. 1756   m 2 <u>Elizabeth Bowne Jumel</u>

Theodosia Burr +<u>Joseph Alston</u>

Aaron Burr Alston d.y.

Edwards-Tryon-Pierpont Family

Rev. James Pierpont+Mary Hooke

William Tryon+Rebecca? Reverend JonathanEdwards+Sarah Pierpont

Samuel Steele+   Thomas+Mary Weld Robinson

WilliamTryonJrm1?m2Mary Steelem3Sarah Saint Robinson LattimerEarl of Essex, Queen Elizabeth I
b. 1645 d1711 db1665 b. 1652 m 1670 db1710 m1688 d1711 favoriteofRoyal HouseofPlantagenet
Bibury,Gloucestershire,Eng//Farmington,Hartford,Conn.// JamesT+Margaret//Robert Shirely+Selina

Abbell Tryon b. 1682+ Abiah Hunnewell //Charles Tryon b1678+Jane Savile 1ˢᵗ Earl Ferrers

AbielTryon+Hannah Northway,WilliamTryonI+Sarah Goodrich//ThomasT+Mary Andrus//CharlesTryon b 1702+Mary Shirley
b. 1710   Bulwick, Northamptonshire, England
Northampton, Mass.   John Tryon+Rhoda Lucas//**Gov.William Tryon**+Margaret Wake
                         John Tryon +Eunice Lay b. 1729-1788 Norbury Park, Surrey, Eng.
Navy Capt. Moses Tryon+Narcis Turner   Col. Moses Ogden+Mary Cozzens

—————————————————————————————————

Matthew Ogden, Robert Ogden+Hannah Crane

Rev Jonathan Edwards, Mary Edw, Lucy Edw., Timothy Edwb1738,Esther Edw, Pierpont Edwards
+Sarah Porter   +Timothy Dwight +Jabliel Woodbridge +Rhoda Ogden +Aaron Burr +Frances Ogden
            Lucy Woodbridge-Jonathan Edwards   Sally B.   Aaron Burr   Henrietta Edw.

1 George W. Edw.   b. 1769   b. 1764 +Tapping Reeves +Theodosia   +Eli Whitney

                                                Theodosia+Joseph Alston

2Jonathan Walter EdwCol Matthias Ogden EdwOgden Matthias Edw Jonathan Edw. Sarah Edw Aaron Burr Alston
+Elizabeth (Betsy) Tryon b. 1777   +Sarah Bradley +Lucy Woodbridge +___Goodrich
            Edwards Tryon Edwards   b. 1796   Benjamin Tappan
3 Sarah Edwards+William Tryon II b. 1736   William Edwards-Rebecca Tappan   +Sarah Holmes
4 William Edw. +Sarah Bidwell   b 1770
                                     Ogden Ellery Edw.   John Tryon+Eunice Lay
                                +Catherine Shepherd Thomas Shepherd +Catherine Tryon
                                                                    b. 1806

                         Timothy Pierpont+
                         John Pierpont+   Joseph Morgan
                                                       +Sarah Spencer
                         Juliet Pierpont+   Juneus Morgan
                         b 1790 Boston   (JP)JohnPierpontMorgan

209

Browne-Coffin Families

Thomas Browne+Abigail Shaw
Joseph (Benjamin) Browne   -OR-   Tristan Coffin+Dionis Stevens
Revolutionary Captain Jonathan Browne+Mary Garland

Newburyport, Mass.   Tristan Coffin+Judith Greenleaf   James Coffin+Mary Severence
                     Stephen Coffin+ Sarah Atkinson   Nathaniel Coffin+Damaris Gayer
                     Stephen Coffin+Sarah Boardman   William Coffin+Anne Holmes
                     Amos Coffin+Sarah Hook

          (Joseph Browne)
          (Bridgeport, Dorset, England)

Catherine De Visme+Joseph Browne?Martha Coffin //   John Coffin+Isabella Child
m. 1782 Hermitage b.1757 (1758-1810(1835)) Rye, N.H. d.3/4/1841 m1841 b 1758 //   b 1729 Boston
Catherine De Visme Browne   Sarah Hook Brown b. 1778   d. 1808 Quebec, Canada
b. 1787 m. 1806 St. Louis, + Robert Wescott d 1808

Robert Edwards Family

WILLIAM THE CONQUEROR (1066-1087) + Matilda of Flanders
I
Henry I + (Edith) Matilda of Scotland
Geoffrey Downing+Elizabeth Wingfield   1st Earl of Gloucester, Robert De Caen (Edwards)
  Geo. Downing +Dorcas Bois   I   Thomas Hall+ Elizabeth Drury, m2Anna Metford-
George Downing +Bellamy   Thomas Edwards+Elizabeth Hall   Quick+m1Wm. Quick
Emmanuel Downing+Lucy Winthrop   Robert Edwards+Margaret Cruelin
     Sir George Downing, Mary Downing, Isabella Downing+Thomas Edwards
          +Francis Howard   +Anthony Stoddard   Robert Edwards, Joshua E., Thomas E.,
Philadelphia Downing+Sir Henry Pickering   I   William E., Leonard E., Jacob E., Martha (Frankie) E.
John Pickering+Elizabeth Prudden   I
     I   Rev. Solomon Stoddard b. 1640   William Edwards+Agnes+Mary Eure
     I   +Esther Warren   Richard Edwards+Elizabeth Tuttle John Pierpont+Thankful Stowe
Timothy Pickering Esther Stoddard+Timothy Edwards Rev. James Pierpont+Mary Hooker+Abigail Davenport
          Rev. Jonathan Edwards+Sarah Pierpont   +Sarah Haynes
               Esther Edwards+Rev. Aaron Burr
Tapping Reeves+Sally Burr, Aaron Burr+ Theodosia Bartow Prevost+Elizabeth Jumel Bowne
               Theodosia Burr+ Joseph Alston
               Aaron Burr Alston

Commentary of Norma Perdue, Researcher for this book.

Norma Perdue considers herself an heir to the Robert Edwards' Land of 80 and 77 acres leased to the Crugers and Aaron Burr in 1778 which now is claimed by Trinity Church Corporation. Through her mother's descendancy from Uriah Hugh Edwards and Samuel Edwards she is a descendant of Thomas Nathaniel and Isabella Downing Edwards. When a great aunt, Lena Caldwell Riddle of Westchester County, Pennsylvania died in 1956 Norma's mother told her of the Edwards family land on Manhattan Island some of which was subleased in 1907-8 by her grandparents Roxanna Caldwell and Alfred Washington Edwards. Great grandfather, Thomas Edwards had married in Noble City, Ohio, Lovinna Knapp of Meigs City, Ohio, daughter of David and Sarah Woods Knapp of Fishkill, Dutchess County, New York, and descendants of the wealthy land holders of the Wade-Knapp Land Company taken over by Olympia and York owned by the Reichmanns of Canada, London and the United States. These companies at one time managed much of Trinity Church Corporation's property on Manhattan Island.

Aunt Lena Riddle was the model for the Reynolds Tobacco Company owned, Garcia Vega Cigar Company. She owned stock in the Culbro Corporation of New York, a holding company for R.J.R. Nabisco, Con Edison Electric, Western Telephone, Goldman Sachs, Bloomingdales and others at the time. The name D.C. (Dewitt Clinton) Reynolds witnessed the 80 acre lease to Aaron Burr and the Cruger brothers, John and George.

Robert Edwards sailed to Wales to assume the Barony of Edwards Hall in 1780, but was lost at sea. The Edwards land in Manhattan settled into the holdings of Trinity Church Corporation about this time despite numerous challenges by rightful and not so rightful heirs.

Mutual friends of Norma and Alan Clark, the author, Ira and Gail Stern, introduced us and the mutual interest in genealogy and American history formed a bond to produce this work. Dr. Clark immediately felt this subterfuge of Manhattan property the tip of a larger iceberg and when he saw the name of Aaron Burr as grantee to the 80 acres of Thomas Edwards, he knew he had a big story because Aaron Burr at the time was an officer in the American army and Thomas Edwards as grantor and a Tory also named a British officer, John Cruger, under General Oliver De Lancey, as co-grantee.

Dr. Clark has skillfully answered many questions about Tory property in Manhattan and in the process has written a book that could change the understanding of early American independence accepted for two hundred years.

This researcher applauds the work Dr. Clark has done in interpreting this historical period in the formation of our country. All the rightful Edwards heirs should be grateful to him for sorting out this very intricate and complicated piece of our Americana. All history buffs of which I am one should be thankful for this fresh perspective on a rather rutted, but well polished history of Burr, Hamilton and Trinity Church.

Through Dr. Clark's efforts this researcher has kept her promise to her mother to find out the why of this disenfranchisement of our family; many accolades to a job well done.

Norma Perdue,
Researcher and Heir

It depends on what your reasons are for writing that will determine its impact. Rarely are historical or for that matter any information books "Best Sellers".

The common person is generally too consumed with trivial gossip and mindless sensationalism. But in time an accurate piece may be picked up in the future and translated to students as a monumental discovery, thereby giving it a greater importance in the long run. Most endeavors of this nature have to be done with a passion for the virtue of truth and selfless giving in order to hit home.

Harry Crouch Jr.

Bibliography

Allan, Sterling D. *Brief introduction to Alphabetics Scripture Code*, www. greaterthings.com,/ Word-Number/intro.htm. Manti, Utah, 2000.

Allen, Thomas B. *George Washington, Spymaster*, Washington, D.C.: National Geographic, 2004.

Alexander, Holmes. *Aaron Burr, The Proud Pretender*, Westport, Conn.: Greenwood Press, 1937.

Bareuther, David I. *New York Wanders Uptown*, New York Sun, 1931.

William Berczy. The Dictionary of Canadian Biography Online, Volume V, 1801-1820, University of Toronto, 2000.

Block, Jr., W. T. *A Tale of Jean Baptiste's Brass Cannon*, www.wtblock.com/ wtblockjr/jean.htm.

Joseph Brant Thayendanegea. The Dictionary of Canadian Biography Online, Volume V, 1801-1820, University of Toronto, 2000.

Brink, Benjamin Myer. *John Vanderlyn*, Olde Ulster Magazine, Vol. IX March, 1913, No. 3.

Burns, Ric and James Sanders, with Lisa Ades. *New York, An Illustrated History*, New York: Alfred A. Knopf, 2003.

Burrows, Edwin G. and Mike Wallace. *Gotham, A History of New York City to 1898*, New York: Oxford University Press, 1999.

Carter, Jimmy. *The Hornet's Nest*, A Novel of the Revolutionary War, New York: Simon and Schuster, 2003.

Chaitkin, Anton. Synarchy Against America. *Executive Intelligence Review*, September 2, 2003.

Chaitkin, Anton and John C. Smith, Jr. *How Britain's Treason Machine Made War Against Mexico*. American Almanac by permission of The New Federalist, November, 1997.

Chernow, Ron. *Alexander Hamilton*, New York: The Penguin Press, 2004.

John Coffin. Dictionary of Canadian Biography Online, Volume IV, 1771-1800, University of Toronto, 2000.

Coghlan, Mrs. *Memoirs of Mrs. Coghlan, daughter of the Late Major Moncrieffe*: New York: T.H. Morrell, 1864.

Asa Danforth. Dictionary of Canadian Biography Online, Volume VI, 1821-1835, University of Toronto, 2000.

Court of Chancery of the State of New York, Report of Cases Argued and Determined in the, before the Honorable Lewis H. Sandford Late Vice-Chancellor of the First Circuit. Nathaniel Bogardus et al vs. The Rector, Churchwardens and Vestrymen of Trinity Church in the City of New York, William Berrian and William Johnson attn., New York: The Lawyers' Co-operative Publishing Company, Book VII, Vol. IV, 1850 p. 1137, 1235

Davis, Matthew L. *Memoirs of Aaron Burr,* With Miscellaneous Selections from His Correspondence, New York: Da Capo Press. Reprint 1971, Vol. I, II.

Davis, Matthew L. editor. *The Private Journal of Aaron Burr during his residence of four years in Europe; with selections from his correspondence.* New York: Harper and Brothers, Cliff-Street, 1838, Vol. I, II.

Descendants of Louis Alexandre Picard, www.freepages.genealogy.rootsweb. com/~picard/LouisAlexandrePicard.

Dunn, Susan. *Jefferson's Second Revolution; The Election Crisis of 1800 and the Triumph of Republicanism.* Boston: Houghton Mifflin Company, 2004.

Ellis, Joseph J. *Founding Brothers,* New York: Vintage Books, 2002.

Ellis, Joseph J. *His Excellency, George Washington.* New York: Alfred A. Knoph, 2004.

Flaherty, Dr. Edward. *Who Owns the Federal Reserve?* , 1999.

Fleming, Thomas. *Duel. Alexander Hamilton, Aaron Burr and the Future of America.* New York: Basic Books, 1999.

Google.com. **World Trade Center 99 year lease.** Search, 2005.

Hall, Jay. *Births, German, and Loyalist Officers in the American Revolution.* British War Office, recompiled 1990.

Hamilton, Stanislaus M. *Writings of James Monroe*, New York: 1878-1903 Vol. I, p.295.

Hamm, Margherita Arlina. *Famous Families of New York,* New York: Putnam, 1902.

Hangley Jr., Bill. *The Loose Tongue of Tom Hickey, or How a Jailhouse Snitch Saved America in 1776.* New York: Explore Articles, Volume: Voices of Lower Manhattan, 2004.

Hartman, Carl. "Naivete cost Hale his life, document reveals", article, *Star Banner*, Ocala, Florida: Sunday, Sept. 21, 2004.

Hause, Eric. *The Outer Banks: The Fate of Theodosia Burr.* North Carolina: Reprint, Our State Magazine.

Haywood, Marshall DeLancey. *Governor William Tryon, and his Administration in the Province of North Carolina, 1765-1771.* Raleigh, North Carolina: E. M. Uzzell, Printer, 1903.

The Hermitage and Its People. Henry Bischoff, Historian URL: The Prevosts, Late Colonial and Revolutionary Period. www.thehermitage.org/prevost_extra. html.

Holcomb, Brent H., compiled, *Marriage and Death Notices from The (Charleston) Times, 1800-1821.* Baltimore: Genealogical Publishing Co., Inc., 1979.

Homberger, Eric. *The Historical Atlas of New York City, A Visual Celebration of Nearly 400 Years of New York City's History.* New York: Henry Holt and Company, 1994.

Kennedy, Roger G. *Burr, Hamilton, and Jefferson. A Study in Character.* New York: Oxford University Press, 2000

Lane, Doris. *Theodosia Burr and the Pirates.* www.starvingwriters.org, 2001.

LaRouche, Lyndon H. *Dope Inc.* New York: New Benjamin Franklin House Publishing Co., 1978.

Leiby, Adrian Coulter. *The Revolutionary War in Hackensack Valley; The Jersey Dutch and the Neutral Ground, 1775-1783.* New Brunswick, N. J. Rutgers University Press, 1962.

Long Island Patriots and Their Stories, http://longislandgenealogy.com/patriots. html.

Lossing, Benson J. *Our Country, Household History for All Readers. 1760 to 1800*, www.publicbookshelf.com, 1877, Volumes I, II.

Lossing, Benson J. *Pictorial Field Book of the Revolution, Book II*, 1850, Chapter XXIII

Louis Alexandre Picard, Dictionary of Canadian Biography Online, Volume IV, 1771-1800, University of Toronto, 2000

Marrs, Jim. *Rule by Secrecy*. New York: Perennial, HarperCollins Publishers, 2000, pages 7, 14, 17.

Melton Jr., Buckner F. *Aaron Burr, Conspiracy to Treason*. New York: John Wiley and Sons, Inc.2002

McCullough, David. *John Adams*, New York: Simon and Schuster, 2001

Richard Montgomery. Dictionary of Canadian Biography Online, Volume IV, 1771-1800 University of Toronto, 2000.

Moorman, J.R.H., *A History of the Church in England, 3rd rev. ed.*, 1973.

Mormon Library. "Deeds and Land Transactions of New York". Microfilm, Salt Lake City: 1956, 1972.

Mullens, Eustice. Articles on the American Banking System. *Widepikea Encyclopedia*.

Mysterious Theodosia. www.theoutlaws.com/people3.htm.

New York City. *The Boston Post Road and Aaron Burr*, A Guide to New York City, 1921.

The New York Historical Manuscripts: Dutch, *Land Papers*, Baltimore: Genealogical Publishing Co., Inc., 1980, vol. GG, HH &II. Translated and Edited by Charles T. Gehring.

The New York Historical Society for the Year 1899, Collections of. *Abstract of Wills, on file in the surrogate's office, City of New York, 1771-1776*. New York: Volume VIII, page 284-5 and for the Year 1902, *Abstracts of Unrecorded Wills Prior to 1790, on file in the Surrogate's Office, City of New York*. Volume XI, page 209-10.

New York Times. February 21, 1856.

Parmet, Herbert S. and Marie B. Hecht. *Aaron Burr, Portrait of an Ambitious Man*, New York: The MacMillan Company, 1967.

Powell, William S. editor. *The Correspondence of William Tryon and other selected Papers Volume II 1768-1818*. Raleigh Division of Archives and History, Department of Cultural Resources, 1981.

Powers, Jr., William J. *The History of the Vanderburgh Family, Lucas Dircksen Vanderburgh and His Descendants*. www.lakedunmorevt.com/vdb, 2002.

Pringle, J.F. Judge County Court. *Lunenburgh, or the Old Eastern District, Return of the Officers of the Corps of Loyal Rangers*, 1890.

Robbins, Alexandra. *Secrets of the Tomb, Skull and Bones, The Ivy League, and the Hidden paths of Power*, Boston: Little Brown and Company, 2002.

Ryerse, Phyllis. *The Ryerse-Ryerson Family Association Newsletter*, Ontario, Canada: The Port Ryerse Journal, Volume 8, Issue 3, October, 2001.

Safire, William. *Scandalmonger: A Novel*. New York: Simon and Schuster, 2000. Prologue: 1792.

Steinberg, Jeffrey. *The Bestial British Intelligence of Shelburne and Bentham*. The Executive Intelligence Review: 1994.

University of Michigan, William L. Clements Library, Ann Arbor, Michigan. *Spy Letters of the American Revolution*.

Vail, Philip. *The Great American Rascal. The Turbulent Life of Aaron Burr*, New York: Hawthorn Books, 1973.

Van Doren, Mark. *Correspondence of Aaron Burr and his Daughter Theodosia*, New York: Stratford Press, 1929.

Vidal, Gore. *Burr*, New York: Vintage Books, 2000 (1971).

Zodhiates, Spiros. *Complete Word Study Dictionary, New Testament*. Chattanooga, Tenn., AMG Publishers, 1992.

Zotti, Ed, Editor. Staff Reports; Straight Dope Science Advisory Board. *Who Wrote the Bible (Part 3)*.www.straightdope.com: Chicago Reader, Inc., Jan., 2002.

Symbols

A

B

Jumel, Eliza Bowen 55, 75, 102, 151, 181, 208, 210
Jumel, Stephen 55
Jumel Mansion 102

K

Kerry, John Forbes 124
Kidnap Washington 80
Kieft, Willem 137, 138
King's College xiv, 12, 17, 28, 40, 46, 78, 79, 195, 206
King's Farm 41, 137, 138, 144, 145, 150
King, Rufus 122, 137, 181
King George III xxx, 161
King James 163
King James II xii, 8
King of England xxix, 7, 9, 12, 56, 58, 94, 136, 142
Kip's Bay Farm 105
Knight 67, 206
Knox, Henry 18, 105

L

LaFayette, General 87, 99
Lafitte, Jean 69, 72
La G xv, 62–64
La R 58, 105, 117
Lee, General Charles 18, 32, 92, 94, 95, 99
Lewis, Morgan 28
Lewis, Susannah 28
Livingston, Brockholst 28, 98, 123
Livingston, Gilbert 28, 144, 206
Livingston, Governor William 28, 79
Livingston, Kitty 95
Livingston, Robert R. 28, 109, 207
Livingston, William 46, 78
London xviii, xxviii, 24, 41, 59, 69, 70, 118, 124, 126, 134, 135, 142, 156
Long Island Spy Ring 82, 83
Louisiana Purchase 58, 69, 114
Louisiana Territory xvii, 21, 44, 51, 55, 61, 73, 96, 115, 117, 118, 120, 132
Louis XVI 95
Lovelace, Governor 138, 139, 145, 154
Lowell, John 122, 125, 203
Loyalist xi, xii, xviii, xxiv, xxv, 3–6, 9, 11, 12, 14, 19, 25–27, 40, 42, 43, 46, 47, 53, 60, 66, 75, 76, 79, 82, 96, 100, 106, 111, 127, 133, 143, 149–151, 163, 166–195, 215
Luther Martin 98, 103

Lynch, Colonel Charles 38, 120

M

Madison, Dolly 97
Madison, James 97, 98, 207
Malcolm, Brigadier General 89
Manhattan Corporation 20, 33
Manhattan Island xxv, xxx, 2, 11, 41, 45, 86, 118, 138, 142
Marion, Francis 70
Mark, Jacob 55, 201
Marrs, Jim 145
Marshall, Justice John 21
McPherson, John 108
Memoirs xvi–xviii, 55, 72, 74–76, 79, 90, 96, 114, 117, 129, 215
Merry, British Minister Anthony 60, 120
Mexican War 125
Mexico xvii, xviii, 21, 37–39, 51, 60–62, 72, 73, 96, 114, 118, 119, 128, 214
Moncrieffe, Major 92, 215
Moncrieffe, Margaret 92
Monroe, James xvii, 23, 25, 46, 69, 72, 79, 94, 95, 98, 99, 100, 117, 151, 160,
    216
Montalto xv, 60, 61, 117
Montgomery, General Richard xii, xv, xvii, 71, 107–110, 113, 184, 207, 217
Monticello xv, 61
Moore, Rev. Benjamin 65, 96, 102, 103, 205
Morgan, George 116
Morgan, J. P. 135, 147, 156
Morgan, John Pierpont 126
Morgan, Juneus 209
Morris, Lewis 48
Morris, Robert 19, 43, 46, 80, 84–87
Morris, Roger 14, 55, 56, 59, 60, 61, 102, 164, 184
Mortier, Abraham 25, 42, 49, 144, 185
Muhlenberg, Frederick Augustus 25
Murdock, Rupert xix, 6, 67, 154, 155, 159
Murray, Mrs. Robert 105
Murray Farm 105

N

Nags Head, North Carolina 69
Napoleon xvii, 4, 21, 114, 117
Nashville 115
National Bank of Commerce 133, 135
Newbury, Massachusetts 71, 112

Portrait 68
Port Authority of New York and New Jersey xix, 150, 151, 152, 157, 159
Prevost, Augustin 204
Prevost, General George 43, 126
Prevost, Jacques 204
Prevost, James Marcus 204
Prevost, John Bartow 99, 120, 204
Prevost, Theodosia 44, 47, 48, 72, 73, 75, 78, 79, 87, 94, 96, 97, 99, 100, 101, 114, 117
Princeton xiv, 18, 125
Princeton College 17, 41, 108, 111, 208
Pulteney Purchase 36
Putnam, General 92, 105
Pyne, Percy 133

Q

Queen's Farm xxx, 10, 40, 41, 138–140, 146, 147, 151–154, 157
Queen Anne 5, 7, 40, 138, 139, 145, 146, 154
Queen Elizabeth 155, 157
Queen Elizabeth II 66
Quick, Anna Medford 143
Quit Rent xxx, 139, 154

R

Rector 11, 14, 65, 138, 145
Reeves, Tapping 208
Report on Manufactures 29
Revolutionary War debt 26
Reynolds' Affair xiii
Reynolds,James 20, 24–27, 29, 144
Reynolds, Maria xiii, 23–26, 28, 29
Richmond Hill xv, 11, 25, 33, 37, 42, 49, 53–56, 59–61, 123, 140, 144, 150, 151, 185
Rivington's press 82, 104
Rivington, James 82, 104
Roberts, Kenneth xxii
Rochambeau, General 85–88
Rockefeller, David 156
Rockefeller, John D. xviii, 133, 135
Rockefeller, William 133
Rockefeller Center 40, 147
Roe, Austin 58, 104
Roe, La 117
Rogers, Richard 119

About the Author

Author, Alan J. Clark, M.D., is a graduate of the class of 1968 from Yale University with classmate, President George W. Bush. He graduated with the honor of cum laude from The Phillips Exeter Academy; among alumni are authors Gore Vidal and Dan Brown. He had the pleasure of knowing his parents' friend Marjorie Mosser Ellis, niece and secretary of author Kenneth Roberts, whose book *Arundel* antedates the account by Clark of the American attack on Quebec in 1775.

A career board certified ophthalmologist Clark interned at the Maine Medical Center in Portland, Maine and completed his residency at the Albany, N.Y. Medical Center receiving his medical degree at Yale Medical School. An early proponent of antioxidant therapy during his career, Clark's practice included many original surgical techniques including temporal wounds to reduce astigmatism in cataract surgery and he embraced early use of outpatient surgery, phacoemulsification and scleral tunnel incisions into his community.

Encouraged to publish the first enumeration of the casualties of the first battle of the French and Indian Wars, the Battle of Lake George in 1755, Clark went on to publish numerous accounts of Loyalist and American ancestors during the American Revolution and War of 1812, both of soldiers and sailors.

This current work represents the first attempt by any author to completely decipher the letters of Aaron Burr and his family and contemporaries revealing a totally new interpretation of the role of American Loyalists during the formation of the United States.

LaVergne, TN USA
15 February 2010
173123LV00002B/25/A